# The Precarious Writing of Ann Quin

# The Precarious Writing of Ann Quin

Nonia Williams

EDINBURGH
University Press

Edinburgh University Press is one of the leading university presses in the UK. We publish academic books and journals in our selected subject areas across the humanities and social sciences, combining cutting-edge scholarship with high editorial and production values to produce academic works of lasting importance. For more information visit our website: edinburghuniversitypress.com

© Nonia Williams 2023, 2025

Edinburgh University Press Ltd
13 Infirmary Street,
Edinburgh, EH1 1LT

First published in hardback by Edinburgh University Press 2023

Typeset in 11/13pt Adobe Sabon by
Cheshire Typesetting Ltd, Cuddington, Cheshire

A CIP record for this book is available from the British Library

ISBN 978 1 4744 6404 8 (hardback)
ISBN 978 1 4744 6405 5 (paperback)
ISBN 978 1 4744 6409 3 (webready PDF)
ISBN 978 1 4744 6412 3 (epub)

The right of Nonia Williams to be identified as the author of this work has been asserted in accordance with the Copyright, Designs and Patents Act 1988, and the Copyright and Related Rights Regulations 2003 (SI No. 2498).

# Contents

| | |
|---|---|
| Acknowledgements | vi |
| Vignette: Quin's dark archive | 1 |
| Introduction: Ways in to Quin | 4 |
| Vignette: A bedsit room of her own | 22 |
| 1. *Berg*: Shifting Perspectives, Sticky Details | 25 |
| Vignette: That same sea | 52 |
| 2. *Three*: A Collage of Possibilities | 55 |
| Vignette: 'Have you tried it with three?' | 84 |
| 3. *Passages*: Unstable Forms of Desire | 87 |
| Vignette: Moving onwards | 115 |
| 4. *Tripticks*: Impoverished Style as Cultural Critique | 118 |
| Vignette: Breakdown, breakthrough | 147 |
| 5. *The Unmapped Country*: Unravelling Stereotypes of Madness | 150 |
| Afterword: Where Next? | 174 |
| Bibliography | 176 |
| Index | 185 |

## *Acknowledgements*

Huge thanks to the lovely team at Edinburgh University Press, especially Jackie Jones, Susannah Butler and Fiona Conn for tirelessly answering my questions. Thanks also to Caroline Richards for careful copyedits and for making my referencing infinitely better.

Thank you to all of my readers along the way, for your perceptive questions and help honing my prose: Victoria Walker, Katie Cooper, Chris Clarke, Hannah Van Hove, Peter Boxall, Clare Connors, Lyndsey Stonebridge and Karen Schaller. Especial thanks to my peer reviewer for such a positive and insightful report.

Thank you to the group of scholars working in the field for sharing enthusiasm about Quin and her fellow writers of the 1960s with me – and for the nice times talking over drinks: Kaye Mitchell, Carole Sweeney, Julia Jordan, Victoria Walker, Denise Rose Hansen, Hannah Van Hove, Alice Butler, Adam Guy, Chris Clarke, Andrew Hodgson and Joe Darlington. Thanks too to John Carter, Frank Bowling, Larry Goodell and others I have spoken to who knew Quin.

Thank you to my colleagues for your support; I know this project has been a long time coming. In particular: Rachel Potter, Katie Cooper, Matt Taunton and Tommy Karshan. Also thanks to Lorna Harris, Kaye Mitchell and Jim Parker for your friendship and for cheerleading the final stages.

A heartfelt thank you to my family for all the childcare and to my children Rosa and Wren for putting up with my absence. This book is dedicated to you.

I am grateful for permission to quote from Quin's letters and manuscript materials. Thank you to Washington University Library, to the Lilly Library, and especially to Ann Quin's Estate. This project would not have been possible in its current form without the generosity of Carol and Alan Burns who I warmly thank in their absence.

I am particularly grateful to Denise Rose Hansen and Ann Quin's Estate for their kind permission to use Denise's wonderful photograph for the cover image. I love how this photo includes both handwritten archive papers and a stunning photograph of Quin, and that these are on her mother's table, where some of her writing took place. I am aware *The Precarious Writing of Ann Quin* might seem to emphasise difficulty and vulnerability, so the choice of this bold photograph is a reminder that precariousness is a state of possibility as well as risk.

Thanks to Catheryn Kilgarriff for kind permission to use the image from the final page of *Tripticks*. I am grateful for permission to rework earlier versions of published material: '"Designing its Own Shadow": Tracing Ann Quin's Reiterative Experimental Processes', in *'Slipping through the Labels': British Experimental Women's Fiction, 1945–1975*, ed. Andrew Radford and Hannah Van Hove (Cham: Palgrave Macmillan, 2021); 'About/Of Madness: Ann Quin's *The Unmapped Country*', *Textual Practice*, 34:6 (2020); 'Ann Quin: 'infuriating' Experiments?', in *British Avant-Garde Fiction of the 1960s*, ed. Kaye Mitchell and Nonia Williams (Edinburgh: Edinburgh University Press, 2019). I am also grateful for the support of a Lilly Library Everett Helm Fellowship early on in my research.

## Editorial Note

Quin's letters to her publishers articulate how the formatting of each of her texts was deliberate, and how this sometimes led to frustration and some wrangling at the typesetting stage. Mindful of this, and because the patterning of writing and space on the page is a notable part of her experimental technique, citations from Quin's work included in this book reproduce formatting as closely as possible to the original layout.

Vignette

# Quin's dark archive

In April 2009, heavily pregnant and right at the beginning of this project, I made a visit to Carol and Alan Burns in the flat they were then living in together (although long separated) in north London. The flat was crammed with stuff and countless shelves of books and papers. There were also several cats. One of them was being sick, I remember, as Carol and I sat talking about Ann Quin at a little table in her kitchen. I'd talked with Alan first, in his separate bedsit area, as he fed me cake and remembered Ann fondly. He showed me photographs and talked of her 'glance, her own particular vision of world'. On later visits it was mainly Carol I spoke with. She shared her collection of Quin's letters and papers with me, allowing me to copy them all and to begin my own 'dark archive'.[1] I know I am not alone among Quin scholars in having a partial, incomplete and unofficial archive of letters and manuscript materials in my possession, kept for a purpose not yet known.

A more recent encounter with another part of Quin's archive in 2018, in a private collection of books, letters and other papers owned by her nephew, also involved being fed cake. (No vomiting cats this time, though.) I made that trip with Chris Clarke, who has described how the items in this particular collection remind us that Quin's archive is as much an absence as a presence. In 1965, she had written to the poet Robert Creeley about keeping his letters in a 'huge trunk in Brighton for Eternity or at least until fifty years after we are all dead!!' Yet when Clarke located the trunk in this private collection, it was empty and revealed nothing.[2] This is perhaps unsurprising. Quin remarks that she has an archive of materials, but she doesn't seem interested in collecting or collating this in any official way and didn't keep carbon copies of her letters to sell on to university libraries as some of her friends and contemporaries did. Instead, her collection of correspondence and papers was and is precarious, vulnerable to a scattering and loss that was, perhaps, partly wilful, and partly to do with how much Quin moved and travelled from place to place. In February 1973, a few months before she died, she described to several friends that 'most of my books, manuscripts and notebooks' were thrown out and burned by 'the Estate Agents' because they were 'covered in cat shit!'.[3]

In terms of what remains, Quin's archive is incomplete, uncollected and strewn across a range of locations, in the institutional archive collections of others – her friends/lovers Robert Creeley and Robert Sward, for example – as well as the papers of her publisher Calder and Boyars, and in private collections of family, and friends like Father Brocard Sewell and Carol Burns. There is no 'Quin archive' as such. Alice Butler captures the elusiveness and dispersal of this well when she says 'little bits of Quin, of her life and her work, have been scattered like ashes'.[4] Writers and scholars interested in recovering her work have embarked on archival quests to track down and locate manuscripts and other materials. Hannah Van Hove and Chris Clarke have recently pointed out how engagement with these has been used to evidence and enhance the critical resurgence of interest in the published writing. Work with her archive may also have been driven by a desire for discovery and encounter, for a frisson that opens up ethical questions; it might have enhanced and contributed to (however unwittingly) descriptions of Quin as a 'revenant' and 'secret'.[5] Perhaps these letters and papers will reveal the secret of Ann Quin as a 'person' to us in a way inaccessible via her published texts, perhaps we will discover and bring to light previously unpublished works, perhaps we will gain an insight into her writing processes and techniques, or perhaps the secret is that whatever it is that we are looking for, nothing will be found. To Robert Sward she jokes about planting clues to 'puzzle our future biographers and all those students' and keep them guessing.[6]

In her published work Quin is a writer of the archive too. The character Berg writes 'NON OMNIS MORIAR' (which can be translated as 'My work will live', or more literally 'I shall not wholly die') on a mirror when contemplating the meaning/meaninglessness of his existence.[7] Elsewhere – in books such as *Three* and *Passages* – the quest for a missing person via dark archives of fragmented, scattered and often inaccessible materials is always frustrated, the person never found. So Quin's writing both warns and entices her reader on with ever elusive and inscrutable archival details.

## Notes

1. I use the term 'dark archive' here after Maryanne Dever, *Paper, Materiality and the Archived Page* (Cham: Palgrave Macmillan, 2015), see p. 84.
2. Quin, letter to Robert Creeley, 14 September 1965, cited in Chris Clarke, '"S" and "M": The Last and Lost Letters Between Ann Quin and Robert Creeley', *Women: A Cultural Review*, special issue: *(Re)turning to Ann Quin*, 33:1 (2022), pp. 33–51 (p. 36).
3. Quin, letter to Brocard Sewell, 10 February 1973, cited in Brocard Sewell, *Like Black Swans: Some People and Themes* (Padstow: Tabb House, 1982), p. 189. Quin also wrote about this to John Carter, 7 February 1973 and Robert Creeley, 10 February 1973.
4. Alice Butler, 'Ann Quin's Night-Time Ink: A Postscript', MA dissertation, The Royal College of Art, London, 2013, p. 4, available at http://www.alicebutler.org.uk/wp-content/uploads/2016/03/Butler_AnnQuin_Book.pdf (accessed 18 November 2022).
5. See Hannah Van Hove, '"The moving towards words & then from them": Circling Passages, Circling Quin'; Clarke, '"S" and "M": The Last and Lost Letters Between Ann Quin and Robert Creeley'; Leigh Wilson, '"So thrilling and so alive and so much its own thing": Talking to Claire-Louise Bennett about Ann Quin'; Nonia Williams, '(Re)turning to Quin: An Introduction', all in *Women: A Cultural Review*, special issue: *(Re)turning to Ann Quin*.
6. Quin, letter to Robert Sward, September 1966, Robert Sward Papers, Washington University Library, Series 1.1, box 8.
7. Ann Quin, *Berg* (Sheffield: And Other Stories, 2019), p. 59.

# Introduction: Ways in to Quin

> It would be progress if we could stop the rhapsodizing of Ann Quin and just read her books without having to defend them. It's hard not to defend them, though. The tweedy male literary world of her generation was not exactly waiting to garland her contribution to literary culture. Few critics gave her books the respect of close reading. It was as if Quin was culturally forbidden to actually possess a coherent literary purpose.
>
> Deborah Levy, 'Ann Quin and Me', p. 119

## Why Quin, Why Now?

This book claims Ann Quin as an important female experimental writer of the twentieth century, shows how the precarious possibility of her writing is its essential attribute, and demonstrates the lasting significance of her work. Via sustained and in-depth readings, I identify the aesthetics, effects and cultural and literary purposes of Quin's writing to show how the range and risk of her vivid and energetic prose – at once deeply personal and wildly experimental – still stirs and startles the reader today.

I open here with Levy's appreciation of Quin in order to position the work of this book, and this introductory chapter in particular, alongside her concerns. Similarly, in *What Ever Happened to Modernism?* Gabriel Josipovici claimed it was high time to reconsider the story of twentieth-century British fiction. He lamented the critical neglect of fiction 'genuinely' interested in experiment and called for the inclusion of a 'whole web of stories'; 'to restore a sense of history being made'.[1] In this way, the story of British writing in the twentieth century could expand to include 'the blind alleys' rather than only the 'achieved successes'.[2] Recent years have seen such critical reconsideration begin to take place, including a resurgence of scholarly work on Quin and her contemporaries which has substantively begun to redress the previous critical 'neglect' of post-1945 experimental British writing.[3] In wider reading culture too, the prevalence, appreciation and growing profile of experimental forms in contemporary British and Irish fiction has been marked by, for example, the 2013 inauguration of the Goldsmith's Prize for innovative writing, won that year by Eimear McBride's *A Girl Is a Half-formed Thing* and more recently by Isabel Waidner's *Sterling Karat Gold*, and books such as Tom McCarthy's *C* and Ali Smith's *How to Be Both* being shortlisted for the Man Booker Prize. At the same time, writing by Quin and her contemporaries, Brigid Brophy for example, has been reissued to a wider readership.[4] In Quin's case, the republication of her books and stories by the independent press And Other Stories since 2018, and the championing of her work by several contemporary writers in addition to Levy – including Kate Zambreno, Claire-Louise Bennett, Joanna Walsh, Juliet Jacques, Danielle Dutton, Jesse Kohn, Joshua Cohen, Lee Rourke, Stewart Home, Ellis Sharp and Ian Patterson, among others – has undoubtedly contributed to her renaissance.

Like many scholarly publications in the field, my previous work on Quin has aimed to recuperate her writing, and to position her among her contemporary British experimental and avant-garde writers of the 1960s and 1970s such as Eva Figes, Brigid Brophy, Christine Brooke-Rose, Anna Kavan, Alan Burns, B. S. Johnson and more. This current book is indebted to that important wider work, which has been necessary to demonstrate and establish the liveliness, variety, and cultural and literary significance of writing in this period, and which has increasingly positioned Quin and her milieu 'as part of a retrospectively coherent, or at least relatively networked, gang of 1960s avant-gardists', as Julia Jordan points out.[5] Yet Jordan and others have also acknowledged how Quin has been 'painted as an isolated and rebarbative voice, perhaps finding herself, in Christine Brooke-Rose's words, as "doubly marginalized as an experimentalist and a woman experimentalist"'.[6] This doubly or even triply marginalised position is an important context for thinking about Quin. Her relative critical neglect has also meant that her life and biography have often been introduced as a precursor to discussions of her writing.[7] However, Carole Sweeney has rightly noted the potentially problematic role of women writers' lives in recuperative scholarly work, especially when it comes to those like Quin and Anna Kavan who both died in dramatic circumstances:

for some critics this has become the primary lens for reading their work.[8]

As I go on to discuss and demonstrate in later sections of this introduction and throughout (and in between) subsequent chapters of this book, my approach here instead reads writing and life alongside each other. The aim of this is not to read Quin's writing *in terms of* her life, but to reveal multidirectional resonances between the two, and to position my work alongside and in dialogue with the auto-fictional nature of hers. This book does not position Quin in relation to the wider field's admirable periodising work, or indeed in terms of categories such as modernism, post-modernism, late modernism, after modernism or mid-century. I do not, however, aim to paint Quin as an isolated, rebarbative voice, but to think about how her work develops particular aesthetic and formal techniques to engage with and respond to the culture and politics of its era. In this, my argument is aligned with Carole Sweeney's interest in how Quin, as a woman writer, goes 'beyond and against the aesthetic and thematic conventions' of her time and writes against notions of the home and domesticity. Sweeney uses the fabulous and insightful term 'vagabondage' to describe the movements of such writing 'into states of transit, transformation and displacement'.[9] As with Sweeney's *Vagabond Fictions*, my work too declares itself as a work of feminist scholarship from the outset. Opening 'Quin's dark archive' with the pregnant woman scholar's body is part of this work – what Maggie Nelson calls 'the spectacle of that wild oxymoron, *the pregnant woman who thinks*' – as is my interest throughout the book in the intersections of Quin's experience, and my discussions of how her writing engages with key questions of gender, sexuality, autonomy and freedom.[10] I do not read Quin via the lens of a particular feminist critical framework, or see women's writing and experimentation as exclusively aligned, but the form, focus and contents of this book are intended to be understood as working in an intersectional feminist mode.[11]

In the title *The Precarious Writing of Ann Quin*, my use of 'precarious' aims to capture the peculiar qualities, modes and preoccupations of her prose, and to provide a way of describing and thinking across her life, archive and published materials. In this, 'precarious' intentionally refers to and includes both Quin's lived experience – such as her volatile material conditions, sexual and emotional life, mental states and more – and the experimentalism of the writing. In Quin's work, precariousness is always both an identity and a literary question, both the condition and the aesthetics of the writing, its politics and its poetics. I use 'writing' to include both the published work – the writings – and Quin's writing activities and processes, as well as being mindful of my own 'writing of Ann Quin' here. By 'precarious writing', I mean to include the wider cultural position of her writing as 'experimental' and marginal; the scattered and uncollected, fragile position of her archive materials; the bodily, sexual and other kinds of vulnerability of the characters in her work; the deliberately unstable techniques and perspectives of her prose. Quin employs such strategies to question and deconstruct pre-existing literary and cultural structures such as marriage and coupledom, the Oedipal triangle and other mythic frameworks, as well as binaries of either/or in relation to gender and sexuality. Its precarious qualities enable the writing to rethink and subvert gendered and othered positions – for instance, Quin's use of the female gaze, or the more particular example of Berg as a queer working-class man.

As I noted in my introduction to the *Women: A Cultural Review* special issue *(Re)turning to Ann Quin*, several discussions of her life and work have attended to questions of class. Brought up by a single working-class Glaswegian mother and sent to convent school, Quin would have experienced being between or both/and working and middle class because of her education, as Leigh Wilson and Claire-Louise Bennett have noted.[12] And the intersections of gender and class – which, if we take her position as a working woman into account, might have quadruply marginalised Quin, as Bennett and others have suggested[13] – are important for thinking about the writing's specific contents and forms. With her experimentalism, Quin was deliberately writing against the modes seen as acceptable for working-class writers, associated at the time with the so-called 'return' to realism, including 'kitchen sink' social realism and the angry young men. It is worth noting that Quin's own position in relation to the question of class was ambivalent, and that her refusal to write in a realist mode could suggest a resistance to class identity as much as an aesthetic protest. Her writing seems to acknowledge its importance – 'Another class, born in a different environment, who could say what the outcome? Surely a matter of luck whether one is swaddled in silk or cotton'[14] – but when talking with Nell Dunn she says, 'Class has never bothered me, only inasmuch that I get sick to death of it.'[15]

While this book does not seek to claim or pin down a particular classed position for Quin, it is certainly the case that her living conditions were difficult and uncertain, and that these were profoundly and inextricably bound up with and in the specific experimental forms of the writing. As Bennett points out, 'a working-class environment may well engender an aesthetic sensibility that quite naturally produces work that is idiosyncratic, polyvocal, and apparently experimental'.[16] And in my chapter on *Berg*, for example, I argue for the significance of how the material effects and aesthetics of working-class environments and experience are reimagined in Quin's precarious prose. My deliberate use of the broader category 'precarious' throughout this book does not in any way mean to ignore Quin's experiences of pressing material need or other class-focused oppressions, but aims instead to offer a more capacious, flexible and nuanced way to think about her life and writing – one that neither denies, nor is wholly grounded in, the political and identity category of class. Precariousness is also particularly useful for expressing how the forms and focus of her texts oscillate between differing modes and moods: on the one hand assertion, risk, bravura, flair, wit, possibility and playfulness, and on the other, fragility, vulnerability, uncertainty, instability and ambivalence. It describes how Quin's work is able to hold opposites such as desire/disgust, presence/absence and sanity/madness in play without having to decide: instead, the precarious qualities of the writing enable it to remain in an in-between, provisional space of possibility as well as risk – a double sense where we quite don't know which way things will go. This ontological and phenomenological uncertainty is a key strength of the prose. It is evident in the shifting pronouns and perspectives across the oeuvre, and more specifically in the fragile push–pull of the woman and man's relationship in *Passages* and the unresolved uncertainty surrounding the character S's death in *Three*.

As the first full scholarly book on Quin, I am fortunate to have space here to pay sustained attention to the aesthetic, formal, technical and political qualities of her writing and to track how these shift, transform and develop across her oeuvre. My primary concerns and questions necessitate a continual return to the detail of her prose. I ask: What is this precarious writing like? What are its textures and rhythms? How does Quin use different literary forms, experimentations and language to express and negotiate being in the world – and what kind of worlds and identities does she depict? Why might the questions, focal points and techniques of her writing bear returning to? In response, my analyses aim to give and open up the experience of reading Quin.

## A Writing of Reiteration, Obliquity and Stutters

> I don't know about making peace with the world – I have yet to make peace with myself, all the selves. I'm concerned more in 'how it is' not with how it should/could be; and even that concern is circled with ambiguities. The possibility of thinking backwards and suddenly insulting one's thought. Sometimes it is enough to watch the rain walk designing its own shadow. Hear the desert wind thru trees absorbed by that yet being raped by the mind's eye into another landscape; emotions; limbs long, want the ocean. See the ocean. Ah that point that opens for the magic usage of things.[17]

The above letter, written in Placitas, New Mexico in July 1966, to her then lover the American poet Robert Sward provides one way in to reading Quin. The sentence 'Sometimes it is enough to watch the rain walk designing its own shadow' offers a compelling description of Quin's writing process – one that is also a performance of it. But the sensory experience of watching the rain is not 'enough'; it is instead reformulated as words on the page. What is seen is translated into what is written, representation substituted for perception. And as the examples below demonstrate, the phrase – 'watch the rain walk designing its own shadow' – is just one version of a reiterative attempt to write the experience:

> I find the landscape absorbing in a very positive way. Like I am continually staggered by the change in colour, the layers of blue in sky, the way the rain walks designing its own shadows over mesas, mountains.[18]

> the world
> where lightning licks
> of the plumed serpent's
> tongue from clouds under
> I look under over the bed
> murdering what I see
> have seen. Have not.
> And see the rain walk
> designing its own shadow.[19]

> After mid-summer's eve cool rains. Soft blue out there. Shape of rain. Walks over mountains. Mesas. Space. Ah space[20]

> Rain walks designing its own shadow. Not here reached but reaching out. Towards. And now moving slowly. Myself. Moving into my own movements. The difficulty really is in finding one's place and

rediscovering communication with one's self. That dialogue within thought. Aie![21]

I deliberately include several examples here to show the variety of versions, texts and contexts in which Quin tests out and reworks the image of 'the rain walk[s] designing its own shadow'. Reading across the variations – 'the rain walks designing its own shadows over mesas, mountains', 'see the rain walk/designing its own shadow', 'Shape of rain. Walks over mountains' and 'Rain walks designing its own shadow' – it is possible to see the reiteration reaching towards forms and phrasing within which to both communicate and create the intense emotional effect of the landscape. This process is a complement of form and content, where the metaphor – 'the rain walk[s] designing its own shadow' – in turn becomes a written construction that 'designs its own shadow' across the writing of the time, 'throwing off ripples of association'.[22] In such materials Quin also directly reflects on her own creative process and articulates the intensity of this in terms of 'murdering what I see / have seen. Have not', and of the sensory experience 'being raped by the mind's eye into another landscape'. Such terms insist that the transformative act performed by 'the mind's eye' is also a violent one which rips things out of context for the writer's artistic purposes.[23]

'Never Trust a Man Who Bathes with His Fingernails' was also written during Quin's time in New Mexico and first published in *El Corno Emplumado 27* in 1968. This story focuses on a man, his wife and another woman who live together in a domestic set-up which is both tense and harmonious. Their *ménage à trois* is challenged and disturbed by the addition of a fourth, a man who does 'odd jobs around the house', and who they go on a day trip with to a local hot spring.[24] The man arrives by motorbike and is written as deeply connected to the story's New Mexico setting – 'he waved. His hand reconstructing the speed, weather, landscape he had passed through'.[25] Throughout, the dramatic and mountainous landscape, rain, clouds and changing weather are recurrent features and they are always closely bound up with this man. He is an ambivalent character in terms of his role in the text itself; he is also a potentially discomfortingly 'exotic' object of sexual desire in terms of how his cultural 'otherness' is written.

Early on in the story the three characters await the man's arrival, the women hoping the weather will be good enough for the proposed day trip to take place. The 'other woman' looks out of the window onto an unfamiliar landscape, at the aspen trees and 'the cloud shadows gathering speed through the valley'.[26] The shift of 'the rain walk[s] designing its own shadow' into this published short story can be read as an example of Quin's askance way of looking at things. Such a position is explicit when the four characters are together at the hot spring: 'The women looked down at the men from the corners of their eyes, while the water bubbled below, and behind them.'[27] This sideways glance is useful for thinking about the direction of Quin's reiterative and associative writing processes, and can be illuminated by reference to Jacques Derrida's comments on how meaning errs and wanders in the 'destinerrant indirection' of the oblique.[28] He elsewhere describes this as 'the ruse of an oblique or indirect gaze. A ruse that consists of sidestepping rather than meeting head on'.[29] The form and content of Quin's writing here (and elsewhere) adopts such a position.[30] The oblique move of the phrase under discussion exemplifies a writing process that differs and defers without ascertainable origin, one that moves outwards and not necessarily onwards, where various reiterations of a phrase remain in reverberating parataxis rather than in a linear progression; there is no best or final form.

In 'Never Trust a Man Who Bathes with His Fingernails', Quin's reiterative process is not only evident in part repetitions of 'watch the rain walk designing its own shadow' (including indirect reimaginings of it, such as the example in the extract below, 'Stilts of rain came slowly down the mountains, faster over the valley'). Oblique patterns of association are also evident at word and sentence level in terms of how, for example, the repetition of sound is utilised:

> Thunder stirred over the distant mountains. A sirocco wind spiralled sand in the desert. Three spirals on their own, that approached, joined up into a whirling tower of sand. Stilts of rain came slowly down the mountains, faster over the valley.[31]

This description is one of resistance as much as of representation: it is a vivid and sensory depiction of extreme weather that includes unexpected, odd detail so that its mimetic effect is made strange. This is bound up with the form of the writing – its pace, rhythm and syncopated metre – as well as its content – the cacophonous distant thunder, spiralling wind, whirling sand, and slanting stilts of rain that move now slowly, now faster, to reach a noisy climax. Across the extract the onomatopoeic 's's – stirred, sirocco, spiralled, sand, spirals, stilts – demand that we listen to the words, and the associative patterning of the writing here creates a 'glossomania' that is based as much on sound repetition as sense.[32] This denies the narration transparency and insists on the materiality of the linguistic surface. The metaphor of 'stilts of rain' is a particularly interesting, dissonant example. As a visual metaphor, it simultaneously suggests and denies the idea of rain as a solid and supporting structure, and the soft yet insistent 's's are dissonant with and performative of the stilting, stuttering attempt at and failure of articulation in the metaphor, announced by the 'st' of stilts.

This insistent phonic patterning, together with the fragmented sentences and disrupted syntax, is a proliferate and essential quality of Quin's writing which can be productively thought about in terms of Gilles Deleuze's suggestive notion of literary stuttering. This is where a straining of language takes place, largely to do with sound patterns but also meaning patterns. When this roughness and disruption replace smoothness and flow, the writer becomes 'a stutterer in language' and new meanings are made rather than pre-existent meanings invoked.[33] This concept is useful for thinking about the striking effects of Quin's language in the extract above; it also provides a way of thinking about the problematic cultural designation of the fourth character. For Deleuze, stuttering comes about as part of an attempt to capture unfamiliar or 'foreign' experiences in the writer's own language but in such a way that the description still comes to life. His example is T. E. Lawrence who, he claims, 'made English stumble in order to extract from it the music and visions of Arabia'.[34] While I question the politics and exoticising sentiment of the phrasing here, the thinking about under what conditions a writer stutters in language remains useful for considering whether and how the forms and techniques of Quin's writing might 'stumble' in its attempts to describe the unfamiliar New Mexico landscape.

The writing also seems to stumble in its reinforcing of cultural stereotypes and uneasy stance towards the fourth character. The husband, for example, uses insulting language – 'Damn it he's just a bum', 'Lazy bastard', and later, 'Ha you think his silences are profound or something – he's dumb';[35] the women watch him 'roused, a little frightened'; the wife is 'flushed from the ride on his motorbike' and 'the other woman waited, wanting to make a third of this situation also'.[36] And the story marks the man in terms of his 'otherness' from the very first page: 'He was a small man. Half Cherokee. His movements, silences were those of the Indian.'[37] While it is unclear whose perspective is being articulated here, the use of the definite article and the implied singular, fixed cultural identity of 'the Indian' has a clearly othering function, marking his 'difference' from the narrator.[38] Yet at the same time, both the husband's critical comments about the man and the women's ambivalent desire for him are clearly called into question by the text. This unstable ambiguity of content is heightened by the writing's stuttering, evident in the compelling aesthetics and reiterative effects which come about precisely because of the attempt to write the unfamiliar landscapes, weather and culture of New Mexico. To think about Quin as a 'stutterer in language' here enables us to assess and articulate how her writing both reaches for and generates renewed articulation precisely through reiteration, and how, at the same time, this might function as a marker of cultural difference and difficulty. In this way, attending to the associative and oblique qualities of Quin's writing enables us to see her prose stuttering into being made.

## How to Approach Quin? Reading Sideways

This book begins with a sideways reading across Quin's unpublished and published material for two main reasons. The first is to demonstrate by example how working with her archive materials can enrich our literary critical work. This is why I open the discussion above, and the book as a whole, by engaging with Quin's private correspondence: to establish the key critical terms and concepts for my readings of her work, and to show that considering archive materials alongside and in dialogue with the published prose enables a particular appreciation of her experimental creative processes. By utilising the same methods for reading unpublished and published writing, I attempt to resist notions of progression or hierarchies that reify published works over and above archive materials. Instead, these materials are read as para-literary texts through which the back-and-forth of Quin's reiterative experimental methods become evident. Such an approach appreciates the ambivalent and ambiguous properties of Quin's prose and demonstrates the critical potency of the archive materials as a vital part of this work.

The second and connected reason I begin in this way is to introduce my reading methods via doing such work rather than describing or theorising it. My approach to Quin aligns itself with Maud Ellmann's in *Elizabeth Bowen: The Shadow Across the Page*. As the title indicates, there are connections between Ellmann's preoccupations and my consideration of Quin's writing 'designing its own shadow' in the examples above. According to Ellmann, Bowen's fiction 'constantly outsmarts the interpretative methods brought to bear on it'.[39] As a reader, her response is to 'attempt to shadow some of Bowen's most significant addictions', to listen to and account for the peculiarities of her writing.[40] My analyses of Quin throughout this book similarly aim to remain aware that her complex and multi-directional experimental work will undoubtedly exceed and outsmart my methods of reading and interpretation, and to be attentive to its 'most significant addictions' in terms of the particular and peculiar qualities of the work. Another suggestive model for my reading method here is Derrida's idea of the oblique as 'a strategy that is still crude', still being made.[41] An oblique reading is not 'an approach', it is not able (and does not want) to offer a definitive interpretation, or one that pretends to mastery. Instead, it recognises that the oblique stance and strategies of the writing – in terms of the askance mode of looking and reiterative processes in the examples above, but also in terms of the unstable literary critical position of Quin at the margins of dominant literary critical narratives – demand a similarly oblique response.

This book is a work of feminist critical recovery, even though, as Quin's precarious and fragmented archive and the ambiguous and deferred quests of her books suggest, her writing is resistant to recuperation. One of her early reviewers described Quin's prose as 'infuriating' and in previous work I have considered the critical usefulness of such a claim due to my interest in recuperative approaches – especially in feminist work which aims to recover marginal women writers – that might acknowledge and include as part of their response the 'negative' as well as 'positive' effects and affects of reading such experimental work.[42] In that essay, I aimed to take the complexity and difficulty of reading Quin's work seriously and to move beyond solely rhapsodising about or being defensive of her books, as Levy urges us to do. At the same time, as Levy also notes, the aims of Quin's experimentations have not always been acknowledged and this needs to be redressed. This current book develops my previous work to more fully and substantively celebrate and argue for the importance of Quin's writing, and to substantiate the cultural and literary purposes of her precarious prose. It seeks to recuperate Quin while acknowledging this can only ever be partial and uncertain, and to resist the urge to create a false narrative (in terms of either her life or writing) of triumph over adversity.

The five main chapters of the book offer sustained readings of each of Quin's major works – *Berg* (1964), *Three* (1966), *Passages* (1969), *Tripticks* (1972) and the unfinished *The Unmapped Country* (1973) – in order to introduce each in turn, and to follow the course of her thinking as it developed and changed. My analyses are extended and deepened by reference to short fiction, non-fiction and archive material. Across the book as a whole I read or refer to nearly all of Quin's published, and some still unpublished, writing, including manuscripts and letters. The inclusion and analysis of this diverse range of textual material works to enhance and enrich my thinking about the effects of her experimental prose. This book does not aim for coverage, however: rather, it attends to the particularly notable, striking and characteristic qualities of each of Quin's books, and hence the form and focus of each chapter differs in response to the work at hand. Throughout, my close attention to the aesthetics and details of her writing aims to open up the work, to be flexible and responsive, and to avoid a 'rigid or set' approach; to draw on Quin's words: 'I find the immediate moment gives one a whole experience, and therefore I hate anything to be very rigid or set.'[43] Read together, the five critical chapters reveal how precariousness is a pertinent and generative overarching notion with which to think about the shifting, unstable, unravelling, destabilising, fragmented, risky possibilities of her writing.

In '*Berg*: Shifting Perspectives, Sticky Details', I show how *Berg* oscillates between indeterminacy and incompletion, and intense particularities. I argue that the book opens up and overturns the Oedipus story via humour and uncertainty, and assess the effects of its unstable narrative frames and perspectives including a slippage of characters and pronouns. I also reveal how Quin's aesthetics of sticky details both express and destabilise the grimy material world of the book's bedsit setting, and consider how the textures of clothes and make-up enable Quin to write ambivalent gender and desire. The chapter finishes by reflecting on the different roles and effects of vulnerable bodies in *Berg*. In '*Three*: A Collage of Possibilities', I evaluate how the indeterminate trinary logic of Quin's writing subverts either/or structures and replaces them with both/and possibilities. I begin by identifying how this book uses confusion and uncertainty to play with and redirect the death drive, and by describing the forms and effects of the book's composite and polyvocal collage form. These, I suggest, are enhanced by Quin's engagement with nouvelle vague techniques to create the particular aesthetics and ontological uncertainty of this text. I also consider how the particular techniques and aesthetics of *Three* work to deconstruct and destabilise social and cultural structures such as coupledom/marriage and class. I finish by assessing the forms and purposes of Quin's writing of sexual violence in this book. Across *Berg* and *Three*, as my readings demonstrate, ideas of the home and of domesticity are refused and shown to be unstable, undesirable, dangerous even.

Both *Three* and *Passages* depict transgressive sex, and both employ different prose techniques and gendered perspectives to raise complex questions about gender and desire. In '*Passages*: Unstable Forms of Desire', I consider Quin's deliberate writing of static sex scenes and the disrupted female gaze to question the possibilities of female desire in the supposedly sexually liberated era of the 1960s, and assess how the book's stuttering and vibrating word-level prose is used to transgressive and energising effect. I argue that this book uses paratactic and fragmented forms to resist readability and mobilise the potential of mythologies such as Medusa and Antigone for thinking further about gender and the gaze, and that *Passages* most directly engages with its historical and cultural context in its writing of the female character's ambivalent desire for the Jewish man. This is a narrative in motion across a Mediterranean landscape and I assess how Quin writes the detail of precisely caught experiences along the way. *Passages* and *Tripticks* are both books of transit and displacement: the journey of the latter is a trip across America. *Tripticks* is also Quin's most overtly political text. Her experimental strategies in this book are deliberately risky and its tone oscillates between bravado and vulnerability. In '*Tripticks*: Impoverished Style as Cultural Critique', I show how Quin uses a surface of screens to mimic the experience of being on the road and in front of a television as a mode of questioning mainstream American culture, and explain how her writing simultaneously critiques 1960s counter-culture to reveal how this had already been co-opted by consumerism. I argue that this book uses cut-up words and pictures and a cacophony of clichés to create a deliberately impoverished style as an insightful mode of cultural critique. At the same time, the effect of this precarious writing in *Tripticks* moves beyond parody into a mode of serious irony that articulates a residual desire for meaning and depth, which is also represented by the book's silent scream.

Finally, my reading of *The Unmapped Country* argues that this text activates the precariousness of madness through Quin's unstable prose. I begin by considering how she was inspired by George Eliot's *Daniel Deronda* to find a way of writing the mind, and specifically the experience of madness. *The Unmapped Country* reveals how attempts to articulate or describe madness from outside the experience, from the reasonable position of a third person narrator, always fail. I show how Quin activates ambivalent stereotypes of psychiatric patients to expose the inability of language to get inside their experience, and how in contrast she writes madness as a paranoid reading of signs, revealing an intimate connectedness between reading and mad experience. I consider how *The Unmapped Country* uses reiterated visions of God to think further about the relationship between stereotypes and possible insights into madness, and argue that, when we attend to its reiterative detail, Quin's writing in this text unknits iterations and clichés of madness to unravel stereotypes and create a kind of maddened form at the stuttering word level of the prose. In this, while this final, unfinished book engages with its era in terms of the topics of madness and cold war paranoia, Quin's interest is also in the question of whether or how language might be able to write madness at all.

One of the challenges posed by writing this book was how to create a structure sensitive to Quin, one that would allow the uncertainties of the writing – its ability to exceed my interpretative methods – to remain. In addition, Quin's auto-fictional mode – gorgeously expressed in *Berg* as 'Threading experience through imaginative material' – makes the relationship between writing and life particularly blurry and unstable.[44] In response, as I have demonstrated in my reading of the letter and story above, I read sideways between the writing and life, and the structure of the book as a whole similarly aims to place the writer's life alongside her work. As such, in between the five main chapters I include six short interchapters or biographical vignettes, one of which, 'Quin's dark archive', opens the book as a whole. This is followed by 'A bedsit room of her own'; 'That same sea'; 'Have you tried it with three?'; 'Moving onwards'; 'Breakdown, breakthrough'. These texts narrate pivotal and pertinent aspects of Quin's life, providing the reader with insights that help to enhance and enrich our thinking about her writing.

This double form is a distinctive and integral aspect of this book. Not only does such an approach mirror and reveal how deeply personal her writing was, but the reader's encounter with this material indirectly alongside – and not subsumed into – the critical chapters compellingly communicates what is striking about Quin's work. It is precisely the non-integration of the biographical vignettes with the literary critical chapters that reveals the points at which Quin's life, writing, range of experimentations and political and cultural contexts are most productively interwoven. The resulting paratactic and fragmented structure deliberately aims to generate suggestive dialogues between writing and life that resist the notion of a 'comprehensive single author study' or 'master narrative'. It enables the book to be sensitive to and to in some ways require similar modes of being read across and between its different parts as those required by reading Quin. The reader might improvise an oblique reading approach – which, I suggest, is fruitful for reading Quin – and choose to read all of the interchapters in sequence, either before or after the literary critical chapters, rather than reading the book in the order it appears. She might note the repeated appearance of cats in connection with both disgust and pleasure across different sections of the book, or the repeated appearance of birds; she might be interested in Quin's immersive writing of the sea, or her writing of archival quests; or in how she writes transient spaces and places, or intense and surprising details. As these suggestions indicate, the overall aim of this hybrid structure is to open up, complicate and invigorate our readings and discussions of the precarious writing of Ann Quin.

## Notes

1. Gabriel Josipovici, *What Ever Happened to Modernism?* (New Haven, CT and London: Yale University Press, 2010), p. 182. Josipovici was one of the fiction writers included in Giles Gordon's *Beyond the Words: Eleven Writers in Search of a New Fiction* (London: Hutchinson, 1975), as was Quin.
2. Josipovici, *What Ever Happened to Modernism?*, p. 182.
3. For example, Sebastian Groes, *British Fictions of the Sixties: The Making of the Swinging Decade* (London and New York: Bloomsbury, 2016); Kaye Mitchell and Nonia Williams, *British Avant-Garde Fiction of the 1960s* (Edinburgh: Edinburgh University Press, 2019); Adam Guy, *The nouveau roman and Writing in Britain after Modernism* (Oxford: Oxford University Press, 2019); Andrew Hodgson, *The Post-War Experimental Novel: British and French Fiction, 1945–75* (London: Bloomsbury Academic, 2020); Julia Jordan, *Late Modernism and the Avant-Garde British Novel: Oblique Strategies* (Oxford: Oxford University Press, 2020); Carole Sweeney, *Vagabond Fictions: Gender and Experiment in British Women's Writing, 1945–1970* (Edinburgh: Edinburgh University Press, 2020); Joe Darlington, *The Experimentalists: The Life and Times of the British Experimental Writers of the 1960s* (London: Bloomsbury Academic, 2021); Andrew Radford and Hannah Van Hove (eds), *'Slipping through the Labels': British Experimental Women's Fiction, 1945–1975* (Cham: Palgrave Macmillan, 2021); Natalie Ferris, *Abstraction in Post-War British Literature 1945–1980* (Oxford: Oxford University Press, 2022).
4. There is perhaps even more readerly appreciation now than at the time. As has been widely noted, B. S. Johnson criticised the 'stultifyingly philistine [. . .] general book culture of this country' in which writers like Quin (and himself) were not appreciated. *Aren't You Rather Young to Be Writing Your Memoirs?* (London: Hutchinson, 1973), p. 29.

5. Jordan, *Oblique Strategies*, p. 143.
6. Ibid. Carole Sweeney discusses Brooke-Rose's 'Three words, Three Difficulties' – That of being a Woman, a Woman Writer, and an Experimental Woman Writer'. *Vagabond Fictions*, p. 2. And as Levy has observed: 'The word "experimental" kept her nicely in her place. All the same, I understand that being described as an "experimental writer" was more dignifying for a woman than some of the rancid versions of femininity available to her'. 'Ann Quin and Me', *Music & Literature No. 7* (Houston, TX: Taylor Davis-Van Atta, 2016), p. 120.
7. For example, my recent introduction to the *Women: A Cultural Review* special issue, *(Re)turning to Ann Quin*, which began with an overview of her life and work. If such an overview would be of use, please see Williams, '(Re)turning to Quin: An Introduction', pp. 2–17.
8. See Sweeney, *Vagabond Fictions*, in particular the section 'The Problems of Biography' in the chapter on Anna Kavan, pp. 38–42.
9. Ibid. pp. 1–2. In this, Sweeney positions Quin alongside Anna Kavan, Brigid Brophy, Christine Brooke-Rose and Eva Figes.
10. Maggie Nelson, *The Argonauts* (London: Melville House UK, 2016), p. 113.
11. Loraine Morley offers a rich and productive feminist reading of Quin and considers why earlier feminist scholars might not have engaged with her work in 'The Love Affair(s) of Ann Quin', *Hungarian Journal of English and American Studies*, 5:2 (1999), pp. 127–41. See in particular pages 127 and 133–5. Sweeney considers the problems of the essentialist move of aligning women's writing with experimentalism made by indisputably important early works in the field such as Ellen G. Friedman and Miriam Fuchs, *Breaking the Sequence: Women's Experimental Fiction* (Princeton, NJ: Princeton University Press, 1989). See *Vagabond Fictions*, particularly the section 'To be an Experimental Woman Writer: "Three words. Three difficulties"', pp. 17–30.
12. See Wilson, '"So thrilling and so alive and so much its own thing"', pp. 18–32.
13. 'Ann Quin was working-class – and an "avant-garde" writer. To be one or the other in addition to being a woman would have been sufficiently indecorous, to be both was downright impudent.' Claire-Louise Bennett, *Checkout 19* (London: Jonathan Cape, 2021), p. 177.
14. Quin, *Berg*, pp. 40–1.
15. Nell Dunn, *Talking to Women* (London: Silver Press, 2018), p. 190.
16. Claire-Louise Bennett, 'Introduction' to *Passages* (Sheffield: And Other Stories, 2021), pp. v–ix (p. v).
17. Quin, letter to Robert Sward, 18 July 1966, Robert Sward Papers, Series 1.1, box 10.
18. Quin, letter to Sward, 26 July 1966, ibid.
19. Quin, untitled poem written for Sward in Iowa, Robert Sward Papers, Series 1.1, box 9.

20. Quin, letter to Carol Burns, undated [but probably late June] 1966, *Carol Burns Private Collection of Papers*. All subsequent letters to Carol Burns are from this collection.
21. Quin, letter to Carol Burns, 18 July 1966.
22. In a conversation with me in 2009, Alan Burns described Quin's 'mode of looking': 'she was noticing out of the corner of her eye. Her glance, her own particular vision of world'.
23. This ambivalent notion of creation as violence calls to mind the wider preoccupations with sexual violence in Quin's writing; for example, S's violent fantasises and Leonard's marital rape of Ruth in *Three* (1966) and the Sadeian sexual fantasies in *Passages* (1969) discussed in my chapters below.
24. Quin, 'Never Trust a Man Who Bathes with His Fingernails', *The Unmapped Country: Stories & Fragments* (Sheffield: And Other Stories, 2018), pp. 95–107 (p. 95).
25. Ibid. p. 96.
26. Ibid. p. 96.
27. Ibid. p. 103.
28. Jacques Derrida, 'Passions: An Oblique Offering', *Derrida: A Critical Reader*, trans. and ed. David Wood (Oxford and Cambridge, MA: Blackwell, 1992), p. 24. J. Hillis Miller describes destinerrance as 'a temporality of differing and deferring, without present or presence, without ascertainable origin or goal'. 'Derrida's Destinerrance', *MLN*, 121:4 (2006), pp. 893–910, pp. 893–4.
29. Derrida, *Memoirs of the Blind: The Self-Portrait and Other Ruins*, trans. Pascale-Anne Brault and Michael Naas (Chicago and London: The University of Chicago Press, 1993), p. 87.
30. Though other critics (for example Julia Jordan's excellent *Oblique Strategies*) have recently considered obliquity in relation to Quin, my discussion here emerges directly out of my own long-standing reading of her writing in this way. See, for example, Nonia Williams-Korteling, '"Designing its own shadow" – Reading Ann Quin', doctoral thesis, University of East Anglia, 2013.
31. Quin, 'Never Trust a Man Who Bathes with His Fingernails', p. 99.
32. Louis Sass discusses glossomania as an aspect of language generated by sound, rhythm and association patterns rather than by sense, in his chapter 'Languages of Inwardness', *Madness and Modernism: Insanity in the Light of Modern Art, Literature, and Thought* (London and Cambridge, MA: Harvard University Press, 1994), pp. 174–81, particularly pp. 178–80. This kind of effect in Quin's writing is something I discuss further in my chapter on *The Unmapped Country*.
33. Gilles Deleuze, 'He Stuttered', *Essays Critical and Clinical*, trans. Daniel Smith and Michael Greco (London and New York: Verso 1998), p. 107.
34. Ibid. p. 110.

35. Quin, 'Never Trust a Man Who Bathes with His Fingernails', pp. 96, 100, 104.
36. Ibid. p. 95.
37. Ibid.
38. Quin's writing of 'others' elsewhere can be similarly challenging and ambivalent, for example the Jewish man and some of the local Mediterranean characters in *Passages*, and the Mexican characters in the story 'Eyes that Watch Behind the Wind'.
39. Maud Ellmann, *Elizabeth Bowen: The Shadow Across the Page* (Edinburgh: Edinburgh University Press, 2003), p. 4.
40. Ibid. p. 2.
41. Derrida, 'Passions: An Oblique Offering', p. 13.
42. See Williams, 'Ann Quin: "infuriating" Experiments?', *British Avant-Garde Fiction of the 1960s*, pp. 143–59. While my term was 'infuriating', taken from reviews of *Passages*, Sebastian Groes describes Quin's writing in *Berg* as 'profoundly, perhaps annoyingly self-reflexive'. *British Fictions of the Sixties*, p. 121.
43. Quin to Nell Dunn, *Talking to Women*, p. 185.
44. Quin, *Berg*, p. 7.

Vignette

# A bedsit room of her own

> Evenings spent in reading; half-heartedly doing homework, preferring to explore books discovered in the Public Library: Greek and Elizabethan dramatists. Dostoievsky (*Crime and Punishment*, and Virginia Woolf's *The Waves* made me aware of the possibilities in writing). Chekhov, Lawrence, Hardy, etc.
>
> Quin, 'Leaving School – XI', p. 16

Like Woolf, but in very different circumstances, Quin's literary education came more from library reading than formal schooling.[1] In 'Leaving School – XI' (1966), she says she 'sleepwalked through' convent school years in Brighton, 'More curious by what the nuns wore in bed. If they were really bald . . . than split infinitives', 'Amo, amas, amat' and irregular verbs. The 'possibilities in writing' of 'books discovered in the Public Library' were far more inspiring, together with Saturday afternoons at 'a seat in the Gods at the Theatre Royal'.[2]

Except for a brief return to education in her late thirties, Quin's schooling ended in 1953, when she was seventeen. Her first job was as an assistant stage manager, where she wrote poems in her lunch breaks and dreamed of becoming an actor, while spending time gathering props, scrubbing the stage, sewing, making tea, laughing at 'camp jokes I didn't understand'. But hopes of acting ended when nerves sabotaged an audition to RADA (Royal Academy of Dramatic Art), and Quin returned 'to the world of books' and to writing. She won a 10 shilling book token prize for her poem 'The Lost Seagull' and vowed: 'I would be a writer: A poet.' But without financial security, Quin was in desperate need of 'a means towards bread and butter', so she took a secretarial course and, 'Armed with shorthand and typewriting certificates I went to a secretarial agency in London.'[3]

From the mid-1950s to early 1960s, Quin was a secretary (and sometimes reader) in various legal, media and publishing offices, as well as at St Dunstan's in Brighton and the Royal College of Art in London, where she worked for three years. The year 1959 found her living in a room in Soho, working for a publishing firm during the day and writing her first novel, *A Slice of the Moon*, at night. Quin's living conditions at this time (and for much of her life) were precarious: as she put it, 'The salary I earned was barely enough for rent and food.'[4] In Soho, she was distracted by watching prostitutes from her window and dreamed of being able to afford books and clothes, a nice place to live in: 'a tower, facing the sea. I'm never so happy as when by the sea'.[5] *A Slice of the Moon* was rejected, as was her next book, 'about a man called Oscar, who kills his monster child – a novel that developed into a telephone directory length of very weird content'.[6] This book and *Berg* were both written while Quin was working in the painting department at the Royal College of Art and living at Lansdowne Road in Notting Hill – 'an attic kind of place, a small skylight, gas ring; partition next to my bed shook at night from the manoeuvrings, snores of my anonymous neighbour': 'There's a man through the wall there, in the next room, and he wakes me up in the morning vomiting, coughing and so on.'[7] The combination of paid work and writing was stressful and demanding for Quin, in material, creative and psychological terms. As she expressed to her publisher John Calder: 'What I don't want to do is to begin worrying about some bloody office job when I'm in the middle of or towards the completion' of a book.[8] Bennett's introduction to *Passages* puts it like this: 'When you are living from one measly pay cheque to the next with no clear sense of a future, day-to-day life is precarious, haphazard, fragmented, permeable, and beyond your control.'[9]

But this was Quin's lived reality, particularly at the beginning and end of her short writing life: unstable, interrupted, insecure. In order to have the private space – a room of her own – in which to write, she had to earn a living, and, aside from a few Arts Council and other grants successes, for the most part this was earned via poorly paid and often short-term secretarial work. Unlike Woolf's hope at the end of *A Room of One's Own*, that women writers of the future would have 'five hundred a year each of us and rooms of our own', Quin's precarious experiences as a working woman, with much time spent trying to earn an income, fretting about money and living in poverty at the same time as trying to write, were closer to those generations of women Woolf imagines at the start, when she thinks of the 'poverty and insecurity' which prevented them from writing and wonders 'what effect poverty has on the mind'.[10] Quin's room of her own was no peaceful, private space in a comfortable family home, but a small, often grotty and sparse living space, a bedsit, sometimes a sub-let, in a boarding house. Her piece 'One Day in the Life of a Writer' communicates how noisy and intruded upon this kind of 'private' space was – the landlady calls up, the window cleaner 'props ladder outside and stares in'. On the day being described, these and other disturbances interrupt Quin's creative process so much that 'the tone is all wrong. I'm no longer capable of writing'.[11]

### Notes

1. As Deborah Levy reminds us, 'It was hard for a working-class woman to get herself an education. Even Virginia Woolf found it a struggle to achieve a formal education, though her father had a well-stocked personal library.' 'Ann Quin and Me', p. 119.
2. Quin, 'Leaving School – XI', *The Unmapped Country: Stories & Fragments* (Sheffield: And Other Stories, 2018), pp. 15–24 (pp. 16, 17).
3. Ibid. pp. 18, 19.
4. Ibid. p. 20.
5. Giles Gordon, 'Introduction' to *Berg* (Chicago: Dalkey Archive Press, 2001), p. xii.
6. Quin, 'Leaving School – XI', p. 23.
7. Ibid. See also Gordon, 'Introduction' to *Berg*, p. xii.
8. Quin, letter to John Calder, 20 November 1964, Calder and Boyars manuscripts, Series II, box 52, folder 2.
9. Bennett, 'Introduction' to *Passages*, p. vi.
10. Virginia Woolf, *A Room of One's Own* (London: Grafton Books, 1987), pp. 108, 24.
11. Quin, 'One Day in the Life of a Writer', *The Unmapped Country: Stories & Fragments*, pp. 209–11, pp. 210, 211.

Chapter 1

# *Berg*: Shifting Perspectives, Sticky Details

## Opening up Oedipus

> A man called Berg, who changed his name to Greb, came to a seaside town intending to kill his father . . .[1]

Many readings of *Berg* have attended to this superb opening. As Kate Zambreno puts it, 'that first line of *Berg*, so stunning in its simplicity as to require its own page'.[2] Danielle Dutton has remarked, 'Rare enough is a book that begins by stating its intention', and Dulan Barber, Quin's editor, claimed that this opening announces the 'plot and essence' of the book and is 'incredibly well designed to lead the reader in and on'.[3] The 'intention', or 'plot and essence' of the book are this: Aly Berg, disguised as Alistair Greb, and inspired by an anxious, uneasy desire to please his mother, Edith, tracks down his estranged father Nathaniel, moves into a bedsit room next door to the one occupied by Nathaniel and his lover Judith, and fantasises about patricide.

That Quin is reworking Oedipus – in terms of both the Greek play and the psychoanalytic 'complex' – is clear, and this offers one way in to reading *Berg*. As Barber rightly points out, though, '*Berg* is an uncompromising, a ferocious Oedipal statement. It is not a retelling of the Oedipal story.'[4] Quin's setting is an out-of-season 'seaside town', and the Oedipus story is subverted via a bawdy camped-up theatre of hair, make-up and character substitution. Take, for example, Berg as Greb. Reversing the letters of Berg's name so that the invented and inverted Greb takes his place means that its protagonist enters the text as an already parodic, back-to-front subject. The name 'Greb' is like a nonsense word, and the narrative plays with the idea of who the 'real' or 'original' version is, Berg or Greb, as well as whether the fantasised patricidal act would enable him to become his 'real' self. As Berg suspects, however, this is a world in which 'not even the most indulgent of all actions "I shall kill" can make me declare "I am"' (31). As this example suggests, and as my readings throughout this chapter show, Quin's brilliant and witty reimagining of Oedipus works to open up and deconstruct both the form and content of the story, to reimagine its triangular geometry, and to refuse closure and heteronormativity, retaining space for uncertainty and, as Loraine Morley puts it, 'uninhibited exploration'.[5]

One way to think about Quin's refusal of Oedipal closure is via a reading of the opening sentence, to reveal the book's provisional stylistics. While this sentence does announce the 'plot' of *Berg*, Quin's play here with syntax and structure, and with modes of expression and narration, also enacts the book's 'essence'. Not only is it incomplete and without dénouement, as also the book itself – no full stop for Berg/*Berg* – but the dot-dot-dot both creates a narrative tension 'designed to lead the reader in an on' and marks the absent figure/s that complicate/s the relationship between pursuer and intended victim. While Berg and his father, Nathaniel, are directly referred to, the motivating force behind the intended murderous act – his mother, Edith – is not. Throughout *Berg*, narrated from Berg's perspective in a mixture of first and close third person, this absent figure dominates much of his thinking, and her voice is directly present in fragments of text that interrupt his perspective. The sentence's omission of the Oedipal third (Edith) and shadowy fourth (Judith) of the opened-up parent-child love triangle that obsesses the narrative is a clue that Quin is interested in refusing Oedipus via absence, incompletion and disruption. The opening sentence's emphasis on 'intending' and the ellipsis at its end dramatise the deferral and failure of Oedipal fulfilment via patricide by the end of the book, when not only is Nathaniel still alive, but he is living and listening in the room next door just as Berg is at the book's start, and Berg has replaced his father as Judith's lover. So rather than killing the father, Berg swaps places with him, almost *becomes* him: in this way Nathaniel's existence endures, and Berg's patricidal desires continue to be deferred and displaced beyond the book's close.

Throughout *Berg*, Berg's Oedipal intentions play out via three substitutions for Nathaniel's death: Berty the budgie, a death which upsets Nathaniel greatly – 'damn you, you know what you've done, killed the only thing I loved' (62); the ventriloquist's dummy; and the dead 'evil-smelling scar-faced bum' (130), the 'eyeless corpse' with a 'scar running from the left ear to the jaw' (143) who Berg identifies as his father to the police: 'Yes there's certainly a scar where you said sir, I am sorry' (149). As this example suggests, *Berg* refuses the tragedy of Oedipus and replaces it with a sometimes dark and sometimes farcical humour. The most drawn out and absurd of these substitutes is the ventriloquist's dummy, which enables a bizarre kind of rehearsal or 'acting out' of the failed patricidal act.[6] Nathaniel is excessively attached to the dummy – 'I made him with my own hands, took me a long time' (69) – it wears one of his best suits and is one half of his double-act; it is a puppet that speaks with Nathaniel's voice, wears his clothes and moves with his body. At the end of a frenzied and confused, drunken night, Berg 'mistakes' the dummy for 'the old man once more draped over the banisters' (71) and strangles it: 'There he is down there, beside the bed, rolled up in the rug' (72). At the same time, Berg knows that the 'body' isn't really Nathaniel, and there are numerous admissions of this, such as 'Strange how light the body was, considering – well considering the old man hadn't been just skin and bones' (78). This uncertainty about Berg's 'so-called action' (72) creates a drama of mistaken identity. Trying to exit the building with the 'body' rolled up in rug and eiderdown, Berg bumps into Judith in the hall of their boarding house, where Judith falls across it, and she asks, 'What's in it Aly, it feels like a body, it isn't, I mean you haven't—Aly what's under that ghastly eiderdown?' (82). This scene, while Berg tries to decide what to do about the body, is full of dramatic irony, for example when Judith says, 'Oh dear I nearly trod on it, I mean him' (84), and the person in the left-luggage office at the train station, 'What's this cor it's mighty heavy... What's rolled up in it eh—a body?' (94). And, even when Nathaniel shows up and Berg has to admit the body rolled up in the rug and eiderdown is the dummy, part of him cannot escape a need for it to be his father: 'I'm still thinking, acting in terms of a dead body, yes, going on as though it had been something real' (139). The comic, double sense of these examples, where Berg both is and is not aware of the failure of patricide, is one technique Quin uses to propel the book's Oedipal critique.

Quin also reworks Oedipus by mobilising and refracting several other versions of the story – such as Sophocles' *Oedipus Rex*, Freud's Oedipus complex and Shakespeare's *Hamlet* – in order to deconstruct and reimagine it. There are knowing references to Sophocles' play, for example Berg's 'absurd, fantastic idea: To take his father's corpse back home to Edith – the trophy of his triumphant love for her! In a Greek play they'd have thought nothing of it' (99) and his comment to Judith that 'it's all a myth' (83). And while some earlier readers of *Berg*, including Barber and Judith Mackrell, describe the narrative's engagement with Freudian ideas as 'unconscious' or 'instinctive',[7] actually by this point Quin had already read some Freud and Jung. In the following jokey letter to Carol Burns, for example, written when *Berg* was just finished, Quin directly refers to Oedipus and psychoanalytical notions of the unconscious:

> I came across (oh yes, of course, in the Oresteian Trilogy – thank you v. much, a delightful surprise!) the fact that Oedipus means sore feet. Do you remember at the end of Berg the father is going to take up chiropody? One could say Jung's collective unconscious at work here I suppose. But the truth of the matter was – my own father, when I last saw him, said he was going to be a chiropodist . . .[8]

This letter both suggests and disavows the notion of an 'unconscious at work' in the book's Oedipal parallels. The overlap, which connects Berg's and Quin's fathers' intended chiropody practice with 'the fact that Oedipus means sore feet', is in part constructed, in part happy coincidence. Quin's later Oedipal and psychoanalytical 'joke' to Carol Burns, referring to her father's death in 1973, evidences a similar play with potential parallels and overlap: 'He's gone . . . What a pity, I had intended doing him in myself!'[9] As Jordan points out, while 'Much of the energy of the dynamic in Quin's novel comes from the Freudian reading', there also, and this is particularly apparent in the dummy as substitute for the father, a 'nexus of anxiety and desire around the parental relationship' which calls psychoanalytical readings of *Berg* into question.[10] My reading here is not interested in attempting a 'Freudian reading' of Quin's book, but in drawing out the reading *Berg* already performs (and calls into question) of itself, in terms of how the 'Oedipus complex' is explicitly present in, and being ironised by, the text. The Oedipal story is not its unconscious but rather an overt consciousness, and Quin's reader does not need to excavate or interpret it because it is written right there on the surface. While for Freud, as Rachel Bowlby reminds us, it is crucial that Oedipal drives are unconscious, in *Berg* Quin consciously names – and therefore refuses and dismantles the usefulness of – Oedipus as a psychoanalytic or literary interpretative tool.[11]

*Berg* also contains more implicit intertextual references to Oedipus, such as the parallels with *Hamlet* when Berg names himself 'a ghost who walks abroad' (59). Hamlet, Freud's archetypal Oedipal character, lets chances pass him by while caught in doubt and indecision: Berg, too, misses parricidal opportunities even as he waits for them. This is dramatised and ironised in the narrative; Nathaniel might almost wink at Berg, and certainly at the reader, when he says,

'Here steady old man, nearly had me over then you know' (51). The Oedipal 'joke' here is on Berg's failure to act, and this is enhanced by the continual return to and divergence from other retellings of the story. His continual hesitation rather than 'ACTION!' (36) and the ultimate failure to commit the patricidal deed might seem to work in tension with the Oedipal framework announced at the start of the book, yet even there the phrase 'intending to kill' announces that in *Berg* Oedipus will be rewritten in terms of uncertainty and incompletion. To draw on Bowlby's thinking about Freud's version of the myth, in *Berg* Oedipus 'refers to desires, not deeds, and it is neither fulfilled nor resisted'.[12] In this way, via reversal, refraction and deferral, Quin opens up and overturns the Oedipal story.

## Unstable Frames and Perspectives

After its brilliantly suggestive opening sentence, *Berg* is framed by windows.[13] The narrative proper begins:

> Window blurred by out of season spray. Above the sea, overlooking the town, a body rolls upon a creaking bed: fish without fins, flat-headed, white-scaled, bound by a corridor room – dimensions rarely touched by the sun – Alistair Berg, hair-restorer, curled webbed toes, strung between heart and clock, nibbles in the half light, and laughter from the dance hall opposite. Shall I go there again, select another one? (8)

And ends:

> A window just cleaned. Above the sea, overlooking a town, a man motionless, bound by a velvet-covered couch, and a woman, whose hands flutter round a butterfly brooch. They stare at the piece of wood, five foot by seven, that shakes now and then – an animal thumping its tail . . . (153)

A comparative reading of these sections is useful for thinking about the complex, multiple, indeterminate and shifting quality of the perspectives in *Berg*. At the start, this is positioned as looking at (whether from without or within) the opening image of the 'Window blurred by out of season spray'. It is significant that this window is 'blurred' rather than being clean or clear, and the lack of definite or indefinite article refuses to tell the reader the window's significance. In this way, the position of this window is both directly stated, and yet also indirect. The missing 'the/a' and 'was' from this first sentence is a micro example of how Quin eschews conventional syntax, grammar and sentence structure, and how her writing utilises sound and rhythm patterns to create a disorientating and intense prose. In the next sentence, this window is located as being 'Above the sea, overlooking' the town. While 'overlooking' could suggest the perspective is from within the room, the distancing and objectifying effects of 'a body rolls upon a creaking bed' seem to position the perspective outside, looking in. Throughout *Berg*, narrative perspective and position is similarly shifting and uncertain. As Dutton says, 'It's often difficult to pinpoint where and when the stance of the narration, the point of view, shifts from within to without.'[14]

Quin's writing of incompletion is developed by the partial repetition of a similar scene at the end of the book, which has the effect of looping back to the book's opening images and of overlaying beginning and end. This means that despite the window being 'just cleaned' at the end, and therefore suggestive of a transparency and clarity that is not present at the start, the nearly exact repetition of 'Above the sea, overlooking the/a town', followed by the part repetition of a body/a man on a creaking bed/velvet-covered couch, blurs the images together and draws attention to the written surface as much as to the fictional world. These windows can be read as a metaphor for the shifting perspectives in *Berg*: the alternating or even co-present blurriness and clarity is an example of how Quin's writing is always a window onto the fictional world that the reader looks at as well as through. And this window is often more opaque than transparent, as the repetitive, overlaid opening and closing windows suggest. Elsewhere in *Berg*, windows also offer a partial view: 'Through a gap in the curtain, made by one stained finger, and if parted wide enough for a spider to slide through' (10). This is a reminder of how the view out of or into a window is always incomplete, limited by the outline of the window's frame and/or how smeary the glass is, as well as what kind of curtains or furnishings might be in the way. In *Berg* then, the framing device of windows draws attention to the position and function as well as the possibilities and limitations of narrative perspective(s) in (Quin's) writing. The book's framing windows, whether 'blurred by out of season spray' or 'just cleaned', call into question the relationship between the written surface and the (fictional) world.

Throughout *Berg* perspectives are similarly unstable and blurry to disorientating and immersive effect. There is the slippage or substitution between characters: for example, Berg 'becomes' his father, Berg 'becomes' Judith; Judith his mother Edith; the ventriloquist's dummy his father; and so on. The speaking voice in and of the narrative is elusive, and the narrative position continually shifts between third, second and first person, which disrupts reading and creates confusion about who is speaking. The first person 'I' has no fixed referent – 'I don't belong to anyone' (35) – and is exposed as a projection, an absence, a space where the shifting 'talk' of the narrative happens. What is experienced instead is a proliferation of multiple voices, where both first and third person make claims to interiority, it is often unclear whether these various voices are oral (therefore aural), or not, and speech aloud is not normally differentiated within the narrative in terms of conventional paragraphing divisions or speech marks.[15]

The result of these unstable frames and perspectives is that in *Berg* there is a complete absence of transparent or 'unwritten' metalanguage through which the fictional world can be clearly viewed. I am using the term 'metalanguage' after Colin MacCabe, where this is described – also via a window metaphor – as a narrative language that regards 'its object discourses as material but itself as transparent. And this transparency allows the identity of things to shine through the window of words.' For MacCabe, in 'classic realism' 'Whereas other discourses within the text are considered as materials which are open to reinterpretation, the narrative discourse functions simply as a window on reality.'[16] In *Berg*, where Quin is deliberately refusing to write precarious or working-class experience in a realist mode, the writing of blurry windows and the absence of metalanguage directly engages with, disrupts and denies the idea (or even the possibility) of transparent language. In this way, Quin's 'narrative discourse' rejects a stable narrative position from which a metalanguage might be spoken and it never 'functions simply as a window on reality'. It is never unwritten; instead the perspective and prose are always waxy, eccentric and vivid.

For example, not only is the position of the narrative perspective uncertain; it is also unclear what exactly is being looked at in the 'corridor room': 'a body rolls upon a creaking bed: fish without fins, flat-headed, white-scaled', it has 'curled webbed toes, strung between heart and clock, nibbles in the half-light'. This grotesque object is then directly named and introduced as Alistair Berg, the book's subject and protagonist, a hair-restorer and unremarkable seedy salesman selling dubious, almost comical, male vanity products. He enters the text as this surreal, fairy-tale creature, as inhuman, freakish and repulsive. The rolling on the bed, out-of-season spray and room overlooking the sea recall the motion of the waves, and the scaly fish-like body and webbed toes suggest some kind of mythical sea or water animal. The following shift to first person with 'Shall I go there again, select another one?' questions who is seeing Berg in this way, and to what extent the preceding description and perspective is internal or external. The view of 'the body' seems to be external, and yet the description is saturated with strange and subjective fantasy.[17] As throughout *Berg*, the physical world is defamiliarised here, partly by the form of the writing with its unusual and choppy syntax, partly because the weird images and details do not seem to make up a human 'body' or to describe a literary protagonist in a clear or recognisable way, and partly because of the indeterminate narrative perspective. In an early and insightful critical response to her work pertinent for thinking about *Berg*, Philip Stevick argues that Quin's writing is preoccupied with 'The texture of mind', and a conviction that 'the mind not only does not ordinarily tell stories – it doesn't even try to'.[18] Stevick points out that the simultaneous presence of such qualities is a significant aspect of the writing; 'it is in the nature of Quin's fiction that it takes place at several levels of discourse simultaneously, alternatively, contrapuntally' and the result expresses 'multileveled experience'.[19]

At the book's end, Berg is framed by the 'just cleaned' window as 'a man motionless, bound by a velvet-covered couch' rather than being 'a body' 'bound' in the corridor room next door, as he is at the book's start. This boundedness is a reminder of his constricted material circumstances and the entrapment of his precarious domestic set-up. The narrowness of the 'corridor' bedsit room, with its 'creaking bed' and 'dimensions rarely touched by the sun', is created by the fact that a larger room in the boarding house has been partitioned into two with 'the piece of wood, five foot by seven' which 'shakes now and then'. Berg begins the book in the 'half light' of the halved room on one side of the partition and ends up in the part room on its other side. The windows framing both scenes symbolise the lack of privacy of Berg's penurious living conditions, and the shaky and impermanent boundary, the partition which creates two cramped living spaces out of one, is insufficient, unstable and insecure, a point of contact as much as it is a border or separation. Both the material living space and perspective are precarious here. This is expressed by how the piece of wood (the partition) is animated, described in the book's final words as 'an animal thumping its tail ...'.[20] While this could be read as if the shaking movement is being caused by an animal, or possibly as a person being described in terms of an animal, in fact it is an example of how, in Quin's writing, the physical world is often activated and fluctuating, and the boundaries between fantasy and (fictional) reality disturbed and uncertain. The list-like details that introduce the human/inhuman 'body' at the book's start renders it strangely inanimate, as if the rolling action and creaking sound comes from the bed rather than the body: at the book's end the man is 'motionless', but the 'wood' is mobile, shaking and thumping. Read together, the incomplete forms and syntax that disrupt and rework the Oedipal frame, and the unstable narrative frames and perspectives, can be seen to perform the book's wider poetics of uncertainty.

## Aesthetics of Sticky Details

The shifting perspectives and unstable phenomenological world in *Berg* work in productive contrast with the intense and sticky details of the book's materially impoverished object-world. In her introduction to *The Unmapped Country: Stories & Fragments*, Jennifer Hodgson describes how 'Quin is particularly attuned to the grotesque details, to what she calls the "eggy mouthcorners" of ordinary life'.[21] For Hodgson, the stories '"A Double Room" and "Every Cripple Has His Own Way of Walking", especially, are redolent of greasy mackintoshes, milk skin, of bare, swinging light bulbs, of chintz and clag'.[22] *Berg*, which is saturated with ephemera and sticky details, is a striking example of such aesthetics, for example:

> ... the room, rumpled bed, the chest of drawers, that refused to close; the half open wardrobe doors, the chipped enamel pot with its faded blue flowers; the wallpaper making everything else collide; this morning's dirty dishes, half a brown loaf – a monk's cowl – perched on the pale yellow plastic table cloth; pin-striped trousers over the rose-chintz chair; pants, string vests; the case full of bottles, wigs, pamphlets. (9–10)

In this sentence describing Berg's cluttered bedsit corridor room, the cumulative list of rumpled, broken, chipped and dirty details accrue to create a grimy aesthetic, the signifying excess of which communicates an uncertain and insecure material world, and the sensory overload of Berg's environment: 'the wallpaper making everything else collide'. The mode of description communicates the peculiar intensity and specificity of Berg's bedsit setting. This is partly created by its tactile qualities, which exemplify the texture of Quin's aesthetic in this book. While the senses of sight, and elsewhere in the narrative, smell, are also important, *Berg* is particularly notable for the sticky, thickened and overly emphasised tactile textures of its written surface. Quin's story 'Every Cripple Has His Own Way of Walking' (1966) has a similar aesthetics and focus on broken and redundant objects. A young girl lives in a stale, cluttered house with strange, ailing and ancient aunts of almost monstrous appearance who wheeze in the night. Descriptions of the house take the form of a fragmented and list-like accrual of incongruous and obsolete objects, the precarious traces of family life such as 'Paper bags within paper bags' and 'Broken spectacles. Medicine bottles. Empty'.[23]

As with the refusal of an 'unwritten' window of narration and the reimagining of Oedipus, the aesthetic qualities of *Berg* are clearly named and expressed by the narrative itself. Throughout, and especially in early descriptions of Berg's material surroundings and childhood memories, words such as 'stained' and 'sticky' are often repeated: 'beer-stained piece of newspaper' (9); 'stained finger' (10); 'held by sticky hands' (10); 'sticky fingers' (14); 'A sticky, sickly child' and 'stained, rat-bitten cuffs' (17); 'stained, threadbare coat' (21). This evocation of Berg's stained and sticky surroundings has a double effect. Such descriptions do not so much aim to create or signify the 'realism' of the fictional world – although the detailed descriptions of Berg's bedsit do communicate the grimy poverty of his living conditions – or to describe the static materiality of an object-world that is just there and at a distance. Instead, the aesthetics of the writing are characterised by stained and sticky objects that express a particular sensitivity to the detail which alerts the reader to the precariousness of the fictional object-world. Here I am using 'precarious' to indicate both the instability of the book's narrative perspective and phenomenological world – the way this world is on the point of falling apart at the seams – and Berg's impoverished surroundings. As Bennett puts it, 'When I read Quin I recognise her fidgeting forensic polyvocal style as a powerful and bona fide expression of an unbearably tense and disorientating paradox that underscores everyday life in a working-class environment.'[24]

This quality of Quin's writing, where precarious experience is expressed via intense details, is particularly exemplified in a later description of the bedsit:

> But what precisely are you proposing to do now, yes you, a pauper who will soon be living off the National Assistance, digging purple toes into a threadbare rug, eyes avoiding the streaks of grease round the gas ring, the dust on the bottles, the chest of drawers, the cracked enamel pot, the crack that runs from one corner to another where the wallpaper ends in a map of Italy. Did these surroundings add up to

anything, had they a separate existence; say I decided to leave, would they mean nothing, absolutely nothing? (56)

This section is another example of shifting and uncertain perspectives in *Berg*, which here moves between addressing Berg as 'you' and 'I', and where, as a result, Berg's 'talk' 'is scarcely "inner" at all, it is rather like actual speech acted out in the theatre of the mind'.[25] It can also be read as a palimpsest of the initial description of the bedsit above, which more directly articulates some of the preoccupations and purposes of the book's sticky and stained aesthetics in terms of how the uncertainty of the material world in Quin's narrative expresses both ontological and phenomenological precariousness. In one sense, this example more directly refers to the material 'reality' of Berg's precarious financial situation and living conditions – he is a 'pauper who will soon be living off the National Assistance' in 'threadbare' surroundings.[26] At the same time, the narrative questions the signifying power of such surroundings vis-à-vis reality: 'had they a separate existence; say I decided to leave, would they mean nothing, absolutely nothing?'

This question, together with the multiple descriptions of the bedsit, alert the reader to how the sticky aesthetic surface both depicts and interrogates the veracity of the book's object-world. Rather than 'setting the scene' and describing the bedsit once, as a static surrounding, the several and variant descriptions of this space create a mobile environment that shifts and changes, partly determined by Berg's mood and preoccupations. Both descriptions of the bedsit include the chest of drawers, the chipped/cracked enamel pot, the wallpaper: both are sticky with 'dirty dishes' and 'streaks of grease'. Yet they also diverge and differ. As with the windows that open and close the book, these variant but overlapping descriptions create uncertainty, call into question what is being looked at, and where from/who by. Dutton reads a common lineage of aesthetics between Woolf and Quin whereby the 'flickering, unstable world of impression, Woolf's "shower of atoms", in *Berg* becomes a whirlpool into which we are sucked and tossed about'.[27] She refers in particular to a description of Judith and Nathaniel's living space, where 'plants, tall, thin, short, fat rubbery plants', create a mobile object-world that 'twisted on either side of him [Berg], sticky, clinging' against a static background of 'furniture, knick-knacks, artificial flowers' (66). Dutton's reading is useful for thinking about the divergent narrative effects that emerge from Quin and Woolf's shared interest in capturing the moment-to-moment movement of mind, and particularly for thinking about the heady and surreal qualities of the phenomenological world in *Berg*.

But as well as thinking about how Quin writes the object-world as animated by the perceiving mind, here I am more specifically interested in how the writing expresses the prosaic material world, and why the focus on broken objects and sticky surfaces. In my reading, the cheap, broken, stained and sticky details in the depictions of Berg's bedsit, and the 'furniture, knick-knacks, artificial flowers' of Nathaniel and Judith's, are significant particularly because of what and how such details signify.[28] As with the animated partition wall of the bedsit, the objects within the bedsit spaces are not static or 'just there', but neither are they wholly a product of mind. Instead, Quin's writing of the object-world has particular phenomenological effects. As Bennett brilliantly puts it, 'the status that things have been accorded is lifted away, and things are loosened and free again' from their ordinary categories.[29] Jordan focuses on the ontological questions raised by Quin's writing, which 'upends the traditional hierarchy between subjects and objects' so that the latter 'stubbornly refuse simple demands to be, simply'.[30]

Questions of what such details 'mean' and whether they are meant to express 'reality' are also bound up with wider literary, historical and contextual purposes. My thinking here is indebted to and engaged with Naomi Schor's idea that the 'sticky feminine world of prosaic details' can be read as a site of historical and political engagement.[31] *Berg* is set in a seamy off-season seaside town, and features tasteless and tacky interiors, disappointing sex and ambivalent desire. Quin works with similar ideas and aesthetics in 'A Double Room' (c. 1966), where two lovers meet at the seaside for a short break and (failed) sex in a second-rate hotel room: 'Yellow wallpaper. Yellow bedspread. Pink carpet. Shiny insect-yellow dressing table. Chintz curtains. But it doesn't even overlook the sea.'[32] In both texts, the setting is probably Brighton, scene of an infamous mods and rocker clash in the mid-1960s; a seaside town in decline, 'not yet come to terms with the fact that the old type of summer visitors and day-trippers from London were no longer coming to Brighton, but spending their holidays on package trips to the costa brava' instead.[33] This decline, together with its geographical position 'on the edge' of England, made Brighton ripe for literary appropriation as a liminal space. The seaside resort, note Peter Stallybrass and Allon White, is placed 'at the outer limit of civil life' and is therefore an ideal setting for literature whose form and/or content transgresses social norms.[34]

In this, the sticky details in *Berg* can be read as an arresting example of a wider aesthetics of decline and transgression also present in Brighton novels such as Graham Greene's *Brighton Rock* (1938) and Patrick Hamilton's *Hangover Square* (1941).[35] All revolve around mania, meaningless violence and murder; action takes place in insalubrious pubs; characters live in grotty bedsits; there are desperate women, and men in cheap suits. In *Berg*, how the seaside town setting is written seems particularly knowing and deliberate, and realism is denied: 'the cliffs, the shore, the façade of off-white lodging houses, the hotels, all discarded props' (32); the train station is 'a discarded film set' (124). Such details are not insignificant, and like the sticky details and surfaces of the interiors in *Berg*, they do not work to signify 'reality' but instead enact a historically and culturally specific mode of engagement with conditions of precariousness, liminality and decline.

## Performing Gender and Desire

The gender politics of the sticky world of prosaic details in *Berg* can be thought about via attention to make-up and clothing – tactile items which are used to hide and emphasise, perform and send up gender difference. Quin uses these to blur boundaries between disgust and desire, and a prime example of this is Nathaniel's lover, Judith. According to Berg, she is 'attractive, he supposed, in the artificial style' (11); 'her cheap but overwhelming scent [is] like incense' (42) and 'behind the dyed hair; the well-powdered face' (19) it is difficult to determine her age. Her first attempt to seduce Berg takes place, late at night, in the bedsit Nathaniel and Judith live in, a room that, as well as containing houseplants, knick-knacks and artificial flowers, is cluttered with heavy Victorian furniture, stuffed animals, wax flowers and fruit, 'draped it seemed entirely in purple velvet, reminiscent of an Egyptian tomb, square and dimly lit' (21). Having invited Berg into the room, Judith goes away to make hot chocolate and re-emerges having 'changed into a housecoat of shiny black material, rearranged her hair, now no longer bound by the net; her eyes carefully outlined into an oriental effect' (22).

As with the drapes of purple velvet, the colour and texture of the shiny housecoat are significant. Both fabrics are tactile and attempt to suggest luxury. In 'Notes for a Theory of 1960s Style', Angela Carter discusses the signification of clothing aesthetics in this time period. She says: 'Velvet is back, skin anti-skin, mimic nakedness . . .

velvet simulates the flesh it conceals, a profoundly tactile fabric', and 'satin invited the stroke, a slithering touch'.[36] Carter claims that velvet and satin bring with them the implicit promise of easy sex, and Quin's narrative plays with such symbolism. At his unexpected arrival at her room, Judith puts on the shiny black housecoat which is highly suggestive of nakedness underneath with its 'slithering' fabric and 'deep crevice in the middle' (23). As Stevick rightly notes, 'Clothes, in Quin, are always erotic.'[37] Judith has let her dyed 'yellow bush of' (21) hair down, unbound and freed it; she has also 'carefully outlined' her eyes. Perhaps she uses kohl, a cosmetic that, according to Carter, 'had the twin advantages of being extremely exotic and very, very cheap'.[38] The tactile fabrics, loose hair and make-up perform a femininity meant to incite Berg's desire. Yet Judith's face is also 'well-powdered', suggesting that she has much to hide, her dyed hair is a flag of artifice, and her scent is cloying. The accumulation of such details present Judith as cheap and tasteless, and in some ways Berg's ambivalent narrative perspective here reduces her seduction attempt to the rather clichéd performance of a 'predatory' middle-aged woman.[39]

In the above scene, Berg both is and is not attracted to Judith. Later in the book, the detail and texture of Judith's make-up and jewellery are similar markers of an ambivalent desire:

> He saw the powder on her cheeks had dried into small particles round her nostrils, and her hair, a blondeness that made one wonder what colour she was elsewhere. An imitation pearl necklace encircled her flushed neck, a few of the beads chipped – decaying teeth against three circles of her neck, above these her scarlet mouth that yawned and yawned wider, nearer. (79)

Here, details such as the 'decaying teeth' of the necklace, the particles of face powder, and the 'scarlet mouth that yawned' evoke both intimacy and disgust. While the image is clearly an erotic one – the dyed blonde hair making Berg 'wonder what colour she was elsewhere' and the gaping 'scarlet mouth that yawned and yawned wider, nearer' suggesting Berg and Judith's desire – it is also repulsive. Judith's face is too close, and her mouth extends in a silent, needy scream, ready to devour. Elsewhere, Judith's mouth 'seemed very near, very wide – large enough to hide my fingers, my hand, large enough to . . .' (66). As with other descriptions of Judith, these examples communicate Berg's simultaneous feelings of repulsion and desire, his lust for contact at the same time as a recoil in which 'disgust is deeply ambivalent', to use Sara Ahmed's words.[40] Ahmed's concept of disgust is useful for thinking about Judith because, as the lover of both Nathaniel and Aly Berg, she embodies the stickiness of a contact which is 'an effect of the histories of contact between bodies, objects and signs'.[41] Judith disturbs the boundaries between father and son; their contact with her in turn suggests a disgusting and ambivalent contact between them both. When Berg finally has sex with her, the whole act for Judith is a comparison, and ultimately a slippage and elision, between father and son. She says both 'Oh Aly make it last, he never could you know' (135) and 'do it again, oh it's lovely. Nathy, oh Nathy my darling' (135) while having sex with the same person (Berg junior). For Judith, the distinction between Alistair and Nathaniel Berg blurs: she desires both men, or rather, desires them as if they are one and the same.

A similarly ambivalent desire is revealed in how Berg's attraction to Judith is fuelled by his obsession with Nathaniel, voiced in an unsent letter to Edith: 'he's been fucking another woman next door, and probably a dozen others besides . . . meanwhile – well I'm going to fuck her too . . .' (58). From the beginning, Berg's campaign to seduce Judith requires not Nathaniel's death, but his continuing presence as voyeur and witness to confirm, or at least be subjected to hearing, Judith and Berg's sexual advances.[42] While she is preparing the hot chocolate and slipping into her shiny housecoat, Berg goes next door, to where Nathaniel lies slumped on his bed after a drinking bout, to check 'had the bastard meanwhile lost all consciousness, cheated me in fact?' (22). The seduction will only bring pleasure if his father hears all through the partition that 'separates' the two rooms. The movements and impermanence of this shaky and precarious border not only render it a somehow animate object; the partition also represents a 'sticky' proximity which intensifies the sense of contact between Berg and Nathaniel. For Ahmed, the stickiness of disgust has to do with borders being disturbed and made contact with, and this kind of effect is directly suggested in Quin's text when Berg (on several occasions) strains and presses himself against the partition.[43]

The sticky contact zone between Berg, Nathaniel and Judith is also suggested by the structure of the hot chocolate seduction scene, which is juxtaposed and split by Berg's moves back and forth between the two spaces. When he checks behind the partition, Nathaniel lies, to his satisfaction, conscious, 'heaving over the bed, mounds of vomit on the eiderdown, on the rug' (22). Here, the sticky surfaces of Berg's grimy bedsit are also sicky, and the disgust of this scene is heightened by further details such as Nathaniel's 'soiled underwear, torn at the back – three bullet holes' (19) and his 'stained threadbare coat, the socks with holes' (20). These could be read as a counterpoint to the sexy, slippery and tactile fabrics of the room next door, yet in Quin's writing – with its interest in texture, tacky surfaces and touch – desire and disgust always intermingle and blur together. This effect is encapsulated in the descriptions of Judith above, as well as throughout the narrative, for example the 'sickly sweet odour of underarms – grass after rain' (23), and Berg's own awareness of 'ambivalence' and 'a wave of nausea' within his desire for Judith (134).[44] These articulate the particular sense of intimacy created by the blurring or co-presence of desire-disgust. For Stevick, who is particularly attuned to the erotics of Quin's writing, 'the phenomenological world tends to appear as if charged with sexual energy'.[45] In *Berg*, the 'sexual energy' of the material world is often explicit, for instance when Judith and Berg meet in the hall over the body of the dummy and Berg's bag of hair tonic splits, they clear it up together, 'sliding in the tonic that spread in its mucus-like way right round them, between them, over them' (81). The pleasure of this scene is expressed overtly via deliberately 'sexual' language and details – 'sticky', 'soft wet tongue', 'biting', 'licking', 'wiping', 'wet fur', 'sneer, a positive leer' (81).

This sticky contact zone of disgust-desire between Berg, Nathaniel and Judith extends to Edith, Berg's mother. As with Aly and Nathaniel, there is slippage between Edith and Judith, in the brooches they both wear – for example, Edith's 'saved-up birthday brooch' (13) and Judith's 'glittering butterfly brooch' (151), the same brooch mentioned in the book's final scene (153) – and when their words begin to overlap and collide: Judith's 'My God Aly you do look a sight, really you do, what's come over you' is directly juxtaposed with Edith's 'Oh look at your lovely new coat all that muck on your trousers too. Oh Aly I told you not to' (144–5). Berg's relationship with his mother is a particularly ambivalent one; his memories of childhood and adolescence are marked by intimacy, unease and sometimes violence. Once, after Berg accidentally knocked off her 'Sunday-best hat' with a 'huge snowball, made entirely by yourself' (112), Edith 'her flushed face as she took you inside, produced the leather strap, the buckle end for you, for naughty boys who never love their mother' (113). Then:

> The white arms with veins, dimples and wrinkles at the elbow; you static over her knees, she rhythmically moving, the pleasure in her eyes, the pleasure that was yours. The sheer delight of not giving in to a single cry, and afterwards running out, blinking back the

tears, whistling, splashing yourself with water. Later her sighs, her soft kisses covering the bruises, the wiping away of blood that took longer, far longer than the cause. (113)

The close focus – 'veins, dimples and wrinkles at the elbow' – conveys repulsion and the 'bruises' and 'blood' violence. At the same time, the shared 'pleasure', 'her sighs', 'soft kisses' and rhythmic movements evoke erotic intimacy. Berg responds to the ambiguity of the contact by distancing himself, from his mother – the 'sheer delight of not giving in' – as well as from himself as a child: 'yourself' 'you static', and 'the pleasure that was yours'.[46] As elsewhere in the book, the pronoun 'I' eludes Berg here even though he is clearly the subject of the recollection as well as the one recollecting. This shift to second person wants to deny, at the same time as confessing, 'pleasure'. The vivid, detailed and intimate nature of this memory, coincident with the disavowal of agency, strikingly communicates the complex push-pull of desire and repulsion, of closeness and detachment, experienced by both Berg and Edith in their relationship throughout the book. In this ambivalent encounter between mother and son, the book's thematic concern with the sticky and porous boundaries between people is used to reimagine and restate the taboo of Oedipal desire.

Above, I have argued that make-up and clothes are a notable aesthetic signifier of ambivalent and sticky desire in *Berg*, and that Judith uses these to invite touch, perform gender and incite desire. Later in the book, these same 'props' are again used to subvert Oedipal desire, as well as to disturb sexual boundaries and binaries of gender and sexuality, in a scene where Berg performs as Judith. Here, Quin exploits theatrical techniques of (pantomime) cross-dressing and the bed-trick to make the taboo sexual tension of desire-disgust between Berg and Nathaniel overt. While hiding from the pursuit of his father and cronies after the 'murder' of the dummy has been discovered, Berg puts on a 'disguise'; he wears Judith's clothes, enjoying the feel of her nylons against his legs, which gives 'him an almost erotic pleasure'. Then:

> Putting one of his [father's] best auburn wigs on, he patted it into place, and arranged the fringe until it came well over his forehead and met his eyebrows. What about makeup? He went back to their room.
> He handled the cosmetics tentatively, then slowly powdered his face, his hands shook so much that at first he made a mess with the mascara. (109)

Berg's disguise in her clothes and his father's wig is completed by Judith's make-up, while he fantasises 'if only the navy were in' (109), a deliberate reference to Berg's homo- or bisexuality.[47] He is 'so taken up with his new appearance' (109) that he does not notice the door open, just as Nathaniel (supposedly) does not notice that 'Judy girlie, my little woman' (109) is in fact Berg in drag. Instead, Nathaniel attempts to seduce 'her': 'love come here, take those things off, here let me help you' (110). Then, with Nathaniel's 'Fingers running up his legs, further and yet further up' (110) Berg thinks: 'This is how it had been, with Edith, with Judith, how they must have revelled in it, giggling, panting, helping the old man's hands, opening their thighs, unsnapping their suspenders, arching their backs, opening up everything, wide—wider' (110), in a description reminiscent of Judith's gaping mouth. From this fantasising *as* his mother and lover/father's lover Judith, Berg then produces his 'flowerless stalk' 'in his [Nathaniel's] face, in his ear, in his eye, let him have it, so he'll remember to the day he dies' (110).

In this way, Berg, in auburn wig, powdered and mascaraed – both female and male at once in a strange amalgamation of Nathaniel, Edith and Judith – performs the narrative's most dramatic example of character slippage. In Quin's techniques here, there is an excess, a blurring and inversion of apparent binaries, and a transgressive humour which enjoys the shock of exposure, of creating discomfort and flouting taboo. The scene is not only another instance of the blurring of desire and disgust present elsewhere in the narrative; it is a particularly good instance of how Quin uses humour to send up and refuse heterosexual and gendered norms in *Berg*.[48] It is a clear example of how the book unravels conventions of masculinity, a thematic and aesthetic concern of the text that is connected to Quin's deconstruction of Oedipus and which, for example, Berg's job as a salesman of male vanity products alerts the reader to from the start. In this context, Berg's performance as Judith can be read as an enactment of the book's sense of gender identity as both performative and unstable. It is illustrative of how Quin's representations of gender and sexuality in *Berg* – as also across her oeuvre – refuses either/or binaries in favour of both/and. As Morley points out, the book 'is characterised by an indiscriminate identification with both male and female protagonists, and "masculine" and "feminine" roles, and by the perpetual rupture and dissolution of these roles'.[49]

## Vulnerable Bodies

In Quin's writing, particularly *Berg* and *Three*, characters lavish affection on pet animals – usually cats – instead of on their partners. These animals are situated as part of domestic scenarios, but they also disturb and disrupt those settings, highlighting a lack of intimacy and emphasising what Berg sees as the nauseous boredom of coupledom: 'this annihilation of domesticity' (136). Nathaniel calls his budgie, Berty, the 'only thing I loved' (62), and Judith complains 'he takes more notice of that blasted budgie than me sometimes, honestly I could scream' (23). Judith's own object of affection is Seby (or Sebastian), a Siamese cat: 'a lovely pussy then, isn't he a dear', 'my darling, my beaufos' (23). Berty and Seby are substitute love objects, recipients of tender words and caresses that incite jealousy in the character who is not their owner. These animals also offer substitutions and outlets for Berg's violent Oedipal desires and extend Quin's tactile and sticky aesthetics.

The killing of Seby, which happens early in the book, is described in dark and disgusting detail. The cat brushes against Berg's legs in the street near the boarding house, then 'began howling, dribbles of brown appeared on the pavement, as the animal half crouched' (29). Then,

> Berg lifted his foot. The cat, oblivious, continued shitting, howling. He stretched his hand out, the creature snarled, yellow fangs bared, and still crouching it started backing. Suddenly it sprang, hanging sloth-like on Berg's arm. He caught hold of its tail, and began swinging the cat out, hardly aware of the thud the creature made as it hit the wall. Only later he heard the cries, the howls. A limp body, twitching at his feet. Berg looked round, wondering if anyone had noticed the episode, the street appeared fortunately to be deserted. He picked the body up, threw it in the gutter. While wiping his hands he noticed how shredded they were, the blood stained his sleeves as well as his shirt-cuffs, with bits of fur clinging to them. (29)

I cite the incident in full here to give a sense of how visceral and detailed the scene is, much more so than the more direct substitutions for patricide – the strangling of the dummy, for example. Berg lifts his foot as if to use it, but the actual killing of the cat is done with his arm, bringing him close to the act even though the death may be accidental. But, while it is unclear how conscious he is as it happens – he is 'hardly aware of the thud' and only later hears the creature's cries – Berg does notice that the street is 'fortunately' deserted, suggesting a level of awareness. The perspective remains distanced from Seby who is referred to as 'the creature', 'A limp body', which snarls, howls, springs, has yellow fangs, metamorphoses into a sloth. Despite these forms of distancing, the scene is brought close by how active and noisy it is, by the sense of touch and sticky texture of Berg's blood-stained clothing – his sleeves and shirt-cuffs, shredded with bits of fur on. The killing of Seby is unexpected and meaningless; it also, inadvertently, serves Berg's ends by creating a rift between Judith and Nathaniel because she blames the cat's death on him. The act also later haunts Berg's interactions with Judith in the form of a repeated 'smell of wet fur' (49), which implies both sexual desire and Seby's violent death. Coming early in the narrative, the incident suggests a capacity for violence in Berg that remains unrealised elsewhere. While this scene is a dark one, there is also a sense in which at the same time 'Berg's violence is a joke', as Dutton points out.[50] Berg is only capable of killing a pet cat and not his father, and the violence in this scene is 'violence' in quotation marks. The scene is sinister and yet absurd, written with an aesthetic instability of bloody, shitting grotesqueness and grim humour.

Berty's fate is more bizarre and disconcerting. The bird ends up as:

> a small yellow object on the table, like one of those tattered powder puffs women produced from their bulging handbags. He [Berg] picked it up. No mistaking this, the same, the only one, the blasted bird, with its brown slits for eyes. (107)

This small yellow object is Nathan's budgie, which has died (whether by Judith's revenge murder for Nathaniel's assumed role in Seby's death or by neglect is unclear), been dropped down the stairs in its cage by Berg, buried by Nathaniel, and then dug up. Here, the exhumed body lies on the table amidst the clutter of Nathan and Judith's flat. The dead budgie no longer resembles an animal, but instead is presented as a tattered powder puff, a vanity tool. The details of the description, the smallness of the 'blasted bird' and the contrasting 'bulging handbags', highlight the meaningless cruelty of the book's characters: 'an unlikeable group of ridiculous people' as Zambreno calls them.[51] The parallel between bird and powder puff is both funny and disturbing in that its intimacy invites the reader to imagine what it would feel like to use this little bird's body to put powder on their face: in this it is a tacticle and immersive connection back to the sticky aesthetics of ambivalent desire signified by make-up in *Berg*; indeed Berg discovers Berty's body just before he makes himself up as Judith.

The connection between violence against animals in terms of their vulnerable bodies and brief lives, and the sticky, grimy details of *Berg*, is even clearer in Berg's killing of a moth in his bedsit. The moth dies by deliberate inaction: 'A moth bumped against the wall, the door, the light. Berg's fingers strayed, lingered on the switch. The moth sizzled against the bulb, now wingless fell' (11).[52] Later, when warming some milk, 'he noticed a brown bur floating about. He scooped the moth out, and pressed it on the edge of the saucer', then 'stirred the milk, and taking a layer of skin off, he put it over the moth in the saucer' (20). The detail of the dead moth is part of the milk-skinned clag of the prose here and works to not only emphasise the sticky and tactile aesthetics of the grimy bedsit, but to reinforce the ontological precariousness and temporariness in *Berg* – of living spaces, perspectives, bodies and genders. It is an example of how Quin's writing uses sticky and intense details to signify dissolution and dispersal.

Berg's experience of his own body oscillates between nausea and disgust at its particularities, and feelings of blissful dissolution – this ambivalence is suggested right from the start when his body is described as a fish without fins rolling on a bed. As with Antoine Roquentin in Sartre's *Nausea*, Berg's feelings come not only from the disgust he feels at the trap of domesticity and his sense of disgust-desire for Judith, but from an absurd awareness of and recoil from his physical body: 'every muscle straining forward, each finger tingled with blood; conscious even of the grey hairs, the dirt between toes, the wart near his navel, the mole under his left arm' (34).[53] This disgust is directly named when he looks in the mirror and notices 'with a slight nausea how yellow his teeth were' (98). The mirror plays a key role in Berg's sense of alienation from himself:

> He caught sight of his reflection; Machiavellian to say the least, rather startling to see the surface revealing in fact so much of what he only partially felt. How macerated the cheeks were, fairly sunken in, making his eyes so huge, his neck mottled, stork-like. (107)

The startling ashen face with sunken-in, macerated cheeks, the protruding eyes, the mottled and bird-like neck, the animal fur adorning his face – all show Berg's alienation from himself and others.

Yet elsewhere Berg experiences a blurring and communion with his surroundings which is often connected with the sea: 'the glorious sensation of weightlessness, moon-controlled, and far below your heart went on exploring' and 'the awareness of becoming part of, merging into something else' (141). For Jordan, such moments have an ethical purpose: 'Quin often seems to suggest that the body's porousness is ethically exemplary: a good way to be. It is generative for us to be open to the world.'[54] These experiences happen when Berg is alone, mostly with nature, and are experienced as a comforting depersonalisation, a kind of ecstasy and freedom from the awkward self-consciousness he experiences in the social world. In them he feels 'welcomed by the natural order, a slow sensuality that circles the sun, rode the wind through the grass-forests, then nothing mattered, because everything comprehended your significance' (17).

> Aware of own shell, skin-texture, sun in eyes, lips, toes, the softness underneath, in between, wondering what miracle made you, the sky, the sea. Conscious of sound, gulls hovering, crying, or silent at rarer intervals, their swift turns before being swallowed by the waves. Then no sound, all suddenly would be soundless, treading softly, diving rocks with fins, and sword-fish fingers plucking away clothes, that were left with your anatomy, huddled like ruffled birds waiting. A chrysalis heart formed on the water's surface, away from the hard-polished pebbles, sand-blowing and elongated shadows. Away, faster than air itself, dragon-whirled. Be given to, the sliding of water, to forget, be forgotten. (140)

Here, the edges of Berg's imagination and perhaps even of his physical body are experienced as if porous and fluid and his feelings of alienation dissolve. The immersive prose is infused with an 'awareness of becoming part of, merging into something else' (141). This effect is achieved by sound and image association. Not only does Berg's 'shell' or outer body merge with the shells on the beach, but the soft sibilant 's's evoke the sea and blur the words and images together, as does the tracking of sound patterns – the movement from 'swift' to 'swallowed' to 'waves' – and part-rhymes – for example, 'eyes'/'sky' and 'fins'/'fingers'. The narrative reminds us to listen to it; to be 'conscious of sound'. In this, Berg's mode of mind seems bound up with a poetics of slippage which the mind's eye and ear are invited to track. According to Mackrell, Quin's writing of this kind of immersive, expansive experience is a particularly effective 'technique . . . to render a faithful impression of the continuous and subjective present of Berg's consciousness'.[55] Indeed, this notion of a continuous present is central to the concept of time in the narrative as a whole, which refuses linear progression and hence also conventional notions of time passing. The seeming fluidity here in fact creates a kind of temporal stasis, a 'frozen' and ecstatic moment, where the description bleeds outwards rather than onwards. Berg's experience is of being without a frame, of dissolving into the surrounding, sensory world. This scene is one example of how, in *Berg*, the wider oscillation between shifting perspectives, slippage and disintegration, and specific, sensory and sticky details is written in particularly evocative ways in relation to the sea.

## Notes

1. Quin, *Berg* (Sheffield: And Other Stories, 2019), n.p. Unless otherwise stated, page references for *Berg* in this chapter will be to this edition and in parenthesis in text.
2. Kate Zambreno, 'The Ventriloquist: A Brief Meditation on Ann Quin', *Music & Literature* No. 7 (2016), p. 147.
3. Danielle Dutton, 'Unpacking Ann Quin's Comic Tragedy', *Music & Literature* No. 7 (2016), p. 149; Dulan Barber, 'Afterword' to *Berg* (London: Quartet Books, 1977), p. 169. The opening of *Berg* has been hailed as impressive, iconic even, by many of its readers, for example Lee Rourke: 'I only had to read the first line to become hooked', review in *The Independent*, 27 August 2010.
4. Barber, 'Afterword', p. 170.
5. Morley, 'The Love Affair(s) of Ann Quin', p. 134.
6. Julia Jordan reads this aspect of the book, where the dummy is substituted for the father, and Berg then 'replaces' his father, as evidence of both the uncertainty and revocation of Berg's father's ontological status and that the artistic notion of creation is itself at stake. *Oblique Strategies*, p. 155.
7. See Barber's 'Afterword', p. 170, and Judith Mackrell, 'Ann Quin', in *British Novelists since 1960, Dictionary of Literary Biography*, ed. Jay Halio (Detroit: Gale Research, 1983), p. 609.
8. Quin, letter to Carol Burns, 29 January 1963. Quin also mentions Freud's 'no. 7 volume 1, on anxiety-neurosis, obsessions and phobias etc.', letter to Carol Burns, 31 March 1962.
9. Carol Burns, piece in memory of Quin, unpublished manuscript, Carol Burns Private Collection of Papers, p. 5.
10. Jordan, *Oblique Strategies*, p. 155.
11. Rachel Bowlby reminds us that 'Oedipus gave Freud not just, perhaps not even primarily, the two crimes of incest and parricide, converted in his theory to universal infantile wishes; it also gave him the unconscious'. *Freudian Mythologies; Greek Tragedy and Modern Identities* (Oxford: Oxford University Press, 2007), p. 6.
12. Ibid. p. 234.
13. The framing effect of windows in *Berg* recalls 'The Window' section in Woolf's *To the Lighthouse*. In that book scenes are framed by windows

and picture frames, what is seen is partial or abstract, and narrative perspective shifts in and out of interiority. Hilary White offers an illuminating reading of *Berg* in terms of the frame in 'The Limits of Looking: Conceptualising the Frame in Ann Quin's *Berg* and Christine Brooke-Rose's *Out*', *Angles*, 13 (2021), doi: 10.4000/angles.4398.
14. Dutton, 'Unpacking Ann Quin's Comic Tragedy', p. 154.
15. R. D. Willmott charmingly puts it thus: that Quin's 'prose style, though it is direct enough, is unconventional and goes against accustomed reading habits'. He himself thinks 'Quin has something original and worthwhile to offer', but he believes some readers 'may feel disinclined to make the effort' of muddling their way through seemingly undifferentiated prose. 'A Bibliography of Works by and About Ann Quin', *Ealing Miscellany, Number 23* (London: Ealing College, 1982), p. 3.
16. Colin MacCabe, *James Joyce and the Revolution of the Word* (London and Basingstoke: Macmillan, 1978), pp. 14, 15. For MacCabe, this relationship between metalanguage and object discourses is a defining feature of 'the *classic realist text*', and George Eliot is his example. I challenge this reading of Eliot in the final chapter on Quin's *The Unmapped Country*.
17. For Jordan, Quin is 'subjective inasmuch as she understands the phenomenal world as responsive to individual perception, and indeed as created by it'. *Oblique Strategies*, p. 142.
18. Philip Stevick, 'Voices in the Head: Style and Consciousness in the Fiction of Ann Quin', in *Breaking the Sequence: Women's Experimental Fiction*, ed. Ellen G. Friedman and Miriam Fuchs (Princeton: Princeton University Press, 1989), pp. 231–9 (p. 237).
19. Ibid. p. 236.
20. This description of the partition echoes and is animated by an earlier description in the book: 'the partition shuddered – an animal in pain', p. 74. The partition is similarly animated in 'Didn't the partition speak for itself?' p. 49. Throughout *Berg* the word 'partition' occurs twenty-five times (my thanks to Antonia Cook for pointing this out).
21. Jennifer Hodgson, 'Introduction' to *The Unmapped Country: Stories & Fragments* (Sheffield: And Other Stories, 2018), pp. 7–12 (p. 10). This is probably a reference to Quin's story 'Ghostworm' (1969) – 'newspapers, eggy mouthcorners, the smell of dirty sheets, toothpaste', *The Unmapped Country: Stories & Fragments*, pp. 125–50 (p. 147) and *Passages* – 'Smudges of egg at the mouth corners', p. 8.
22. Hodgson, 'Introduction', p. 10.
23. Quin, 'Every Cripple Has His Own Way of Walking', *The Unmapped Country: Stories & Fragments*, pp. 51–64 (p. 51). References to Berg's grandma and great-aunt in *Berg* (pp. 96–7) are very similar to some of the descriptions of the grandma and great-aunts in 'Every Cripple Has His Own Way of Walking'. A similar childhood environment with great 'Auntie M' is also remembered by the character S in Quin's *Three*,

which also includes the specific detail of 'paper bags'; *Three* (Sheffield: And Other Stories, 2020), pp. 27–9 and p. 69.
24. Bennett, *Checkout 19*, p. 178. See also Bennett, 'Introduction' to *Passages*, p. vi.
25. Stevick, 'Voices in the Head'. He continues: 'quite far from seeming a gratuitous experimentalism, Quin's fictional technique comes to seem a perfectly natural way of rendering a mode of mind', p. 232.
26. In a childhood memory, Berg remembers how he was taunted with 'hasn't got a dad, his mum pawns herself to pay the fees', *Berg*, p. 16.
27. Dutton, 'Unpacking Ann Quin's Comic Tragedy', p. 153.
28. Elsewhere I have considered how broken, lost and forgotten objects might create a reality effect that exceeds the text. See Williams, "LOST! HANSOME GOLE BROOCH': Broken, Lost and Forgotten Objects in Woolf, Mansfield and Stein', in *Modernist Objects,* ed. Noelle Cuny and Xavier Kalck (Clemson, SC: Clemson University Press, 2020), pp. 209–24.
29. Wilson, '"So thrilling and so alive and so much its own thing", p. 25.
30. Jordan, *Oblique Strategies*, p. 153.
31. See Naomi Schor, 'Reading in Detail: Hegel's *Aesthetics* and the Feminine', in *Feminist Interpretations of Hegel*, ed. Patricia Jagentowicz Mills (University Park: Pennsylvania State University Press, 1996), pp. 119–47 (p. 145).
32. Quin, 'A Double Room', *The Unmapped Country: Stories & Fragments*, pp. 31–50 (p. 35).
33. Stanley Cohen, *Folk Devils and Moral Panics: The Creation of Mods and Rockers* (Oxford and New York: Basil Blackwell, 1987), p. 195.
34. Peter Stallybrass and Allon White, *The Politics and Poetics of Transgression* (Ithaca, NY: Cornell University Press, 1986), p. 191.
35. In a rather dismissive and patronising review of Quin's work, Robert Nye described *Berg* as: 'chiefly remarkable for its evocation of Brighton . . . its emotional intensity nearer the early work of Graham Greene than the fashionable French new-wavers its author . . . imagined she was imitating'. 'Against the Barbarians', *The Guardian*, 27 April 1972.
36. Angela Carter, 'Notes for a Theory of 1960s Style', *Nothing Sacred: Selected Writings* (London: Virago, 1992), p. 85.
37. Stevick, 'Voices in the Head', p. 235.
38. Carter, 'The Wound in the Face', in *Nothing Sacred*, p. 97.
39. Elsewhere Berg expresses a rather sneery and sexist view of Judith: 'how women's voices altered to suit the occasion, to gratify their ends', p. 21; 'nag, nag, nag – women', p. 52; 'the nonsensical babble of this whore, a bitch-goddess', p. 89; 'bitch-goddess', p. 105, etc.
40. Sara Ahmed, *The Cultural Politics of Emotion* (Edinburgh: Edinburgh University Press, 2004), p. 84. See also pp. 84–8.
41. Ibid. p. 90.

42. In fact, his father's continuing presence is so bound up with his desire for Judith that Berg worries, 'he had to admit it, there was the possibility she would not prove so fascinating after his father's death', p. 65.
43. See Ahmed, *The Cultural Politics of Emotion*, pp. 88–9; *Berg*, pp. 15, 25, etc.
44. Berg's nausea is 'caused by an acute attack of boredom, the futility of everything, especially the game of human relationships', p. 134. Once the obsession with Judith's sexual allure has begun to fade, their resulting domestic relationship provokes scorn: 'Yes let's have a proper meal, with a proper woman sitting opposite, with a proper plastic table cloth, a proper pink, with proper yellow cups and saucers, and a proper clock ticking over with the proper time', p. 148. The repetition of 'proper' here, and the idea of the 'game of human relationships', deflates desire and ridicules domesticity. The colours of this description are reminiscent of the yellows of the hotel room in 'A Double Room', p. 35.
45. Stevick, 'Voices in the Head', p. 234.
46. As Ahmed reminds us, disgust requires both proximity and knowledge for the recoiling and distancing that follow. *The Cultural Politics of Emotion*, p. 85.
47. Berg's homosexuality is suggested elsewhere in *Berg*, for example in his memories of being called a 'cissy', p. 16, and of 'Letters, Proust-like to a friend, George into Georgina', p. 126; in Edith's 'dreadful shame' at what she calls his 'evil lust', p. 16; in the question 'you're not one of those' and the problematic 'warning' that he might 'turn queer', p. 125. There is also a sense in which Berg is almost epicene, with a 'Longing to be castrated', p. 10.
48. For an interesting reading of this aspect of the book, see Noriko Nishino, '"Fish without Fins" in the Heteronormative Sea: Ann Quin's Queer Experiment in *Berg*', in 'Between Fluidity and Stability: Reading Ann Quin's Experimental Novels', doctoral thesis, University of Tokyo, 2021, pp. 22–59.
49. Morley, 'The Love Affair(s) of Ann Quin', p. 134.
50. Dutton, 'Unpacking Ann Quin's Comic Tragedy', p. 149.
51. Zambreno, 'The Ventriloquist', p. 150.
52. In a letter to her friend Paddy Kitchen Quin wrote: 'I never seem happy to settle down anywhere for long – like a moth searching for the light and maybe when I touch the light it will burn me up', quoted in Kitchen, 'Catherine Wheel: Recollections of Ann Quin', *London Magazine*, 19 (June 1979), pp. 50–7, (p. 53). Clarke has thought about the connection between Quin's imagining herself as a moth and her experiences of being a female writer in '"S" and "M": The Last and Lost Letters Between Ann Quin and Robert Creeley', see pp. 36–8. I can't help but read the moth's death in *Berg* as somehow aware of Woolf's essay 'The Death of the Moth' given Quin's familiarity with her writing.

53. Quin wrote: 'Sartre said it all much better in NAUSEA – I mean the futility a man feels about his existence' and 'BERG turning out to be a comedy now'. Letter to Carol Burns, 15 May 1962.
54. Jordan, *Oblique Strategies*, p. 162.
55. Mackrell, 'Ann Quin', p. 609.

Vignette

# That same sea

> ... the sea is referred to so often in her writing, the sound of it, the smell of it, the waves, the weed, the rocks, that it's quite clear she had some kind of relationship with the sea, to the extent that she felt she was of it perhaps ...
>
> Claire-Louise Bennett, *Checkout 19*, p. 176

Quin's writing is fascinated by water and especially the sea; with the textures of seaweed and sand, the briny tang and uneven contours of the beach, the feeling of being in the water. For Stevick, this sensory writing of the sea is also a sensual one: 'No one makes water more sexual than Quin: the sea, the river, the wash basin, the hot-spring pool, the hotel shower, the swimming pool.'[1] In *Berg* the sensuality of being immersed in water is directly expressed when Berg and Judith are having sex, as 'Entering the sea. The sea alone. Alone by the sea. By the sea. Alone. By yourself. Oh it's nice when you do that, do it again, oh it's lovely.'[2] While elsewhere their sexual encounters are ambivalent or disappointing, Berg's experience with Judith here is 'lovely', like entering water, as if it is the sea he is having sex with, a suggestion enhanced by the rhythmic part repetitions of mainly monosyllabic words, which also mimics the rippling rhythms of the water. In *Passages*, the male protagonist asks, 'Is it her body I hold in my arms or the sea?'[3] Bennett's idea of Quin's intimate 'kind of relationship with the sea, to the extent that she felt she was of it perhaps', is suggested by these descriptions of sensations of immersion and blurring between bodies and the water.

Quin grew up by the sea and was a strong swimmer; she also died by drowning off the same coast that she had lived by as a child. As Bennett puts it, 'Ann Quin went into that same sea and did not come out again.'[4] Unlike Woolf, who left a suicide note and deliberately drowned herself in a river, the causes of Quin's death at sea are unknown. On a hot August Bank holiday weekend in 1973, aged thirty-seven, Quin took off her clothes and walked slowly into the sea at Black Rock, Brighton, watched by a man fishing. She then swam too far out, with slow, deliberate strokes, and drowned. It is not clear what her purpose was. Was she seeing visions or being called by the mystical voice of the ocean? Was she echoing Woolf with suicide by drowning, or was it a horrible accident? Quin's body washed ashore at Shoreham a week later, and the coroner's report gave an open verdict, the death certificate recording 'death by drowning'.[5]

Quin's writing of the sea is not only fascinated by blissful sensations of being in the water, but by the possibility of drowning and oblivion too. The macabre story 'Nude and Seascape' (undated) suggests an intimate connection between death, the sea and aesthetics. A man grapples with and drags a woman's dead body across a beach, arranging it in different positions and eventually cutting off the head in his attempt to make art. He is disappointed in the result, deciding that the severed head 'seemed too perfect, far too beautiful', but that 'in a certain light and shade, in the corner, where he had left it, forgotten, the body looked better than it ever had before'.[6] The story ends with the man wading out into the sea. In the 1950s, Quin had written to her friend Paddy Kitchen saying that 'woman is halfway in mid-stream and can never quite reach the bank but has one leg in the estuary and misses the boat out to sea [. . .] men do but at least they are given the opportunity of drowning in the ocean and not in a mere river'.[7] Here, drowning at sea is a metaphor for being taken seriously as an artist, as Quin expresses her frustrations about a gendered lack of opportunities for women writers. In 'Eyes that Watch Behind the Wind' (1968), an intense short story about the painful end of a love affair, set in New Mexico, the female protagonist seems close to drowning in the ocean when she enters wild and dangerous 'Waves she was for the first time in her life frightened of' and:

> threw her body, no longer her body, but just a body hurled out of the ground, into the mountains of water, she bent her head under, rose up, bent again, and struggled out [. . .]
> And if she returned?
> If she chose not to, but moved on out into the ocean until perhaps the areas she had so nearly reached could be touched upon.[8]

This last sentence recalls Berg's ecstatic and expansive feelings of floating in the sea, to 'Be given to, the sliding of water, to forget, be forgotten', a peaceful desire for oblivion that contrasts with the desperate yet thrilling struggle with the 'mountains of water' at the start of the extract.[9] And *Three*, which Quin began more than ten years before her death, while living in her turret room at Lansdowne Road and working at the Royal College of Art, revolves around the mystery of the central protagonist's drowning, a drowning that perhaps foreshadows its writer's own, final, journey into the sea. This potential prolepsis, which has been noted in several critical responses to her work, has in some cases led to too much emphasis on her death as a framework for introducing and understanding Quin's life and work. While boundaries between this writer's life and her writing are particularly porous, and (her) death by drowning is undoubtedly intriguing and mysterious to the writer or scholar engaged with her work, some have gone so far as to unequivocally presume suicide. Yet such an assumption positions her death in terms of an already problematic stereotype of women writers and suicide, and ignores the sensory and aesthetic complexity and suggestiveness of Quin's writing about and relationship with the sea.

## Notes

1. Stevick, 'Voices in the Head', p. 235.
2. Quin, *Berg*, p. 135.
3. Quin, *Passages*, p. 89.
4. Bennett, *Checkout 19*, p. 179.
5. Several of Quin's friends, as well as her mother, attended the funeral on 14 September. Brocard Sewell remembers: 'We drank two bottles of wine to Ann's memory, which was perhaps a form of ritual salute to her, a tribute to her achievement as a writer, and gesture of farewell, that she would have appreciated.' *Like Black Swans*, p. 192.
6. Quin, 'Nude and Seascape', *The Unmapped Country: Stories & Fragments*, pp. 25–30 (p. 30).
7. Quin, letter to Paddy Kitchen, quoted in Kitchen, 'Catherine Wheel: Recollections of Ann Quin', p. 54.
8. Quin, 'Eyes that Watch Behind the Wind', *The Unmapped Country: Stories & Fragments*, pp. 108–24 (pp. 117–18).
9. Quin, *Berg*, p. 140.

Chapter 2

# *Three*: A Collage of Possibilities

## Redirecting the Death Drive

*Three* begins after one of the three protagonists, only ever known as 'S', is dead, and ends just before her death. Though it is not a mystery story as such, the book revolves around the question of S's mysterious death, perhaps by drowning in uncertain circumstances. *Three* is composed of alternating sections, some of which are in S's words, and some of which narrate the conversations and activities of the book's other main characters, Leonard and Ruth. An example of the former is S's written diary, which is preoccupied with the relationship between her, 'L' and 'R' (Leonard and Ruth), with her growing desire to visit a lake in the middle of the mountains, and with thoughts of death and drowning: 'How easy for a body to drift out, caught up in a current, and never be discovered, or for anyone ever to be certain.'[1]

The text of S's diary and the book as a whole end with:

> Today the first signs of sharpness in the air. The mist rises up from the ground lying in thin frost. The boat is ready, as planned. And all that's necessary now is a note. I know nothing will change. (143)

S has made preparations for a boat trip to the lake in the mountains: 'The boat is ready, as planned. And all that's necessary now is a note.' S's fantasy about drowning and the note mentioned here suggest suicidal ideation – as does the despair of 'I know nothing will change' – but it is just a suggestion, and on the opening page of the book Ruth admits 'we can't really be sure could so easily have been an accident the note just a melodramatic touch' (1). Pervading uncertainty about S's death means it is only ever a possible suicide – 'could so easily have been an accident' – and as Juliet Jacques rightly remarks, the multiple form(s) and resulting ambivalent narrative of *Three* insist that what seems to be suicidal 'ideation does not necessarily mean that S's death *was* self-inflicted'.[2] When thinking about her own death, S observes, 'My certainty shall be their confusion' (53); other characters and the reader remain uncertain about whatever this supposed 'certainty' is, and the narrative as a whole remains in unresolved 'confusion'. As Ruth says later in the book: 'I thought she might have talked about suicide given us something definite but there's nothing absolutely nothing there maybe the journals yes perhaps there . . .' (p. 116). And this uncertainty of 'maybe' and 'perhaps' extends beyond whether or not S commits suicide to the question of how she dies. In his introduction to the recent reissue of *Three*, Joshua Cohen reminds us that it is not even clear whether S does die by drowning, although this is one possible option; 'or perhaps she's stabbed to death by a gang of nameless faceless men before her body washes up onshore . . . or perhaps the stabbed-dead-body that washes up on shore is someone else'.[3] As Cohen's revealing discussion of the geometry and logic of *Three* points out, the 'trinary logic' of the book – its undecided and precarious perhaps – works to deconstruct and refuse either/or dichotomies, and in the case of S's death means that 'Future violence by the tideline cannot be true, it cannot be false, it can only be contingent, possible or probable.'[4] The readings in this chapter will engage with and return to the notion of trinary logic because of how this provides a framework for thinking about the plurality of possibilities of *Three*.

In *Three*, as in *Berg* and across her writing, Quin is not primarily interested in storytelling. At the same time, the drive of this book's story and plot, as much as there is one, is towards S's death, the absent but formative event that shapes and generates the energy of the text as a whole. The basic 'storyline' of *Three* is this. A young woman, S, goes to stay/live with a married couple, Leonard and Ruth, after having an abortion. There is an ambiguous relationship between the three of them with S playing roles such as boarder/daughter/sister/lover. Then S disappears and dies, and Leonard and Ruth talk and obsess about what happened. While *Berg* could be read as a narrative that explores the drive towards a death that never happens, *Three* drives towards a death that has happened already. This death is anticipated in the book's final words and foreshadowed in repeated references to the lake in the middle of the mountains in S's earlier diary entries.[5] Given this, it is possible to read *Three* as cognisant of, and perhaps in some senses as directly working to deconstruct, the 'death drive' – as *Berg* does with Oedipus. With the death drive, as articulated by Freud in 'Beyond the Pleasure Principle', *'the goal of all life is death'*.[6] According to Freud, life is a distraction, structured on a repetitive attempt at mastery, on the way to one's own permanent absence in death. Peter Brooks thinks about this in relation to literary narrative and plot, and claims that deep within the plotting of many literary texts, 'at the heart of structures of repetition, the death drive is "found out" by betraying itself *in* repetition',[7] hence narratives that reiterate or foreshadow a trajectory towards death.[8] *Three* plays with, diverges from and deconstructs the death drive plot with its non-linear trajectory and with multiple textual forms which are structured in an alternating and reiterative format. As a result, the narrative drive towards and desire for knowledge about S's death are circular, both ante (narrated in S's words) and post (in third person sections that focus on Leonard and Ruth) 'event'. These repeated before and after references to S's death send out echoes throughout the text like an inverted déjà vu, and because of this, *Three* can precisely be read as a text where the 'death drive is "found out" by betraying itself *in* repetition' in terms of how it is both overtly present and at the same time called into question, particularly in how the structure of the book subverts and refuses a linear plot trajectory ending with death.

S's written diary entries narrate and foreshadow her own absence. She writes 'I become almost a shadow. The kind that extends up the wall, across the ceiling, dwindles gradually into other shadows. In my room. Theirs' (62), a claim which positions her somewhere between absence and presence – 'I became almost a shadow'. Her metamorphosis from 'I' into an 'almost' shadow that 'dwindles gradually into other shadows' is towards an absent signifier of previous presence. Elsewhere, S seems to desire death as a self-determined and articulate act, a form of authorship with her own life; 'to write it down would almost be like performing the action itself' (139).[9] Such a desire could be read in terms of narrative agency and self-actualisation, and the mystery of her death, which only S has 'certainty' of, perhaps adds to this sense of control. However, the ambiguity of 'perhaps', and the 'confusion' surrounding S's death across the narrative of *Three* as a whole complicates such a reading. As with, for example, Lise's supposedly self-determined death in Muriel Spark's superb *The Driver's Seat* (1970) – a text where the death drive is also 'found out' and interrogated in terms of its role in relation to narrative plotting and fantasies of female agency – Quin's text is ambivalent about and sceptical of the notion of a woman's self-destruction as articulation and self-actualisation.[10] And as Morley's insightful triple reading of S's death suggests, while a feminist reading of S's death might interpret it as 'a grim edict on the fate of women under patriarchy', it could also be read as the deliberate 'failure to maintain the female consciousness/voice that the novel initially appears to seek to establish', or even as the 'dismantlement of a feminine identity no longer of service to Quin's work'.[11]

S's desire for death as self-authorship in written diaries that are read as archival artefacts in her absence acts as a reminder of the radical difficulty death presents for understanding or articulation. Elisabeth Bronfen reminds us that writing always confirms absence while at the same time negating that through partial presencing in the act of representation. And with death there is a particular gap between language and the linguistic signifier.[12] Death, as dissolution of the self, can only be articulated in relation to the self either in presence, when looking forward to death – something Quin tackles by the direct inclusion of S's words – or retrospectively in absentia, interpreted by the surviving subjects – present in *Three* via conversations between Leonard and Ruth and their engagement with S's 'archive'. In her diary, S's wish for and writing of her own absence works to presence her voice throughout the book: in the third person sections where S is already dead, Leonard and Ruth's desire for contact works to presence her when they listen to tapes of her speaking, read her diary and watch videos of her.[13] In this way, the different textual forms of *Three* destabilise and redirect the death drive, and express the particular ambivalence created by presence/absence when it comes to (S's uncertain) death and the written word.

## A Composite Collage Form

*Three* is a collage of prose and free verse journal forms, audio tapes and videos of S, and free indirect third person narrative blended with dialogue: together these create the polyvocal, unstable and fragmented form of the book as a whole.[14] Its composition from different types of textual material is clear from the start. The narrative opens with – and is framed by – an extract from a newspaper story about a man who *'fell to his death from a sixth-floor window'* (1). To some extent, these initial lines serve a similar function to the opening of *Berg*, in that they announce a preoccupation of the narrative – here (a possibly accidental) death – which, as I have suggested in 'Redirecting the Death Drive' above, the book then works to deconstruct and reimagine. In *Three*, unlike *Berg*, these framing words are positioned at the top of the first page of the narrative proper and are therefore directly juxtaposed and brought into dialogue with the first section of third person narrative, which begins, 'Ruth startled from the newspaper by Leonard framed in the doorway' (1). The missing verb in this opening sentence, together with the choppy syntax and minimal description, is a fitting example of Quin's startling prose style in *Three*. Leonard and Ruth's ensuing conversation about the newspaper article – 'What's the latest then? Fellow thrown himself out of a window. Ghastly way to choose' – immediately shifts to discussion of their uncertainty about whether S's death was also a choice – 'But Leon hers wasn't like that' (1).

In this, the first page of *Three* not only introduces a central preoccupation of the book – S's death – but notable aspects of the book's style and shifting, multiple forms too. As in *Berg*, the aesthetics of the third person narrative sections of *Three* appeal to the senses, particularly sound and touch – or at least the desire for touch – and the focus of the prose shifts between an intense focus on objects in the material world and unstable perspectives of memory/fantasy.[15] But, while in *Berg* it is not always clear whether speech happens in or outside of Berg's head, the third person sections of *Three* offer minimal access to Ruth and Leonard's subjectivities and talk is nearly always aloud. Their dialogue on the opening page continues:

> He shuffled a few shells, pebbles, covered his ears with two. Used to wonder whether it was really the sound of the sea. I knew it never could be. Ever practical Ruthey. We should have gone with her Leon. She liked rowing out on her own. You went with her sometimes. Only once or twice then felt I intruded. But didn't she ask you to go the evening before? We had shopping to do. And it was stormy in the morning even she remarked how the clouds were low-lying mountains couldn't be seen either. (1)

The handling of shells and pebbles and listening for the sea in the shells seem to anchor this moment of the narrative in tactile and aural responses to the material world; at the same time, Leonard's actions here introduce the wider allure of the sea and mountain lake that S (and the text as a whole) is drawn by. Perhaps he desires contact with S by this invocation of the sea, or perhaps he is attempting to shut out and divert conversation away from rumination about her death with a childhood idea – 'Used to wonder whether it was really the sound of the sea'. Leonard's whimsy is dismissed by the 'Ever practical Ruthey', who responds to his question with 'I knew it never could be' and returns their conversation to guilt and regret about S: 'We should have gone with her'. As this section demonstrates, the lack of speech distinguishers in *Three* creates indeterminacy about who is speaking. While Quin uses a similar technique in *Berg*, in this second book the unmarked shifts of speaker seem to be used to create familiarity and intimacy between characters. At the same time, the condensed and undifferentiated nature of the third person narrative sections in *Three* is disorientating, and the lack of space in this technique creates gaps in comprehension that suggest what is lost in conversation. The momentum created by the lack of speech markers, together with the continual return to worrying about S's death, creates an elusive narrative that is infused with loss and misunderstanding where reading must slow, circle and repeat as it reaches for understanding.

Across the book as a whole a collage of different forms are juxtaposed. *Three* is composed of eight sections of three types of prose: four take the form of Ruth and Leonard's dialogue interspersed with third person perspective (such as in the example above), and two of S's written diary. The remaining two are transcripts of S's recorded voice, which create a kind of aural journal.[16] The arrangement of these eight sections alternate between third person and S's perspectives so that although S is technically 'absent' from the narrative because she is dead, at least half of the book is expressed in her voice. While her written journal takes a relatively familiar diary form, the two sections of free verse 'poetry' that represent the taped recordings of S speaking are the most visibly and explicitly 'experimental' sections of the book. S describes impressions of life with Leonard and Ruth as well as narrating childhood memories and sexual fantasies. There are also moments of 'direct' sensory perception, for example the scenery seen on a journey 'By car. Roof off':

> Colonnade of trees.
> Fall over ridges.
> Trees
> Stacked in valleys.
> Mountains
> appear. Move forward. When one is static.
> Retreat when approached.
> Fold of hills. Held by shadows. Dead seas. Fortresses
> of stone triads.
> Armies
> of cromlechs. Face east. Sounds of hooves. Marching feet. Through
> white flowers
> swept

one way. Stones into sheep. Water endlessly stretches.
Gulls moan. Flap
cry across. But silent near. Around. The house.
Surrounded by trees. No sign of anything living. But bend closer.
Turn up stones.
Separate
plants.
Leaves.
Branches. These stir. Rotate. Forests stride in the night. Neglected
orchards. Where blossom deceives.
A composite of silhouettes in a yellow field (23–4).[17]

Line breaks juxtapose and separate ideas or images, but it is unclear whether this patterning is motivated by metre, rhyme or sense, or whether these breaks and spaces indicate moments of silence between the sounds Leonard and Ruth hear. Perhaps both. Registering the absence of sound with visual space on the page serves to presence S's acoustic voice as well as the lacunae between her words: a direct contrast with the lack of space in Leonard and Ruth's run on conversations. The space and pauses here suggest that S's thoughts and feelings are half-formed, and can only be conveyed to the reader impressionistically, through unusual or repeated word pattern and image, or by focus on the sound and rhythm in and between words.[18] The free associative, pre-articulate momentum and listing of sensory impressions here do not work to communicate a recognisably inner self. Instead, the fragmented prose mimics the spontaneity, shifting perspectives and improvised articulations of the object-world as seen from a moving car.

In his study of diary fiction, Andrew Hassam proposes that Quin's poetic-prose in these sections communicates the 'surrealism of contemporary reality'.[19] And in some senses, their composition and effects also seem to recall surrealist automatic writing practices and the poetic forms of the Black Mountain poets, which both aimed to get as close as possible to direct sensory experience. More specifically, the line breaks in S's transcripts seem to '[cut] into a flow of associations almost arbitrarily', to use Peter Nicolls's words about surrealism in English literature, and this creates 'displacements and metonymies which disembody the human and throw familiar objects into ominously unfamiliar perspectives'.[20] In the example above, what is seen/objects in the material world are made strange: some shift and metamorphose (mountains move, forests stride) and some are verbally photographed and rendered static (the sea is dead, stones become sheep). But while the supposed 'free' association recalls the spontaneous qualities of automatic writing, the recordings of S's speech are, albeit in fractured and transitory form, also always a constructed verbal performance that anticipates a listener or audience. In the section above, for example, the spoken words/written transcript directs the listening ear/reading eye to stir, rotate and separate leaves and branches, to discover what is behind or beyond the seemingly static image. S's speaking presences both the absent character and her audience, the fact that this speech is recorded on tape (and therefore anticipates a listener) seems in tension with the spontaneity suggested by its apparently direct spoken form, and the fragmented and disrupted layout of the written transcript on the page draws visual attention to the composition of these sections as a device. Yet in this the transcript perhaps 'operates mimetically', in that the consciously 'poetic' style of S's performance may be precisely the point here.[21]

Leonard's journal, extracts of which are included in the third person narrative sections, appears on the page as a conventional and familiar diary form: 'poignantly traditional', as Cohen calls this and S's written diaries, with the inclusion of days/dates and 'discussions of weather'.[22] Leonard's journal also seems to anticipate an audience/reader and to refuse interiority, which resists and complicates the notion of diaries as confessional or revealing texts. His tone is excessively flat, repressing feelings in favour of an 'undifferentiated' record of events:

> October 18th   Boat found capsized. Coat identified. Also note in pocket—looks like suicide.
> October 19th   Two hours questioning by police sergeant. River and coastline dragged.
> October 20th   R in bed all day. Translation completed.
> October 21st   Dinner with the Blakeleys. A good hock.
> October 22nd   Orchids making progress especially Barbatum. (41)

This example is typical of a journal in which events are recorded seemingly at random: 'looks like suicide', 'coastline dragged', 'Dinner', 'good hock'. Here, the response to the central event of *Three* does not want to reveal knowledge of either Leonard, or of his feelings about S's death. At the same time, despite its form and surface, Leonard's journal seems 'less about preserving facts than about asserting, even performing, a self'.[23] The reader suspects that his deliberately callous and shallow performance, which pretends not to differentiate between – or care about – the experiences of being questioned by the police and dinner with friends, is false. While it is not necessarily out of place for Leonard to be dismissive of Ruth, the performance of indifference is unconvincing when it comes to the seemingly impassive record – 'looks like suicide' – of S's death. Leonard's reported intimacy with S elsewhere in both third person and S's (written and spoken) journal sections of the book, and in his videoing of her and secretive watching of those videos, belie his apparent dispassion. And the journal itself exposes its minimalist form as a self-conscious performance that anticipates and enjoys resisting its reader: it is full of 'little black marks' denoting 'Far more personal' (42) events that Leonard takes pleasure in refusing to explain to Ruth.[24]

Quin's inclusion of S's 'archive' materials and 'reproduction of her character's artifacts',[25] form a substantive part of the composite collage of *Three*, and are essential for communicating its cultural and literary preoccupations. The divergent realities created by the direct inclusion of multiple character voices and perspectives, together with the range of textual forms that these are expressed in, creates a 'confusion' that deliberately prohibits the possibility of creating a coherent narrative of events.[26] For Morley, the overall effect is a 'fragmented, disparate and complex text, at times in conflict with itself, at times difficult and confusing for the reader, and in this way conveying the jouissance and pain of the riven female body and consciousness (of) which it speaks'.[27] The polyvocal, composite form of *Three* is essential not only for communicating the uncertainty surrounding S's death, but for expressing the complexity and ambiguity of the book's other main preoccupations: marriage, class and female sexuality. The collage form is one way that Quin began 'to find a shape' (56) with which to explore and express these; another was to draw on the experimental techniques of the nouveau roman and nouvelle vague.

### Nouvelle Vague Techniques

> Bergman's latest THROUGH A GLASS DARKLY – affected me like hell – felt like death when walking out; incest and ALL THAT BUT beautifully photographed and acted; very Ibsenesque – sins of the father etc., family searching for life/God in each other, through each other, and the twilight or pale sunlight of the Swedish landscape penetrating in its indifference [...] like the way Bergman uses the mythical to get across the anguish of the present day.[28]

Quin was an enthusiastic viewer of European art house cinema. In *Three*, the cinematic aesthetics and techniques of the nouvelle vague are reimagined and repurposed for written form, and this is clear in Quin's reworking of the styles and stances of the genre's cinematography, *mise en scène* and precisely directed performance, as well as her interest in questions of time, repetition, movement, sound and silence. Andras Balint Kovacs points out that at this time there was a particularly 'sharp opposition between art cinema and entertainment cinema'.[29] For many cinema goers, the aspiration to art was 'the cultural Imaginary of the middle-class' and too often 'involved an internal distancing from the popular which was complex and often contradictory in its effects'.[30] But for Quin, such effects were precisely what appealed. The letter above is keenly aware and appreciative of form, structure and symbolism in *Through a Glass Darkly* (1961); for instance, the admiration of the 'penetrating' 'indifference' of the scenery, and how 'Bergman uses the mythical to get across the anguish of the present day'.

Quin's interest in the creative possibilities of art house cinema is evident in *Three*, which directly engages with *Last Year in Marienbad* (also 1961), written by Alain Robbe-Grillet and directed by Alain Resnais. The film's setting is a large, ornate hotel where wealthy couples are gathered. It is filmed in black and white, is a composite of tracking, travelling shots and static images, and there are three characters caught up in an ambivalent triangle of desire: A, a woman, and two men, X and M. X tries to convince A that they met and spent time together at the hotel the year before, but A has no recollection of their meeting. M, who may or may not be the woman's husband, repeatedly asserts his dominance over X by beating him several times in a game. The repeated game playing seems to represent each man's desire to win, but in fact represents a desire to keep on playing.[31] Quin makes several references to the film in letters to Carol Burns, and dismisses François Truffaut's *Jules et Jim* (1962) (also a narrative of three) as 'a slight skit on Marienbad'.[32] *Last Year in Marienbad* is a combination of Robbe-Grillet's nouveau roman obsession with close detail stripped of temporality and Resnais' new wave – 'la nouvelle vague' – continuum between the real and imaginary.[33] As I have shown in the chapter on *Berg*, Quin's writing also oscillates between intense particularities and blurred, shifting perspectives. She was particularly impressed by the film's sense of impenetrability and internal distancing, as well as the connection between photographic stasis and atemporality: 'a photo holds the image, is static, and therefore imprints itself more firmly by not having side-effects, or the infringement of past and future, isn't this was [sic] Last Year at Marienbad tried to bring off?'.[34]

Like *Last Year in Marienbad*, *Three* is polyphonic, and each character's version of events is different and irresolvable. In both texts, the perspectives of the different characters at times overlap and therefore seem to corroborate, but more often they widely diverge and compete for credulity. The viewer/reader cannot work out which of the versions corresponds most closely with 'actual' events, because these competing imaginaries and voices work to complicate rather than elucidate. What is achieved is an almost phenomenological faithfulness to the different subjective experiences of the characters, which refuses and rejects the usefulness, or even the possibility, of an overall 'master' narrative. In *Last Year in Marienbad* 'the factual status of the past event is made uncertain' and 'subject to mental manipulation by the characters': there is a sense in which 'even the "past" and the "trauma" are created by the mere textual process of the narrative'.[35] In *Three*, where the central traumatic event is S's supposed suicide, the fluctuating narrative modes, disordered chronology, and range of alternative versions of her death mean that the circumstances of her death become less and less clear as the narrative progresses. Resolution is not possible, or even desirable, because Quin's interest is in the continuation and proliferation of uncertainty: it is specifically the unresolved nature of the trauma that holds Leonard and Ruth together, and precisely this quality that enables the book to so compellingly express (to draw on Cohen's description of the effects of the book's trinary logic) 'the messiness of being human'.[36]

In both *Last Year in Marienbad* and *Three*, narrative uncertainty is enhanced by an unreality of setting created by strange and specific aesthetics. One of the most memorable aspects of the film is the visually striking garden of the hotel. The garden, which contains several classical statues, has a geometric design with cubist effect, leading on and splicing the viewer's gaze into segments. This setting, filled with familiar things, becomes unfamiliar, made strange because of the angles it is seen from, and the confusing play of light and shadow. The setting of *Three* is Leonard and Ruth's country retreat, 'the Grey House' belonging to his father, which has a similar garden: 'between the trees, statues. The shadows of statues on the lawns stretched to the cliff edge' (3), 'statues gleamed, elongated shadows across the grass' (16). Quin consciously and carefully – the clue is in the repetition of stretched and elongated shadows here – creates a visual effect akin to the garden of *Last Year in Marienbad*, one which directs the reader's gaze outwards.[37] There is a similar description on the book's opening page, where 'A mirror extended the window. Gardens' (1), an image which leads the reading eye to the outer edges and almost beyond the frame of the mirror, window and page itself. Sylvia Bruce's review of the book brilliantly captures this quality: 'with deliberation designed, <u>Three</u>, when viewed from the appropriate distance, resolves itself into a model of tautness and precision (sculptural, yet also cinematic)'.[38] The geometric arrangement of statues of classical Greek figures in the garden announce form and formality, both in terms of being consciously crafted depictions of sculptural objects, and in terms of how they invoke and deconstruct the authority and forms of the past by being unstable and incomplete, 'broken, unbroken, unfinished' (4).

The statues in *Three* are a useful example of how Quin is, like Bergman, interested in using 'the mythical to get across the anguish of the present day' (to use her words). The statues in *Three* are often odd or perverse: 'Hallucination Aphrodite father's favourite. Certainly not mine so grotesque didn't even have a head I mean was it a man or a woman that thing sticking out of what looked like breasts?' (9). Here, the suggestive potency of the mythical is juxtaposed with Ruth's disgust – 'so grotesque' – at the surreal ambivalence of gender and sexuality in the 'thing sticking out of what looked like breasts?' For Ruth, the uncanny familiarity and yet unfamiliarity of these 'classical' statues has a distorting and disturbing effect. The Hallucination Aphrodite is a deliberate and irreverent transgression of the classical with the lewd, it is inverted into the form of an incongruous, multiple self. Leonard's father and Leonard himself – 'I rather like a few of them lend something to the place a great pity they had to break up Hallucination Aphrodite' (9) – are rather drawn to the statues, as are the guests at one of their parties: S notes, 'The same person who had kissed my feet, I later saw embrace a headless statue, pour drink over heavy stone breasts' (138). But Ruth's response to the statues is one of repulsion at their ontological, as well as gendered and sexual, ambiguity:

> Those ghastly statues of your father's too disembodied pieces of bronze stone and bits scraps of metal you tried making into flesh and blood participators or audience of your little charades frankly grotesque Leon quite quite horrible ugh. (7)

Here, the line between 'disembodied pieces of bronze stone and bits' and 'flesh and blood participators' is blurry and precarious, and the statues seem to shift between lifeless and alive, subject and object. A similar uncertainty is noted by S in her diary: 'Even the statues seem human' (136). Jordan offers an illuminating meditation on subjects and objects in *Three* and *Berg* which focuses on the ventriloquist's dummy and the statues. She claims that the statues' 'obscenity is sexual as well as ontological, as if the ambiguity itself might be what disturbs and titillates', and that Quin's 'statues, and dummies, and effigies' distastefully reveal 'the ambivalence by which they exist'.[39]

## Deconstructing Coupledom

In *Three* and *Last Year in Marienbad*, three protagonists are caught up in a triangle of ambivalent desire which is revealed in their engagement in role play. This, together with the multiple, divergent and interwoven perspectives, create complex layers of interplay between the three without attempting to reduce their relationship into a coherent narrative. In both film and book the role play performances initially seem to offer a framework for interpretation. *Last Year in Marienbad* opens with a simplified melodrama, a possible allegory for the more complex nuances of a three-way relationship in the film as a whole. The garden of 'the Grey House' in *Three* contains an empty swimming pool among the statues that is used by Leonard, Ruth and S as a theatre in which to perform. S writes: 'At my suggestion L made a platform, with steps leading from either side, in the empty swimming pool. We both write little scenarios which R half-heartedly joins in' (66). On this 'stage' the three of them enact dramas, usually in mime form, wearing masks and costumes to conceal their identities. S comments, 'My favourite one with masks is just the three of us, two reject one, or one rejects two, or all three reject each other, or equally accept' (66).

In *Three*, the relationship between the several scenarios played out in the empty swimming pool and the characters' 'real' relationships with each other is particularly enigmatic, and what kind of interpretative frame such performances might offer is unclear. Leonard and Ruth's discussions reveal mixed feelings of repulsion/desire in relation to the role play 'games', as well as exposing the explicit and implicit layers of role play at work in their relationship:

> She certainly had talent for those mime plays for instance. Oh those I must say I never had much time for them. You joined in readily enough Ruth. What could I do remain passive outsider to all your games then? You seemed to enjoy them rather I thought. Well – well I'd hardly thought you were aware whether I did or not. They looked at each other, quickly away, at their drinks. (6)

Even though, according to Leonard, Ruth 'joined in readily enough' and 'seemed to enjoy' 'those mime plays', Ruth rejects the idea that she participated willingly. She describes herself as a 'passive outsider' who 'never had much time for them' and conforms to her role of the prim wife. Leonard and Ruth remain 'in role', in terms of his enjoyment of the performances and her resistance. If Leonard enjoys the mime, Ruth must disapprove; these are the positions that, on the surface, their relationship allows. At the same time, their interaction suggests more complex feelings when they 'looked at each other, quickly away'. Here (as elsewhere) the roles of 'playful husband' and 'disapproving wife' provide stereotypes of an unhappily matched couple that Quin plays with, exposes and interrogates.[40] In this way, one of the effects of the repeated mime plays in *Three* is ironic, to show that apparently 'natural' and intimate interpersonal interaction is also always a kind of role play. As S recognises: 'R plays a role when he is with us. Except I wonder if it is not a certain role she plays with me, when we are on our own' (142). The characters 'play out' selves in the domestic setting of 'the Grey House' as much as they do on the empty swimming pool stage.

In *Three* and *Last Year in Marienbad*, most characters are referred to by letter rather than name – although Leonard's and Ruth's names are known, they are referred to as L and R in the diary sections. Quin uses this technique to particular effect vis-à-vis the book's *ménage à trois*, for example in S's aural journal where letters are used to replace (and obscure) the characters' names/identities:

> Three points *A B* and *C* on a rigid body in a straight line. When the points *A* and *C* being given *B* is chosen such that the sum of distances *AB* and *BC* is a short as possible.
> Suggestion *A* walks past *B* and *C*. *A* might turn. Stop. Shrug. Walk on. *B* and *C* watch. Perhaps follow *A*. Or separate. Possibly disappear together. Variations endless. (21)

This scenario takes the mathematical form of a logic puzzle which identifies various results depending on the 'sum of distances', the 'perhaps' and the 'possibly'. In this, the range of potential outcomes/forms of relationship generated by the book's three-way relationship, or 'trinary logic' and geometry, is made clear – 'Variations endless'. As Cohen explains; 'In trinary logic, a statement can either be True or False or some indeterminate, or indeterminable, third value: ???'[41] And, as with the reworking of the Oedipal triangle in *Berg*, the precarious and uncertain triangle in *Three* is shown to be a desiring rather than deciding one. While *Berg* opens up the heteronormative parent–child triangle of Oedipus, in *Three* Quin uses trinary logic to deconstruct the (also heteronormative at this point in time) monogamous institution of marriage. S, a single and sexually imaginative young woman, is the third who both troubles and shapes Ruth and Leonard's marriage. S seems to reject institutions such as marriage – 'a bourgeois stronghold' (61), as she describes it – but she also admits more mixed feelings: 'So often scorned before, but soon understood, almost succumbed to: an ambiguous luxury' (61).

Even once absent via her death, S remains a key part of the dynamic of Leonard and Ruth's coupledom. Together and alone, they are obsessed with her, the necessary third who energises and enables their continuation as a couple while at the same time disrupting its linear narrative. The mystery of S's absence, following the disturbing effects of her presence, offers them focus and energises their marriage.[42] Despite uncertainty about whether she and Leonard had sex or not and the resulting anxiety felt by Ruth, S's role as absent (possible) transgressor of their married two subsequently works to hold their relationship together. In this S is 'The absent protagonist or anti-heroine-hypotenuse of this love-triangle tale' who expands the couple into a 'throuple'.[43] The trinary logic of Quin's book insists that a three-way relationship offers more interesting and challenging possibilities than a dyad. Leonard and Ruth's coupledom is depicted in terms of 'toleration politeness that brings a basic relationship a certain smoothness in day to day living. But never laughter' (124); 'nights of self-pity, wishing in a way he would leave' (125). This humourless 'smoothness in day to day living' suggests a surface without depth of affection, as do the toleration and politeness. Rather than love or desire for each other, Leonard and Ruth seem bound together by their fascination with S and by the routine of the 'habits they parcel up/ hand to each other' (102).

The claustrophobic form of the third person narrative sections particularly reveal and critique the oppressive effects of the habits of Leonard and Ruth's married life: 'She picked the plates up, rattled them together, scraped the remains and put them down for the cat' (15); 'Have you been tidying my desk Ruth? A bit someone's got to tea's getting cold do come and sit down and stop fluttering around honestly you're like an old woman sometimes Leon' (85). The humourlessness here (even where the effect is of a sort of grim humour), together with endless and petty negotiations about whose turn it is to pour various beverages and stilted mealtime conversations, build to create a repetitive and confining narrative without space which belies the intimacy it seems to perform, for example:

More potatoes darling? Don't mind. Yes or no? She stood beside him, over him. He leaned back, twisted his neck. If there are some left thanks no no more that's plenty. How can you watch that programme just don't know I don't think it's funny one bit. He pronged a potato, held halfway, and laughed until his eyes watered. She looked at the cat, made noises, clicked, sucked, her nose wriggled. Make the coffee Leon. When this is over ohhhhhhhhh ahhhhhhhhhh oh that's good. (15)

Here, as throughout the third person sections (see my discussion of the opening page of *Three* in 'A Composite Collage Form' above, for example), the omission of speech markers blurs the distinction between what is thought and what is said. The specific purpose of this technique in *Three* is to emulate the interactions of a married couple without distinction or space. Each utterance follows closely on the heels of another, and the effect is oppressive. In this, the form of the third person narrative sections are, as Cohen puts it – and 'vicious' is the right word to articulate the ferocity of Quin's critique of marriage in the book – 'a vicious condensation of third-person description' and '"interior" – house-bound – dialogue'.[44] In the passage above, as well as the haranguing and threatening tone and stifling form of their dialogue, Leonard and Ruth's power struggle is fittingly and viscerally expressed via the magnification and crowding of sounds. The pronging, clicking and sucking, and the extended 'ohhhhhhhhh ahhhhhhhhh' communicate the tension and conflict of a scene in which Ruth's 'darling' comes across as both habitual and ironic. The onomatopoeia here reaches behind, beyond, before, underneath what is said, into inarticulate sounds which express more than their words. Ruth's stance 'over him' and Leonard's twisted neck add unspoken body language to the cacophony and the cumulative result vividly exposes the tensions and conflict between them. In contrast to this fraught coupledom, the third position offered by S – as well as the collage form and nouveau roman techniques of the book – posit a more open and ambiguous relationship which rejects either/or structures in favour of both/and. It is not that a three-way relationship is without unhappiness, boredom, suspicion, misunderstanding or tension, but that *Three* insists it is at the same time more redolent with possibility.

## Destabilising Classism

As part of its cultural critique, *Three* interrogates class structures as well as marriage and monogamy. S depicts Leonard and Ruth as imprisoned by being middle class and limited by all its nice things and nasty prejudices, and positions herself as an irreverent outsider who exposes and rejects the trappings and hierarchies of social position. Her listing (and ridicule) of Leonard and Ruth's plethora of gadgetry and objects disparages their bourgeois status:

> Sofa. Flora-impregnated.
> Chippendale chairs. Unchipped. Upholstered in blue.
> They call turquoise.
> Persian rugs. Second skins. For them.
> Warm napkins
> Silverware pawns. Salt-cellar dominates.
> Rooms soundproofed.
> Paintings
> not hung
> too small. Not small enough. But still-lifes she used to do.
> Burglar-proofed.
> China plates
> On the wall. Glass doors. Concealed lighting. White curtains (20–1)

The luxurious material surroundings and objects in the domestic space of 'the Grey House' directly contrast with the cheap, sticky and broken objects in the bedsit settings of *Berg*. This difference is marked from the start of *Three* with the description of 'A wicker arm-chair opposite the Japanese table. Screen. Sliding doors' (1) as opposed to the 'Squatting furniture', 'imitation Japanese table' and shaky wooden partition of *Berg*.[45] In S's description above, the chairs are 'Unchipped', unlike the chipped and cracked objects in Berg's room, and the rugs are 'Persian' instead of threadbare. As with *Berg* this description appeals to touch, but here the surfaces are smooth and warm, like 'Second skins'. S's appraisal of Leonard and Ruth's domestic life here renders it little more than a list of branded and luxurious, superfluous, objects; elsewhere, she depicts their life together in terms of paid-for services – 'specialists/ psychiatrists/ analysts/ masseurs/ osteopaths/ palmists/ clairvoyants' (26).

The form of these lists surrounded by white space on the page contrast with the spaceless form of the third person narrative sections, but both express and expose the performance of married intimacy, as also do Leonard and Ruth's (discussions of) role play. Jacques notes how Quin's rendering of the details of their lives, as in the example above, is a vital part of her class critique: 'Quin's eye for the minutiae of bourgeois life is acute, and utterly ruthless.'[46] The objects in 'the Grey House' are props of a middle-class domesticity and snobbery that set the stage for the behaviour of guests at Ruth and Leonard's dinner parties, for example those who speak 'with calculated eloquence. In French, in Italian. Cigars pampered, liqueur glasses stroked – the stems' (57). These guests are pretentious, and the 'calculated eloquence' of their performance confirms it is all for show. Such examples add to the sense in which, in *Three*, ideas of what is role play and what 'real' are blurred and inverted. The middle-class characters are 'Chameleons in company' (21), performing a range of roles and selves for social and cultural purposes.[47]

S's critique of bourgeois behaviour is extended by the third person narrative's rendering of, in particular, Ruth's classist prejudice. When she is rude about Leonard's father for having sugar in his tea – 'why it's almost a working-class habit' (80) – the narrative mocks her attitude. Her attitude elsewhere articulates bigotry and paranoia about working-class people:

> such peasants here too never can trust them tell them to do something and when your back's turned have to watch while they do it and show them. Yes like beasts and how they stare too Leon have you noticed when we drive past that woman and her kids honestly given half the chance I think they'd quite happily see us dead? They're all right if you talk to them. But what on earth can one say they wouldn't understand just go on staring and once we're through the gateway I can hear them laugh. (9)

Quin's depictions of Ruth's assumptions here engage with, and take a position on, a wider cultural question of the time. When discussing the fear of vandals which emerged in Britain in the 1950s and 1960s, Stanley Cohen identifies what he calls 'deviancy amplification' in an attempt to describe and explain the intensity of the media and middle-class attitudes.[48] Deviancy amplification includes a distortion of terminology, where repeated and emotive phrasing provides a narrative for events that are yet to happen – for instance Ruth's 'I think they'd quite happily see us dead'. Misperception and fear of working-class youths drives Leonard and Ruth's anxiety about trespassers and their desire for a 'Burglar-proofed' home. Not only do they put up notices, but Leonard 'plans to stop them bloody well will too get a high wall built all the way round that'll put an end to their vandalism. They'll still find a way over. Have cut glass on the top and wire yes that's it an electric wire will soon cure them' (10). The paranoia of this violent fantasy communicates Quin's class critique in *Three*, positioning them both as prey to the broader 'folk devil' fear of youth culture so that Ruth and Leonard's prejudices and anxiety participate in and enact a wider antagonism. According to Cohen, class tensions at this time were underpinned by the 'recurrent theme of *winning space.* Territoriality, solidarity, aggressive masculinity, stylistic innovation'.[49] More important than their actual behaviour, he points out, working-class youths 'have occupied a constant position as folk devils', to be feared, banned and barred.[50]

In *Three*, Leonard's signs and fences are not enough to keep the vandalism and violence of the feared working-class 'others' out. As S puts it in her aural journal:

> Then they came. In the middle of
> a storm. One night. Waving torches.
> Throwing
> fireworks
> into the swimming pool. Stampeded
> round the statues. While he stood quivering. In the summer-
> house. In the dark. They screamed. Tore flowers out. She buried
> her face in cushions. Crying. Hands covered her ears. Then they
> left. When the storm passed. A trail of torn flowers left.
> Plants. Broken bronze pieces.
> Littered paths. (103)

What happens is uncertain, confused and ambiguous – for example, who is the 'they' that screamed? What is clear is that Leonard and Ruth have been expecting 'them' to come, and when they do, he stands quivering and she buries her face 'in cushions', cries and covers her ears. Not only are property and inanimate objects violated and damaged, but Leonard, too: 'His blood. After they came / down. Hurled themselves. Pieces of metal at him' (104). The scene is partially rewritten in S's written diary, which has the effect of adding to the confusion of the scene. In that account, during the enactment of a mime, 'I noticed them first, half a dozen or so faces over the edge of the pool' (136). Then things are thrown down, 'three of the statues moved' and Ruth screams, followed by a flurry of movement:

> I couldn't make out anything, hardly see, as earth, metal pieces, broken bits of bronze fell around. When finally I could see, L lay flat on the ground. He was being beaten up by three men, whose faces, arms, legs were whitewashed [. . .] They looked like clowns giving vent to years of repressed feelings, as they punched, and kicked L. (136–7)

Appearing as 'clowns' waving torches, the perpetrators are 'whitewashed', their real identities masked. They are only partially seen rather than fully apprehended, a blur of faces, arms and legs which enables them to remain in the text as abstract others, 'folk devils' and objects of moral panic.

But S's critique of Leonard and Ruth's middle-class status and the narrative's mocking of Ruth's classism alert us to the fact that *Three* is not complicit in but questioning of an attitude which aligns violence and trespass with othered working-class youths or 'peasants', as Ruth calls the people who live on a council estate. After the incident above, S becomes aware of being watched from across the water by 'several of the men who had beaten up L. They played some game with knives on the sand, and beckoned me over' (139). Their game is threatening, and the previous attack confirms their capacity to carry out such a threat. Yet at the same time S sees Leonard watching from across the water and the text suggests that his presence also signifies the threat of violent transgression. When 'an unidentified young woman, with stab wounds in back and abdomen, was found yesterday by a lake near the Sugarloaf mountain' (131) is read together with, for example, Leonard's marital rape of Ruth (discussed below), or his deliberate killing of a crab – 'L, still laughing, jumped on the crab and moved his foot several times, before looking down at the broken remains of shell, claws, greenish fluid' (133) – his enjoyment of force and brutality is exposed and Leonard is shown to be just as, if not more, threatening than the working-class youths he and Ruth vilify. Here as throughout *Three*, Quin contests, exposes, destabilises and deconstructs a range of classist stereotypes as part of a complex engagement with pressing social questions of her time.

## Writing Sexual Violence

My discussions of marriage and class above have shown that in *Three* the threat of violence and trespass is located both outside and inside the domestic space – it is expressed in the tension of Ruth and Leonard's daily interactions, for example, and in Leonard's presence alongside the attackers. Violence is also complicatedly bound up with the book's representations of pleasure, sensuality and sex. Leonard and Ruth lavish love and sensual caresses on things other than each other – he on his orchids, which are erotically written with a focus on their 'moistness' (11), 'dampness' (12), 'tips of purple and red' (12), and when Leonard 'parted leaves. Thrust through. He poked about with his little finger. He murmured with pleasure, sometimes sighed' (12). Ruth's object of affection is her cat, Bobo: 'She looked at the cat, made noises, clicked, sucked, her nose wriggled' (15). Her cutesy language – 'come on Bobo bedbeds' (15) – and continual stroking of and fussing over him recalls Judith's behaviour with Seby in *Berg*. In both books, the displacement of affection onto plants/pets exposes the lack of intimacy and affection between the couple and creates antagonism – to Leonard, Bobo is a 'Fucking stinking animal' (14) who he treats with aggressive contempt, recalling the violence towards Seby and Berty in *Berg*.

As well as their difference of opinion about Bobo, Leonard and Ruth seem incompatible in other ways: in taste and preference, intellectually and sexually. While Ruth 'wriggled about, explored herself with an oval bar of lilac soap' (43) when in the bath with Leonard and, when alone with Bobo, 'Touched herself, the cat', 'took her nightdress off, inspected her breasts, held the mirror to them, licked a finger and rubbed a nipple' (76), she repeatedly refuses Leonard's sexual advances, always attempting deferral: 'Just tired so exhausted after everything' (16); 'don't darling not now' (51); 'perhaps tomorrow – tomorrow darling' (52). When they do have sex, the depiction is disappointing and unpleasant, more reminiscent of death than pleasure: 'He twitched several times, then sank down. She lay motionless, tears ran into her mouth' (79). As my readings of Leonard and Ruth's conversations have shown, Quin's writing of their various forms of marital intercourse are pretty damning. Even when their physical interaction is positive and suggestive of intimacy such as when they bathe together, it is at the same time marked by anti-climax and a lack of intimacy: when Leonard gets an erection, Ruth rejects him and 'He watched the purple tip disappear, swallowed up by the grey water' (44).[51]

Later in the book, sex is depicted as an act of violent marital rape[52] which I include in full here in order to consider its composition and significance:

> He pulled her dress up, slid the underwear apart, and went into her quickly, as she cried out, her arms above, hands clawed the wall. Her body sank into the bed, as he moved above her. Not like this oh God Leon not . . . He panted as he strove faster, deeper. You're hurting oh Christ it's hurting me don't – no Leon are you mad? She tried bringing her legs together. His knees pressed them further apart, his hands planted either side of her arms. She dug her nails in until her fingers were covered in his blood. Going to fuck you fuck you fuck you until . . . She screamed out as he went deeper in. She tore at his hair, face. He paused, turned his head away, began again, moved faster, until her bare thighs, belly smacked against him, and the springs of the bed creaked. Her body limp, head alone moved, twisted, came up, sank back, her mouth open, but no scream came. (127–8)

This disturbing and violent scene is the ultimate acting out of the antagonism that underpins Leonard and Ruth's marriage. As with their mealtime interaction of 'more potatoes darling?' (discussed above), the proliferation of sound and movement is used for visceral effect here. The onomatopoeia of 'belly smacked' and 'bed creaked' creates immersion in the tension and distress of the scene, and 'screamed out' recalls the expressive power of inarticulate sounds at the mealtime. In both scenes bodies twist, but here the physical movements are pained and desperate – 'clawed', 'tore', 'smacked' – and there is an accumulation of noise and action. The rhythm, momentum and arc of the passage, created by the predominance of monosyllables, short clauses, repetition and part-repetition, underpin the content of the scene and perform its transgressive and forceful action. At the end, Ruth's body is 'limp' (recalling her lying 'motionless' at the end of their earlier sex) with her 'mouth open, no scream came' – a silent scream which disturbingly inverts Judith's gaping lust in *Berg*.[53]

In these ways, the echoes between this scene and others of domestic intercourse – both in terms of conversation and sex – integrate the violence and shock of this act with the fabric of Leonard and Ruth's married lives. Part of the purpose of the marital rape scene, then, is to ramp up the critique of marriage in *Three*; yet this does not quite explain the form of the scene, why it is so up-close and detailed. As my reading of *Passages* also demonstrates, Quin's writing is undoubtedly interested in transgression and taboo; in terms of experimenting with what can be depicted, and via what techniques, specifically when it comes to sex, and with how far writing can push into the messy complexity of all forms of experience. Elsewhere in *Three*, for example, forceful intercourse and violent language are written as desirable. When Leonard says 'I want to fuck you' (88), Ruth recoils in horror. S's sexual fantasies, on the other hand, find violence titillating: 'Pretend I'm tied to the bed', 'Whip me with your hair', 'Hair on his chest burnt with a cigarette', 'When will you fuck me next?' (142).[54] Leonard and Ruth's sexual intercourse is something he does to her, whereas S is an actively engaged sexual partner.[55] When read together with the marital rape, however, S's transgressive desires are undoubtedly ambivalent in terms of how male violence and female agency, desire and libertarian libido are entangled, despite the distinction between consensual and non-consensual sex – I return to Quin's wrangling with such questions in my discussion of *Passages* below in 'The Female Gaze'.

In *Three*, a text suffused with (often violent and frustrated) sexual desire, S is the primary focus of nostalgia, longing and fascination for both Leonard and Ruth. Ruth's sexual desire does not focus on Leonard at all, but on herself, Bobo and S. She is titillated by wearing S's clothes, necklaces and beads – 'She licked the beads, replaced them on the extended nipples, her head thrown back, knees parted pressed into the carpet, feet together' (12–13). The sexual intimacy of this scene is heightened – if that were needed – by its being juxtaposed and intercut with the erotics of Leonard's activities in his orchid summerhouse, where he 'peered into centres, ran a finger along stems, pink against pink laid there. Turrets of intense purple. Wings. Tongues' (12). Ruth is not able to admit her desire for S to either herself or Leonard. She 'Picked up the clothes and pushed them into a cupboard' (13) when she hears him coming back into the house and denies masturbation: 'just got rather hot in the night' (77). And S's aural journal records that when in bed with a bad period Ruth pleads:

> Do stay with me. An orange light
> interior of some exotic flower
> hovered
> over walls. Smell of heavy perfume
> Bodies. Hers. Only the shape moulded from the sheet. Will you
> brush my hair?
> Long
> Thick
> over shoulders. (112)

Ruth's desire for physical contact with S in this request for hairbrushing is embellished by the scent of heavy perfume, the interior of the exotic flower (which recalls Leonard's fingering of the orchids) and the dimmed light, and such details imply a room fusty with the smell of bodies and sex. Leonard also desires intimacy with S. After her death, he voyeuristically watches her on film in an attempt at contact and intimacy. He sits alone in the dark, hand over his face after watching: 'A girl, naked, emerged from the sea, hair over her face', who 'danced away to edge of the sea, where she flung towel and mask down, dived into a huge wave, bobbed up, hair and seaweed caught in spray' (90). As with Berg's experience when having sex with Judith, the sensory and sensual relationship with the sea is a key part of the depiction of sexual desire here.

S's wish to test and transgress the limits of Leonard and Ruth's coupledom – 'a situation I long to wade in right up to the very limits of imagination if possible. Gain another level, and added dimension, preferably bringing them both with me' (62) – is driven by the trinary logic of possibility. This possibility is always also precarious and fraught with difficulty; their 'throuple' is unequal and contingent, bringing with it anxieties that unbalance and disrupt the narrative at the same time as it underpins and binds it together. For instance, Ruth compulsively listens to a section of the taped journal that she believes implies a sexual encounter between Leonard and S:

> first faint light. In a darkened room. Hurt me hurt
> me hurt me
> there
> here
> anywhere. This way. If you like. Talk to me talk.
> Talk
> to
> me
> Was it like this with
> Never before. Not like this. No one has touched me ever
> never never
> like this. Before. Like waves. The coming
> slowly. Dual roles
> realised. Yes yes
> yes. (114)[56]

Ruth is already anxious about their relationship, and here she replays the tape, listening and fast-forwarding it in the search for 'truth'. The fragments of tape that Ruth hears and skips past are not quite exact repetitions of segments elsewhere in the transcript and these slight differences create a divergent emphasis that ironises her repeated attempts to find out about S and Leonard: 'hell hell if only I knew – knew' (117). But the ambiguity of S's aural journal resists this desire and what actually happened between them remains uncertain and unresolved. It is unclear whether references to sex between them are imagined or real, and when S describes having ecstatic and often violent sex in her written diary, it is unclear whether this is with Leonard or not. The circular form of the spool of tape complements and exaggerates the repetitive nature of Ruth's action, communicating the fragility, the fallacy, of her desire for clarity and understanding, something she later admits, 'But this now brings no such certainty. What would it mean to her if . . . She switched off. Listened to the hum of the recorder only' (120).[57] The inarticulate sound refuses to either confirm or deny Ruth's suspicion, and this connects with the radical uncertainty and confusion that also surrounds S's death. Both are key examples of how Quin uses the polyvocal forms and trinary logic of *Three* to insist upon the irreducible complexity, messiness and precariousness of interpersonal experiences – as well as of wider cultural questions. The text refuses to decide about, explain or judge the situations it depicts, instead preferring and delighting in a collage of ambivalent, divergent and productive possibilities.

## Notes

1. Quin, *Three* (Sheffield: And Other Stories, 2020), p. 139. Subsequent page references for *Three* in this chapter are in parenthesis in the text. S fantasises about 'a body' drifting out and away, to 'never be discovered', as Berg wishes to disappear 'into the very centre of the ocean'. Quin, *Berg*, p. 140.
2. Juliet Jacques, 'Fundamental Uncertainties: On *Three*', *Music & Literature No. 7* (2016), p. 157.
3. Joshua Cohen, 'Introduction' to *Three*, pp. v–x (p. v). See also *Three*, p. 131.
4. Ibid. p. ix. As John Hall puts it in 'The Mighty Quin', her prose 'is a landscape strewn with three-corned dances; the shape is the prime figure of Quin's geometry'. *The Guardian*, 29 April 1972, p. 8.
5. Quin, *Three*; for example, pp. 24, 104, 106.
6. Sigmund Freud, 'Beyond the Pleasure Principle', *Beyond the Pleasure Principle and Other Writing*, trans. John Reddick (London: Penguin, 2003), p. 78. Italics in original. For Freud, in the case of self-destruction, the self takes a 'short cut to its life's goal (to short-circuit the system as it were)' and the attempt at mastery is synonymous with absence, p. 79.
7. Peter Brooks, *Reading for the Plot: Design and Intention in Narrative* (Cambridge, MA and London: Harvard University Press, 1984), p. 156.
8. A wonderfully explicit example of this from a writer Quin read is found in *Tess of the D'Urbervilles*, where Tess imagines her death-day: 'a day which lay sly and unseen among all the other days of the year', that recurs with the regularity of a birthday and is already somehow marked out from the beginning of her life. Thomas Hardy, *Tess of the D'Urbervilles* (London: Penguin, 1979), p. 149.
9. This connection between death and articulation recalls Walter Benjamin's claims that 'Death is the sanction of everything that the storyteller can tell. He has borrowed his authority from death'; 'life – and this is the stuff that stories are made of – first assumes transmissible form at the moment of his death'. 'The Storyteller', *Illuminations*, trans. Harry Zorn (London: Pimlico, 1999), p. 93. For further consideration of the annihilation of the self in writing, see Richard Poirier, 'Writing Off the Self', *Raritan*, Summer (1981), pp. 106–33.

10. For a consideration of the problematic idea of a woman's death as self-authorship, see Elisabeth Bronfen's *Over Her Dead Body: Death, Femininity and the Aesthetic* (Manchester: Manchester University Press, 1990), in particular pp. 141–67.
11. Morley, 'The Love Affair(s) of Ann Quin', pp. 131–2.
12. Bronfen, *Over Her Dead Body*, p. 30. Bronfen's argument here recalls Derrida's observation, in *Memoirs of the Blind*, that the act of representation always takes place during 'the suspension of the gaze', p. 117.
13. Roland Barthes suggests that an expression of absence works to presence the other, because of the desire for contact: 'you have gone (which I lament), you are here (since I am addressing you)'. *A Lover's Discourse*, trans. Richard Howard (London: Penguin, 1990), p. 15.
14. Collage was Quin's method too: 'My ménage book is bit by bit progressing – in fact it's becoming a collage, from collections of other peoples' letters (that's where you, Alan, Frank, Paddy, Myra and James come in...), receipts, bills, etc'. Quin, letter to Carol Burns, 13 February 1963.
15. For Denise Rose Hansen, 'Quin's particular aesthetic of touch is alert to what is close at hand, but equally to what is not, quite, there.' For Hansen's compelling discussion of touch in *Three*, see 'Little Tin Openers: Ann Quin's Aesthetic of Touch', *Women: A Cultural Review (Re)turning to Ann Quin*, 33:1 (2022), pp. 52–72 (p. 69).
16. I refer to spoken sections of S's text as aural rather than oral because they are experienced as *heard*, rather than spoken. For an attentive reading of the aurality of S's taped voice and the historical significance of reel-to-reel tape in *Three*, see Adam Guy, 'Ann Quin on Tape: Three's Auralities', *Women: A Cultural Review, (Re)turning to Ann Quin*, 33:1 (2022), pp. 73–92. Sections of *Three* can be heard, read aloud in Quin's (taped) voice and made available by Larry Goodell: https://duende.bandcamp.com/album/ann-quin-reads-from-three-1965. Track 2 includes Quin reading the section above.
17. This 'spoken' free verse form recalls Quin's engagement with the Black Mountain poets, who aimed to create poetic forms able to communicate direct experience and perception as closely as possible. In particular, Quin refers to Charles Olson and Robert Creeley, who edited the *Black Mountain Poetry Review*. She met Creeley in 1964 at a Calder event and they remained friends: *Three* is dedicated to 'Bobbie and Bobb' Creeley. Andrew Hassam claims Quin's particular diary forms in *Three* evidence a 'North American influence on the younger British writers of the time'. *Writing and Reality: A Study of Modern British Diary Fiction* (London and Westport, CT: Greenwood Press, 1993), p. 5.
18. Natalie Sarraute describes pre- or inter-linguistic pauses in speech as 'numerous, entangled movements that have come up from the depths',

in 'Conversation and Sub-conversation', *The Age of Suspicion*, trans. Maria Jolas (New York: George Braziller, 1963), p. 116. Sarraute's ideas are relevant for thinking about Quin's aural journal because she is discussing speech rather than writing. Quin read Sarraute in the early 1960s and said, of *Portrait of a Man Unknown*, 'without being too profane it reminded me a little of my own work'. Quin, letter to Carol Burns, undated, 1961.
19. Hassam, *Writing and Reality*, p. 5.
20. Peter Nicholls, 'Surrealism in England', in *The Cambridge History of Twentieth Century English Literature*, ed. Laura Marcus and Peter Nicholls (Cambridge: Cambridge University Press, 2004), pp. 400–1.
21. Glyn White discusses a similar effect in B. S. Johnson's *Albert Angelo*. *Reading the Graphic Surface: The Presence of the Book in Prose Fiction* (Manchester and New York: Manchester University Press, 2005), p. 97.
22. Cohen, 'Introduction' to *Three*, p. vii.
23. Brian Evenson, 'Introduction' to *Three* (Chicago: Dalkey Archive Press, 2001), p. x.
24. S's written diary describes finding 'L's diary': 'Nothing very much apart from some little black crosses, which seem to be some kind of code.' *Three*, p. 65.
25. Cohen, 'Introduction' to *Three*, p. vii.
26. A more thorough examination of the dispersive and disruptive effects and effectiveness of journal forms of *Three* can be found in Hassam's *Writing and Reality*, pp. 132–7, where he draws on comparisons with Doris Lessing's *The Golden Notebook* (1962).
27. Morley, 'The Love Affair(s) of Ann Quin', p. 131.
28. Quin, letter to Carol Burns, November 1962.
29. Andras Balint Kovacs, *Screening Modernism: European Art Cinema, 1950–1980* (Chicago and London: The University of Chicago Press, 2007), p. 115.
30. Stallybrass and White, *The Politics and Poetics of Transgression*, p. 193.
31. This brings the triangle in *Berg* to mind, in terms of Alistair and Nathaniel Berg's play for Judith, where the continuation of the rivalry is, in the end, more important than an assertion of dominance.
32. Quin, letter to Carol Burns, 26 May 1962. The film is also named as key to Quin's work – 'wouldn't you know it "Last Year at Marienbad"' – in Hall, 'The Mighty Quin', p. 8.
33. For further and detailed discussion of this combination, see Gilles Deleuze, 'Peaks of Present and Sheets of Past: Fourth Commentary on Bergson', *Cinema 2: The Time-Image,* trans. Hugh Tomlinson and Robert Galeta (London: Athlone Press, 1985), pp. 98–125.
34. Quin, letter to Carol Burns, 28 September 1962.
35. Kovacs, *Screening Modernism*, pp. 105–6.
36. Cohen, 'Introduction' to *Three*, p. ix.

37. The phrase 'elongated shadows' also occurs in Berg's visionary experience on the beach. *Berg*, p. 140.
38. Sylvia Bruce, review of *Three*, unpublished manuscript, p. 1. Carol Burns Private Collection of Papers.
39. Jordan, *Oblique Strategies*, pp. 152, 153. For Jordan's fuller discussion, see pp. 149–58.
40. The various 'games' and roles played by married couples had been outlined and discussed by Eric Berne in *Games People Play* (London: Penguin, 1964); see 'Marital Games', pp. 80–95.
41. Cohen, 'Introduction' to *Three*, p. ix.
42. This is reminiscent of the effect Ellmann identifies of Bowen's geometry: 'On one level these supernumerary presences pose an impediment to love, but on a deeper level they generate its energy'. *The Shadow Across the Page*, p. 70.
43. Cohen, 'Introduction' to *Three*, pp. v, vi.
44. Ibid. p. vi.
45. Quin, *Berg*, pp. 21, 23.
46. Jacques, 'Fundamental Uncertainties: On *Three*', p. 156.
47. 'The Chameleon' was at one stage a working title for *Three*. In discussion with Dunn, Quin refers to women in social situations as having to be chameleons. *Talking to Women*, pp. 193–4.
48. Stanley Cohen introduces this phrase in *Folk Devils and Moral Panics*, p. 177.
49. Ibid. p. x. For Cohen, the 'moral panic' that followed working-class youths' need to win space largely focused on style. Teddy boys, for example, wore style and brutality as a group identity: their attitude included a callous threat of violence which, while exaggerated by the media, was nevertheless there.
50. Ibid. p. 10.
51. This is reminiscent of the sexual disappointments depicted by Quin in 'A Double Room'.
52. Although 'marital rape' did not of course exist in UK law until 1992.
53. The soundless scream and inarticulate sound recur in Quin's writing. I consider their similar/different effects in my chapters on *Tripticks* and *The Unmapped Country*.
54. The ambivalence and political significance of Quin's writing of sex in *Three* is discussed in more detail in Nell Osborne's insightful article on sexual violence, female agency and consent: '"I'm telling you to stop": Staging the Drama of Rape, Experiment and Sexual Consent in Ann Quin's *Three* and Muriel Spark's *The Driver's Seat*', *Angles* 13 (2021), doi: 10.4000/angles.3818.
55. The relationship between social status/class and disgust at sex is considered in Stallybrass and White's discussion of the bourgeois rejection of carnival in chapter 5 of *The Politics and Poetics of Transgression*, pp. 171–90.

56. This section is partially repeated on p. 118: 'Was it like this with / Never before like this. Before. Like waves. The coming. / Slowly. Then the rush of it. Demanding more. But without asking. / Dual roles. Realised. Yes yes / Yes.'
57. Guy considers the communicative potential of this hum in 'Ann Quin on Tape: *Three*'s Auralities', pp. 87–90.

Vignette

# 'Have you tried it with three?'[1]

> What role do you think sexual fantasy played in her writing? Three, that's it. Three. Three. Three.[2]
>
> Do if you possibly can go & see Marat/Sade it is fascinating – a dream within a dream (well mine anyway!).[3]

When life in London became too intense, Quin escaped and caught the train to Axminster, in retreat to Carol and Alan Burns's Swain's Lane cottage in Dorset. The cottage had no running water or electricity, water was drawn from a well, and there were oil lamps and a garden with an apple orchard. Here, Quin dreamt of meeting a farm labourer like Mellors from D. H. Lawrence's *Lady Chatterley's Lover*, spent time with her married friends Carol and Alan, reading and talking, walked for miles along the coast, and saw her then lover Henry Williamson.[4]

Quin was promiscuous and sexually adventurous, and her permissive libertine fantasies and desires often transgressed boundaries. Her role as third to several of her married friends' twos – including Carol and Alan Burns, Robert and Diane Sward, and Bob and Bobbie Creeley, for example (the latter of whom *Three* is dedicated to) – reveals a wish to access and open up the boundaries of intimate relationships and the perceived intimacy of two, and to experiment with different forms of sexuality and sexual experiences. When in conversation with John Hall, Quin describes herself as bisexual, but her interest in the performativity of gender and her resistance to binaries could be seen to position her as queer.[5] Throughout her life Quin's desire was mobile and sometimes taboo: as a young adult she met with her father in London and 'pretended he was my lover'; her first and long-lasting love was for her half-brother who she met at fourteen and fell 'desperately in love with'; and towards the end of her life she fell in love with her nephew, his son.[6] Like S, then, in her intimate and fantasy life Quin was interested in playing at and blurring distinctions between roles such daughter/sister/lover/other. As she expressed it to Brocard Sewell: 'I have often found myself at my best, a kind of security when with two other people, most of my friends are couples, & I suppose automatically I play the role of the child.'[7]

Yet despite the 1960s supposedly being an era of increased sexual freedom for both women and men, Quin's desire for a *ménage à trois* – whether her role in this was as lover and/or child – still challenged accepted structures of monogamy and committed coupledom. So, while Quin's friendship with the Burnses was supportive and creatively productive, it was also not without tension, and they refused her request to dedicate *Three* to them. And her longing for liberated and even libertine intimacy was complicated by Quin's own simultaneous desire for – and fear of being trapped by – domesticity, especially as a woman. When talking with Nell Dunn in 1965, she says: 'if I married I would hate to think that they expected me to have a meal there every time they wanted a meal. I would really loathe that and I think women can get very bogged down and they can get bugged up about it'.[8] Yes, the stability of marriage or coupledom might be alluring, but this would, Quin felt, inevitably become ordinary, uptight and compromised, especially for the female partner. Worse, a traditional domestic set-up could well interrupt and limit the freedom to write: 'I seek stillness, as that is the vital reservoir needed for creating, and only by living on my own am I able to achieve that.'[9] At the same time Quin admitted that to 'share one's life can bring a whole area of experience. I've often thought what I really need is a wife'.[10] This joke about the appeal of homosexual marriage challenges traditional gender and marital roles, and admits and ironises a continuing tension between the position of the working (female) writer and the desire for both intimacy and sexual freedom.

## Notes

1. Quin, *Three*, p. 142.
2. Sward, email to Nonia Williams, 17 November 2008.
3. Quin, letter to Carol Burns, 23 September 1964. Patricia Waugh discusses the impact of the play's staging of the two opposing ideological positions of rationalism and libertinism in *Harvest of the 1960s: English Literature and Its Background 1960 to 1990* (Oxford: Oxford University Press, 1995), see pp. 58–60 and 111–12.
4. Henry Williamson (1895–1977), Quin's much older lover, was the writer known most famously for *Tarka the Otter* and supported her,

though rather begrudgingly, with the Harkness and D. H. Lawrence Fellowship applications.
5. Hall, 'The Mighty Quin', p. 8.
6. Quin, 'Leaving School – XI', p. 17.
7. Quin, letter to Brocard Sewell, cited in *Like Black Swans*, p. 183.
8. Dunn, *Talking to Women*, p. 186.
9. Quin, letter to Brocard Sewell, cited in *Like Black Swans*, p. 183.
10. Dunn, *Talking to Women*, p. 185.

# Chapter 3

# *Passages*: Unstable Forms of Desire

## The Female Gaze

> Not that I've dismissed the possibility my brother is dead. We have discussed what is possible, what is not. They say there's every chance. No chance at all.[1]

In *Passages*, Quin's logic of three re-emerges as a woman and her male lover search for her lost brother across a Mediterranean landscape. That this book's position will be one of ambivalent 'possibility' is evident from these opening sentences with the push and pull between opposite statements that 'there's every chance. No chance at all' 'my brother is dead'. This structure, where apparently opposing positions or perspectives in fact coexist, underlies the quest narrative in *Passages*. Like *Three* – and indeed *Berg* – the direction of the narrative resists linear trajectory and either/or binaries to offer up a more expansive both/and space of 'possibility', of 'what is possible', where statements or an outcome can be true, false and/or indeterminable at once.[2]

*Passages* ends mid-sentence with the possibility of 'the sea that soon perhaps we will cross' (108) and no full stop, like *Berg*. And, like *Three*, *Passages* is a split form text.[3] It is divided into four sections: two told from the woman's perspective in run-on prose that moves between first person and third person free indirect style, and two in the form of the man's annotated journals. Although these perspectives and forms are distinct and separated out, they also echo and reverberate with each other – like the several diary forms of *Three* – to offer multiple and often conflicting versions of the same events. In *Three*, Leonard and Ruth pore over an archive of documents, recordings and objects left behind by S in their unsuccessful search for the 'truth' of what happened and their desire for some kind of contact with her. But rather than the static location of *Three* in 'the Grey House' in England where Ruth and Leonard have been left by S, *Passages* is a text of transit and the shifting locations of hotels and trains. In *Passages*, the clues or documents relating to the missing brother are so few that even the existence of such materials is unclear – 'I remember where I came across his signature, that perhaps wasn't there at all' (2) – and his voice is absent from the text, so that here the desired third character entirely eludes the narrative and cannot be located at all. While in *Three* the focus of the text and of Leonard and Ruth's desires are directed towards S, the role of the missing brother in *Passages* is less clear, and the drive of this text instead focuses on the woman and man's fantasies, libidos and desires for self-discovery.

In *Three* depictions of sex and desire are used to critique the disappointment of married coupledom and the forced violence of marital rape: in *Passages* depictions of sex and sexual fantasy explore the possibilities and limitations of 1960s libertinism and promiscuous 'free love', especially for women. For Bennett, *Passages* offers 'one of the most veracious and moving depictions of the tensions and conflicts, the push and pull, that beset a fervid love affair'.[4] This love affair between the woman and man is intense and non monogamous. The man has sex with some women at a party, as well as with local women they meet. The woman's desire for others seems connected to her missing brother: the man observes that she 'makes love with men younger than herself (the age her brother disappeared?)' (37).[5] The man has sex with some women at a party, as well as with local women they meet. Both characters are aware of, and watch (and are even perhaps aware of the other watching) each other's sexual encounters with other people. In this, the gendered, male voyeurism present in *Berg* in Berg's watching of the dance hall opposite and in *Three* in Leonard's viewing of videos of S is reimagined in *Passages*, where the gaze is positioned as both male and female: my reading here is particularly interested in Quin's writing of the latter.

Towards the end of the first section of the woman's narrative, for instance, she describes watching the man in a threesome at a party:

the three
   lay there, their legs, arms linked in the formation of a dance. Under the chandelier they moved slowly. He in the middle hardly moved, watching the two women circle. Their backs arched, breasts thrust high, forward. The leather strap he passed through suspenders. Black slithered across white, between the less black. His head raised, then bent. Arms spread out from the white sleeves. He balanced a whip in

each hand. The girl strapped to the chair. Her head swayed over the back, hair hung down. Legs apart, fruit placed between. He drank, but did not swallow. On his knees he thrust his face between. Sound of whip meeting flesh, into a rhythm, slow at first. Merged with the music, as she danced on the table, danced with her shadow, bent back as though to perform a backward somersault, while the other woman behind stretched out both her hands as if to catch the flying figure. (21)

In his diary the man writes: 'I was aware of her, in fact felt sure I saw her', 'saw a face flattened against the window, when looking past the two women lying either side of me' (53).[6] The woman's description seems dispassionate and distanced as she itemises details and observes the movement, contrasts and shapes created by the three bodies who merge and dance together, swaying, bending, arching, slithering. And the props – whips, suspenders, fruit – and the presence of the watching woman, together with the nature of the scene seen – the 'legs apart, fruit placed between' – suggest a choreographed and staged performance that anticipates an audience.[7]

While Quin called this her 'pornographic book' and described the 'gt. orgy scene more or less ending 1st pt.' in letters to Sward, its sex scenes are in fact few and their artificial manner is suggestive of erotic set pieces as the example above shows.[8] For one of the book's early reviewers, these ultimately rather static sex scenes were disappointing: 'the temperature of even the most torrid moments of sex passages never rise above 4 degrees'.[9] Yet such an appraisal misses how such scenes are directly reminiscent of the formulaic and structured eroticism of writers like Georges Bataille and the Marquis de Sade, whose transgressive literature flouts tableaux, parody and pastiche – all of which are clearly employed by Quin here too. And though Anaïs Nin's books of erotica – *Delta of Venus* (1977) and *Little Birds* (1979) – were yet to be published, these had in fact been written much earlier, in the 1940s, and their caricatured and theatrical sexual content is foreshadowed and echoed in some Nin's other fiction, which Quin had read.[10] *Passages* suggests an awareness of the limitations of such writing when the man observes: 'Perhaps the orgy my imagination composes is better than the actual thing' (106).

Elsewhere Quin's writing *is* erotic and 'charged with sexual energy' – Leonard's fingering of the orchids in *Three*, for example, or the hammering in 'Never Trust a Man Who Bathes with His Fingernails'.[11] But in *Passages*, as in *Berg* and *Three*, the sex scenes themselves are often deliberately lacking in eroticism and intimacy. Rather than reading such scenes as failed eroticism, I interpret them as an example of Quin's wider interest in disappointing and transgressive sex scenes. In *The Sadeian Woman*, Angela Carter articulates how the supposed acceptance of female as well as male libido and promiscuity had created a kind of stereotype. 'In this period', Carter writes, libertine sex was an 'act', a rite of passage, and '"promiscuous abandon" seemed the only type of free exchange', but this ignored how 'pornography [itself] must always have the false simplicity of the fable', because it 'deals in false universals'.[12] *Passages* can be seen to play with stereotypes of libertinism and the 'false simplicity' and 'false universals' of pornography in the fable-like, distancing quality of its framed and static sex scenes.

For Carter, what seemed to be an era of increased sexual freedom was in fact also one that renewed and required the re-enactment of sexual and gendered stereotypes, and Quin offers a complex response to this context with her writing of the female gaze in the woman's sections of *Passages*. Quin demonstrates awareness of the idea of the desiring male gaze when she says to Dunn, 'I think eroticism is more visual – men go much more in a way for visual eroticism.'[13] In contrast, according to Mary Ann Doane in her consideration of mid-century cinema, the female spectator has been assigned a certain 'naiveté'.[14] In this, a distinction has been made not only between the supposedly active male gaze and passive female image, but also between an assumed objective male gaze compared to the 'overinvolved female spectator'.[15] Doane identifies 'recurrent suggestions of deficiency, inadequacy, and failure in the woman's appropriation of the gaze'.[16] For John Berger, the cultural norm where 'Men look at women. Women watch themselves being looked at' results in 'The surveyor of woman in herself [being] male'.[17] Both identify limitations that have been associated with the female gaze, and Berger's point in particular is that it is the position or type of looking that is gendered and not the gender of the watcher herself. In *Passages*, the gaze of the woman's sections can be read as a desire to reclaim an active looking in which distance and self-awareness is maintained: one where the woman 'watches herself watching' (27).

This position is exemplified by the woman's location behind glass. The threesome scene above is framed by a window, and this framing of the female gaze foregrounds the activity of her looking as much as the scene being looked at:

> Again behind glass I saw
>   what did I see, for when that scene reappears it merges with a dream, fallen back into slowly, connected yet not connected in parts.

> So what I saw then was as much a voyeur's sense. And since has become heightened. Succession of images, controlled by choice. I chose then to remain outside. Later I entered, allowed other entries. In that room a series of pictures thrown on the walls, ceiling, floor, some upsidedown. Only afterwards could I see things. (20)

Here, the narrating 'I' returns to and enters a place, where, screened behind glass, the woman previously saw something with 'a voyeur's sense'. This 'sense' is both in the manner of/like a voyeur and in the act of looking, of sight. In turn this foregrounds the reader's eye, which, from various different positions, watches the watching narrator. I have suggested that the tone and form of how the threesome is described suggests an uninvolved and distanced watcher. At the same time, here there is ambivalence about whether the woman's gaze might also be a desiring one: what the woman sees 'since has become heightened', 'in specific detail' (20); it is a scene she remained outside of, looking in, but later 'entered, allowed other entries'.

This uncertainty of position is complemented by the form of the narrative here, a sequence of 'connected yet not connected' images. The confused and confusing time structure and order of events interrupts the readability of the prose, and the narrative returns to a purposefully undefined moment – 'that scene', the 'then' – from several angles.[18] This effect calls to mind Bruce Morrissette's discussion of the temporal non-specificity of nouveau roman forms.[19] The blurring of 'associative time', where memories are revived by the shifting states of a narrator or character – for instance Quin's 'behind the glass I saw/what did I see, for when that scene reappears it merges with a dream', with 'restructured time', creates a 'new fictional topology'.[20] As Morrissette points out, such nouveau roman structures are closer to music than conventional literary time patterns. Quin regularly listened to jazz musicians such as Thelonius Monk and Miles Davis; she was also directly influenced by the music and writing of John Cage.[21] It is unsurprising, then, that the movement, timing and rhythm of her writing is reminiscent of nouveau roman forms close to music. Quin herself described the technique in these sections of *Passages* as 'moving towards words and then from them v. much like jazz improvisations'.[22] Or, as it is articulated in the text, its movement is led by 'Improvisation' (27): 'Jazz filled the room, shaped shapes from spaces I could not then see' (19).

In these ways, Quin's writing of the woman's watching of the threesome scene reassesses and complicates connections between gender, the gaze, desire and ideas of sexual liberation. The position of the watching woman suggests an agentic and distanced female gaze while the static mode of the scene evokes the 'false universals' of pornography; this ambivalence recalls the paradox Carter identifies between supposed 1960s liberation on the one hand and a shoring up of gendered stereotypes on the other. Quin's writing of such stereotypes is knowing, and the deliberate absence of the erotic in the 'orgy' scenes of *Passages* calls the politics and possibilities of sexual liberation into question. At the same time, the disrupted temporality of jazz forms suggests a more ambivalent and fluid relationship between the woman's desires and what she is looking at, shaped 'from spaces I could not then see', 'only afterwards could I see things'. Here, seeing comes after sensations of form and sound, and in this, by disrupting the primacy of the woman's watching with writing inspired by the movements of jazz, Quin suggests the limitations of 'visual eroticism' (which she says 'men go much more in a way for') and the gaze when it comes to the possibilities, fantasies and writing of the female libido.

## Vibrating Prose

Quin's rethinking of the female gaze and desire in *Passages* is extended by the transgressive potential of patterns of association across the vibrating line of the woman's words. Rather than telling a story *about* the characters or their search, the divergent flow of associations and episodic prose of the woman's sections move 'like jazz improvisations' in a quest for revitalised forms of writing with which to capture intense sensory experiences and desire. This is evident in the sequencing, slippage and continuity across the line of words in the following:

> His hands round the glass, veins pressed under hairs, lighter from cuffs to knuckles. Hands above his head, marking the design of some unfamiliar birds. Slant of wings to the slant of their bodies under, caught the light of falling. They turned from a straight course into a curved one, remained at the same height, wings on the convex side of their curving movements, moved in line. Lines
>    under his eyes, mouth. His mouth betrayed the eyes' attention on the play we saw that night. (12)

This section moves around, under, above, under, between man and birds, and the line break between 'Lines' and 'under' directly performs and draws attention to such a movement. Man and birds become closely associated by the trajectory of the prose: slanting, falling, straight, curved, moving together. The connecting instance, when the man's action mimics the movement of the birds, is proliferated by repetitions and patterns in the language. The seemingly chance gesture that connects them – 'hands above his head, marking the design of some familiar birds' – is also one which marks and declares the text's patterning and design, its interest in a movement that unfolds and follows from image to image. The birds move in an ordered chain, they turn and slant; so too does the line of words that moves with and weaves around them.[23]

My reading of the very particular effects of Quin's prose in the woman's sections of *Passages* can be extended and deepened by engaging with Roland Barthes' captivating and generative analysis of Georges Bataille's erotic book *Story of the Eye* (1928) in his essay 'The Metaphor of the Eye'. There, Barthes claims that *Story of the Eye* is not a story of characters but a story of the object itself (the eye), which moves 'from *image to image*':

> its story is that of migration, the cycle of the avatars it passes through, far removed from its original being, down the path of a particular imagination that distorts but never drops it.[24]

Quin writes of the woman's watching as a 'Succession of images', and the movement of words and birds in the extract above not only coincides with Barthes' use of the concept of 'migration', but their arrangement also corresponds with his term 'syntagma'. This refers to 'the plane of concatenation and combination of signs at the level of actual discourse (e.g. the *line* of words)' where 'narrative is simply a kind of flow of matter' driven by the search for ever invigorated forms of linguistic interchange.[25] The syncopated rhythms and reiterative patterning of Quin's words in the woman's sections similarly migrate back and forth between images and ideas. According to Barthes – and this is where his analysis is most suggestive for my reading of Quin – *the point* of the restrictive form of Bataille's book is to bring out the terms of the various metaphors, resulting in a 'wavy meaning' in which 'the whole of *Story of the Eye* signifies in the manner of a vibration'.[26] Barthes' terms here – 'wavy' and 'vibration' – are useful for the way that they participate in the qualities and effects of Bataille's writing, and they are critically productive for thinking about the woman's sections of *Passages* because of their energy and mobility. Neither *Passages* nor *Story of the Eye* is concerned with realistic story or content: both are instead interested in developing techniques with which to express the intensity of experience and ambivalence of sexual desire. And in both texts this works at word and sentence level – the line of words – by freeing 'the contiguities of terms' so that metaphors and meanings make contact, liaise and cross, and 'The world becomes *blurred*; properties are no longer separate.'[27]

In Barthes' reading, the chain of metaphors in *Story of the Eye* always carries a residue that ensures a unifying substance across different versions of the same idea, and this 'contagion of qualities' is the root of Bataille's eroticism: 'the transgression of values that is the avowed principle of eroticism is matched by – if not based on – a technical transgression of the forms of language, for the metonymy is nothing but a forced syntagma'.[28] This articulates how closely content and form are bound up in texts such as *Story of the Eye* and *Passages*, where 'the transgression of values' is 'matched by – if not based on – a technical transgression'. The idea of 'contagion' here calls to mind Ahmed's theory of disgust, and her claim that certain ideas get stuck together through a history of association: 'Such objects [ideas or words] become sticky or saturated with affect, as sites of personal and social tension.'[29] As Ahmed identifies, and as I have discussed in relation to *Berg*, this stickiness connects as much as recoils, creating 'boundaries that allow the distinction between subjects and objects' to be 'undone in the moment of their making'.[30] In *Passages*, 'technical transgression[s] of the forms of language' undo boundaries to create the vibrating prose that characterises the woman's sections. In this, as with *Story of the Eye*, whether or not Quin's writing of fantasy and desire in *Passages* is transgressive is not so much connected to how explicit (or not) the sex scenes are, but to the 'forced syntagma' and 'violation of a limit to the signifying space' of her vibrating prose.

In the woman's sections of *Passages* disparate elements of the narration are inextricably connected and interwoven. Language spills over and exceeds itself, its properties cannot remain separate – for example, in this extract which again begins with the man's gesture and which sets a chain of associations going:

> Grains in wood his fingers traced, she entered. Land many oceans spilled into. The way landscapes entered a room. Rooms she went through, corridors. Doors she opened onto carpets that grew towards trees, branches through walls, windows. Soft green light she touched, and was touched by. The scuttling of a crab or some other sea creature passed between them, over the wood. Movement under sand. Shifting of sand in front, behind. Flying fish between waves, those that fell out of the sea, fell back. (65)

Here, interior and exterior are blurred, and the writing overlaps close observation of sensory experiences at the beach – things felt, seen and heard – with the woman's imagined movements through and beyond interior spaces framed by doors and windows. The woman enters and opens into the scene: she passages along corridors and through doors, the rooms she goes through expand and grow towards trees, their branches come through the walls.

The resultant 'meaning' is wavy and blurred, for example when 'she entered', does this mean the scene where 'his fingers' trace the grains in the wood or the land oceans spill into? Instead of telling a story, Quin's prose here traces and sets in motion a flow of associations. Its composition and rhythm oscillates in a wave-like back-and-forth movement – 'his fingers traced, she entered', 'she touched, and was touched by', 'in front, behind', 'fell out of the sea, fell back'. This writing announces its own qualities – a movement which spills and shifts across a contiguous series of images, where descriptions blur into each other and it becomes hard to follow their sense or 'meaning'. Each focal point is effaced in favour of the next: land, landscapes, room, rooms, corridors, doors, trees, shifting sand, waves, and so on. The energy and vibration of this extract is heightened by simultaneous coincidence and divergence of sound and meaning repetitions: for example, the juxtaposition of 'corridors. Doors'. In one sense this proximity is mundane, but the surrounding content of the beach scene, together with the stuttering sound repetition, makes the familiar strange. A similar disruption of expectation and convention is present when the landscapes enter the room. Yes, branches can (eventually) grow through (crumbling) walls, but the implied simultaneity created by the momentum across images here renders the idea unfamiliar and uncertain.

The above extracts are good examples of how the writing in the woman's sections of *Passages* disturbs ordinarily expected linguistic associations to disrupt and invigorate language, making it stutter into new meanings. My Introduction argued that Quin's prose 'stutters' when attempting to express the experience of being in new and unfamiliar landscapes and environments. According to Deleuze, stuttering in writing 'make[s] the language take flight' by 'ceaselessly placing it [language] in a state of disequilibrium, making it bifurcate and vary in each of its terms, following an incessant modulation'.[31] The strange and unfamiliar use of ordinary words in the example above, and the reiterative, disruptive effects of sound across its syntagma, are examples of how, in *Passages*, Quin's prose makes language 'take flight'. 'Land many oceans spilled into' is an example of this. The sentence construction is unusual, beginning with the (seeming) object – which lacks the expected definite article – and ending with the verb and preposition. While the proximity of 'land' and 'oceans' is apparent, the verb 'spilled' is perhaps unexpected. Elsewhere in the woman's sections, 'Unmade roads curled above chasms' (7) and 'fish [are] unchained at the water's edge' (3). Repeatedly in the woman's sections, unusual sequencing and unexpected words interrupt readability and Quin's language stutters and vibrates so that, rather than invoking pre-existing ones, new and alternative meanings are made, 'unmade' and 'unchained'. Across the woman's sections of *Passages* then, the unstable forms of Quin's writing work to explore and express linguistic and sexual desire – to disrupt and rethink the female gaze, and to play with the transgressive and suggestive potential of patterns of association at the word level of the dynamic prose.

### Mobilising Mythologies

Here, I turn attention to the man's journal sections of *Passages*, to analyse the reading effects of their paratactic and oblique forms, and to consider how the mythical content of these sections continues the book's reconsideration of the gaze. The man's journal is particularly visually striking for the form of its fragmented parallel columns of text, which initially seem more static and less 'wavy' than the woman's sections of prose, and that are mostly composed of marginal notes and source material on the left-hand side of the page, with diary passages and notes to self on the right.

My discussions of Oedipus in *Berg* and the classical statues in *Three* have shown how Quin was interested in both engaging with the structures and suggestiveness of myth, and in deconstructing and reimagining mythic forms and ideas: how she was clearly well versed in, for example, stories of Greek mythology and religion, and was interested in their potential for interpreting the modern world.[32] Such potential is clearly suggested by both the form and content of the man's journal in *Passages*:

| | |
|---|---|
| To make an order out of the myth/ the past | I would like to exhaust the limits of the possible. (88) |

This example places the man's desire 'to make an order out of myth/ the past' alongside a wish to 'exhaust the limits of the possible', in terms of what might be articulated, and how, and in the pursuit of intense experiences. Reference to 'the limits of the possible' here recalls how Quin's writing in *Berg*, *Three* and *Passages* is located in a logic of possibility and uncertainty.[33] The techniques of *Passages* aim to more fully articulate and inhabit this. To do so, the man's sections of the book generate a productive tension between the seeming pattern or order offered by myth and the past and Quin's drive towards ever more experimental forms. Barber's review of the book rightly claims that 'The tremendous energy of *Passages* derives from its extraordinary alliance of classicism and chaos.'[34] Yet for others, the close and unacknowledged use of source material, for example Jane Harrison's *Prolegomena to the Study of Greek Religion* (1903), was a problem. Robert Nye, for example, claimed that Quin's book was 'too rigorously informed by' Harrison's; 'choice bits of which', he said, 'float about undigested'.[35] And Quin does include 'bits of' Harrison's descriptions and interpretations of ancient Greek artefacts without context or the visual aid of the photographs included in the *Prolegomena*. But my analyses of the man's sections of *Passages* disagree with Nye to show how the energy of Quin's prose is in fact enhanced by the inclusion of sources such as Harrison.

The incongruity of the relationship between fragments of the *Prolegomena* and other parts of the text adds to how the parallel columns of the man's journal sections deliberately disrupt sequential readability.[36] The reader must improvise a reading approach, and this is always ambivalent and uncertain, merely one possible way of reading across and between the columns and fragments. The text itself remains in parataxis – or disequilibrium – and this energises and enhances as well as frustrates and interrupts reading. My approach here draws on Barthes' grappling with Genesis 32:22–32 in his essay 'The Struggle with the Angel', where he suggests that the reader 'savour [the] friction between two intelligibilities':[37]

| | |
|---|---|
| Drawing of a third Siren's eye by two strokes only without the pupil: the sightless eye, eye in death/sleep/blindness | Sometimes she talks in her sleep. Names I don't know. Some secret language. She says I talk Hebrew in my sleep, yet I only know a few words in that language. There are moments when she looks at me startled, not really seeing me, perhaps thinking I am someone else. The walls shift in patterns, colour, shapes behind her head, and I think I am somewhere else. At home perhaps, where the murmurs are Mother's, made from her bed, the light shining from the kitchen, stopping in a blade of light at the foot of the |

| | |
|---|---|
| Image of myself as Bar-Lgura, the Semitic demon sitting on the roof and leaping down on them all. | bed. How I hated Mother then. Day after day (and nights, long nights) of pain. Windows closed, curtains pulled, thin-walled box rooms. Death, the smell of it, the sickness permeated everything. Nurses, doctors came and went, she thought they were family. I made her hot drinks and thought of pissing in them. (33) |

As the eye passages to and fro across the page here, there are plenty of what seem to be connections between the two columns of text. For example, the annotations on the left do appear to comment on and give meaning to the memories narrated on the right, where the Jewish man describes the experience of watching his mother dying. The marginal notes include a description of a drawing which illustrates the sightless eye of a third siren, as well as the narrator's self-identification with the image of Bar-Lgura, an occult Semitic demon. The content of the parallels here creates a reading between Hellenic and Judaic traditions. For example, a connection is suggested between the 'Drawing of a third Siren's eye', taken from a description in the *Prolegomena*, and the mother's death.[38] In this way, the imagery and connotations of 'eye', 'sleep' 'blindness' and 'death' do seem to connect the marginal notes and journal text. While it is unclear what their exact relationship is, whether interpretative or coincidental, the cultural ambivalence created by the alongside-ness of the two traditions here creates a multiple and open-ended 'improvised' reading of both together rather than of either/or.

Eye-sleep-blindness-death connotations echo across the man's journal sections. The closed eye of the siren above evokes the myth of Medusa. Elsewhere in the man's journal Medusa is directly present in a dream: she is indeed encountered, as she only can be, while the man's eyes are closed. The description of the dream (as well as its 'cut-up') is accompanied by an excerpt from Harrison describing a 'black-figured olpe' which portrays 'the slaying of Medusa by Perseus', and Quin's depictions of Medusa in the dream(s) focus on the 'evil' power of her eyes. For example, the '*Dream*' of Medusa, as it is titled in the man's journal, begins:

> Medusa entered my room. I felt uneasy, certain she had only evil intentions. I had the revolver ready. I could just see her eyes, great glowing ovals; I would aim at those – just two shots. (98)

This dream narrative is followed by several passages of the '*Cut-up dream*', which begins:

Medusa entered a room that opened out onto the balcony. I had evil intentions. She had the revolver ready. I saw three women, great glowing ovals, on a mattress, in an arc. (98)

This second narrative continues with a grotesque, fairy-tale like sexual fantasy, involving two 'monstrous guardians' and a girl, all of whom have 'large warts covering their bodies' (98).[39] Both dream narrative and cut-up begin with the entrance of Medusa, whose 'evil' eyes must be annihilated. The metamorphosis of 'her eyes, great glowing ovals' into 'three women, great glowing ovals' recalls not only Medusa's position as one of three Gorgon sisters, but also the syntagma of the woman's narrative sections: the two eyes are ovals that become three women.[40] The powerful and destructive effects of Medusa's (female) gaze, the subject who cannot be looked at or objectified by the male gaze, not only connects with and destabilises the focus on visual desire and looking in the man's sections of *Passages*; it energises and is energised by the complex and ambivalent female gaze in the woman's sections of the book. It is only ever during the suspension of the gaze, when looking is instead oblique and diverted, that Medusa can be encountered.[41] The ambiguous role of the cut-up '*Dream*', where partially repeated content is complicated rather than elucidated by the parataxis of the three versions of the story, adds to this by directly calling attention to Quin's writing process.[42] Reading *Passages*, particularly the man's sections, is therefore always an improvised and indirect process that allows for ongoing ambivalence and friction between different ways of making the text intelligible. The presence of Medusa – who represents the female gaze but cannot be looked at directly – as well as the parallel fragments of material which divert readability and send it sideways, recall Barthes' claim that when a text remains 'oblique, readability is *diverted*' and must remain open-ended.[43]

By reading and rewriting Harrison's own rereading of Greek myth, *Passages* is itself involved in an already open-ended process of reinterpretation. Harrison, a progressive feminist scholar and close associate of Virginia Woolf, wrote the *Prolegomena* to redress 'a fundamental error in method': 'the habit of viewing Greek religion exclusively through the medium of Greek literature'.[44] In particular, as Rachel Bowlby points out, Harrison insists on the ambiguity of myth in relation to the female body, and shows how in pre-patriarchal communities, fertility rites centred on women's bodies and nature.[45] Greek religion appropriated and recast such beliefs in terms of its own mythology and cultural structures, while maintaining the intensity of feeling and loyalty granted the earlier rites. In this way, Harrison's writing is already engaged in a process of interpreting, describing and enacting narrative and cultural evolution: the *Prolegomena* reinterprets Greek myths as already being 'modern' developments of older beliefs. So rather than reading the repositioning of myth and of Harrison's text in *Passages* as Nye does, as something Quin is doing without reason and without productive effect, this can instead be read as deliberately engaging in an already ongoing process of retelling – both in terms of Harrison's work and in relation to Quin's engagement with myth in her earlier books. And Quin's reading of books such as H.D.'s *Helen in Egypt* (1961) reveals her knowledge of other avant-garde and feminist reworkings of myth too.[46] *Helen in Egypt*, a poetic recreation of classical versions of Helen's story, has an experimental split-form and paratactic structure somewhat similar to *Passages*. The several sections of H.D.'s book intercut illustrative reasoning about Helen's situation with passages of poetry. These different forms of text act in tension with each other: although there are similarities, they are also highly divergent in both content and form, and the relationship between the two remains unexplained.

In similar ways then, the *Prolegomena*, *Helen in Egypt* and *Passages* aim to open up reading and free source texts from static meaning. Bowlby reminds us that while myths might seem to be unchanging archetypes, they in fact 'alter their possible or likely meanings according to the changing cultural contexts in which they are retold'.[47] She explains her decision to use the plural 'mythologies' in these terms: 'because, unlike 'ideology' or 'theory', the word implies a narrative movement of telling and retelling that at once sustains and changes the likely or fabulous ideas and stories in circulation'.[48] Another example of this in *Passages* is in the woman's search and desire for her brother, which recalls the Antigone myth: the man says of the woman, 'She's playing at Antigone' (30).[49] This remark connects with the idea of an archetype: the woman plays out the role of suffering sister, here for the effect of alluring other men (according to her lover). However, as Judith Butler points out in her reading of the myth, Antigone is a character whose grief is an ambiguous act of defiance which cannot be reduced to an only symbolic one. According to Butler, the Antigone myth specifically refuses readings that want to reduce it to fixed archetype and abstraction.[50] The man's sections of *Passages* likewise refuse archetype and abstraction by mobilising and energising mythologies in relation to contemporary experience. This works through the unstable and open-ended form of the text, the inclusion of fragments of source material such as Harrison's *Prolegomena* (which itself already participates in retellings of mythic stories) and the parallel columns of text that demand an oblique and improvised reading approach; and in particular through Quin's rewriting of Medusa and Antigone, which specifically locate the engagement with myth in terms of female experiences of desire and the gaze.[51]

## Ambivalent Desire

> Jewish couple next door. Her large nose, dark hairline above the mouth, slender body. He shorter, plump, coughs a lot at night. They walk one behind the other in the park opposite the hotel. Their tumbled bed in the morning.
>
> The American couple opposite play cards, watch television all day, half the night. Their neatly made beds in the morning (26).
>
> Strange kind of insular feeling one has in this country, cut off from all the violence, wars etc. Films of Vietnam, the Congo, Israel etc., followed by the guy who does the weather forecast 'our immediate concern is now the weather'.[52]

The man's diary sections claim that the woman is fascinated by his Jewishness. The ambivalence of her desire for him and the references to Jewish people and customs in *Passages* are some of the most politically and historically charged aspects of the book. In this context, the extracts above are relevant because of how they highlight and call into question both the assumed 'otherness' of the 'Jewish couple next door', and the 'insular' and 'cut off' feeling of Britain in the 1960s. In the letter to Sward here, Quin claims that the most urgent Jewish question of the time (Israel) is one of the situations – together with those in the Congo and Vietnam – treated as distant and distinct from 'our immediate concern' in 'this country'. The wry inverted commas communicate her heightened awareness, having recently returned from living and travelling in America, of a British tendency to distance itself from world politics.

Even though from the Jewish man's perspective, the stereotyped description of the Jewish couple above makes for uncomfortable reading. Given the timing of *Passages* – written during the same decade that the widely reported Eichmann trial took place in Jerusalem[53] – it is worth asking how deliberate or unwitting such remarks are, and what their purpose might be. In her letters to the Jewish Carol Burns, Quin seems to evidence and perpetuate a casual anti-Semitism as she jokes about 'yids eating and farting'.[54] While this repeats a phrase Carol herself uses, when the comment comes from Quin's pen, its meaning is ambiguous and potentially offensive. Yet it is clear from the letters of the time that Quin felt herself to be philosemitic. This ambivalence, between a tendency to stereotyping at the same time as the expression of intrigue or desire, is important in terms of the book's historical context and because of how *Passages* participates in the unstable position of the long-standing British literary fascination with Jewish characters.[55] In the example above, the short, plump, coughing male Jewish body recalls nineteenth-century stereotypes about the 'degenerate' as opposed to 'muscle Jew'. The former was a feminised character with a weak and inferior physique supposedly subservient to his intellect.[56] In Quin's writing here, the man's feminisation is heightened by the contrast with the Jewish woman's stereotypically masculine characteristics of a large nose and dark hairline above the mouth. This fascination with and stereotyping of the otherness of the hairy Jewish woman recalls, for example, the ambivalent desire for Honor Klein in Iris Murdoch's *A Severed Head*, who the protagonist initially finds repulsive and unfeminine, but later irresistible.[57]

While in the example above the Jewish couple are clearly figures of interest, intrigue and difference, what is less clear is whether they are intended as objects of disgust and/or desire. If their physical characteristics do not make them appealing, arguably the tumbled bed in the morning does. This implies a warmth and intimacy that is emphasised by contrast with the American couple's passive television watching and neatly made bed. The Jewish couple might be physically unattractive, the narrative suggests, but they are also passionate and interesting. Of course, the appeal of the implied passion of their tumbled bed could be seen to itself enact another stereotype, which is that of the animalistic passions of the exotic other. The ambiguity of this attraction/repulsion reflects what scholars such as Nadia Valman, Bryan Cheyette and Tony Kushner have argued is a wider, and specifically English, attitude towards Jews. They find a continuing ambivalence towards Jews in the English literary imaginary, in which anti- and philosemitism become indistinguishable and Cheyette points out such 'perceptions of Jewish Otherness [. . .] are deeply ingrained in British culture'.[58] In illustration, he offers a story about Martin and Kingsley Amis which exemplifies this position: 'Both father and son [. . .] considered Jews to be "exotic and different". As a result, Martin Amis ended up liking Jews whereas Kingsley Amis disliked them. One should not underestimate this statement.'[59]

It is not so much the professed like or dislike of Jews that is important here, but the problem inherent with both father and son's positioning of the Jew as wholly other. Zygmunt Bauman has called this 'practice of setting the Jews apart as a people radically different from all the others' 'allosemitism'.[60] This position 'is essentially non-committal [...] it does not unambiguously determine either hatred or love of Jews, but contains the seeds of both'.[61] Not only is this allosemitism, or radically ambivalent attitude towards the (perceived) other, potentially present in the attitude towards the Jewish couple above – as well as throughout *Passages* – it certainly seems to characterise Barber's review of the book which calls the man 'a satyr, maimed by his own duality – in a sense, by his alien Jewishness'.[62]

To some extent, representations of Jewishness in *Passages* – for example the Jewish couple above – could be read to express allosemitism. This position also seems to be expressed in the female character's attitude to the man's Jewish heritage.[63] Her ambivalent desire and fascination is evident where one minute she criticises 'you and your middle-class Jewish upbringing [...] never a step out of place that's your trouble' (89) and the next admires it:

> She envies my Jewish blood, no reason, at least she said there wasn't any specific one. Envy for the historical sense of it all, a meaning for feeling persecuted? Strangely enough I've felt more Jewish with her curiosity that I've ever felt before. Though usually I feel no more Jewish than

|  | | |
|---|---|---|
| | lover | |
| | husband | |
| Can be any one of these, according to whim/projection. What is it/shall it be for today | brother father guardian prophet | 'The scape-goat all skin and bone |
| | mystic writer addict | While moral business, not his own, Was bound about this head'. |
| = | demi-god | |
| = | beast | Hebrew Conception: The scape-goat was not a sacrifice proper: its sending away was preceded by sacrifice |

'And the goat shall bear upon him all their iniquities into a land not inhabited' (33–4)

Here, the attitude and expectations of the non-Jewish woman are placed in parataxis – and arguably in tension – with the thoughts of the Jewish man, as perceptions of other and otherness are pitted against each other. His characterising of himself as variously 'lover', 'brother', 'prophet', 'mystic' and 'demi-god' delineates the range of roles supposedly available to him. When read in conjunction with both the three meditations on the 'scape-goat' and the woman's curiosity about him as Jewish, these roles seem narrowed and recast in terms of ideas of religious inheritance. What is interesting here is that the narrative explicitly suggests that what makes the man feel the most Jewish is the woman's curiosity about him.[64] This notion of the otherness of the Jewish person as being something always created by others recalls Sartre's discussion in *Anti-Semite and Jew* (1965), which claims that the Jew's identity as 'a Jew' is always one presumed or imposed from without.[65]

By suggesting that the woman's curiosity is reductive, *Passages* can be seen to raise and engage with important questions about where the woman's ideas about Jewishness come from: the fragmented form of the narrative in the example above asks who exactly the other is in such a representation and reveals how an allosemitic fascination with otherness skews and disrupts representation and understanding. The woman's 'Envy for the historical sense of it all, a meaning for feeling persecuted' is placed alongside the threefold representation of ideas about the 'scape-goat', and both of these, through mimicry and repetition, interrogate the idea that the Jewish role in history is fixed. Such an assumption is based on a stereotyped, outdated and mythical idea of the Torah as unchanging and legalistic, as well as an eschatological view in terms of the Jew as eternal victim after the Holocaust. Such a misrepresentation perpetuates the misconceived tension between the supposed flexibility, spontaneity and progression of Hellenism and an assumed strictness of conscience of Hebraism – a tension which Quin's form in these sections of the book deliberately energises and disrupts.[66]

The problem, as *Passages* itself suggests, with the woman's 'historical' sense of Jewishness and ambivalent desire for the Jewish man is that it is framed in terms of a fixed mythology. As Cheyette claims: 'We need to dismantle a view of anti-Semitism as a freefloating eternal hatred and locate discourse about Jews, certainly in the modern and contemporary era, within specific contexts and events.'[67] Given this, I want finally here to briefly think further about Jewishness in *Passages* specifically in terms of its historical context. Written in the late 1960s during a crucial era in terms of Jewish identity in a post-Holocaust world, the book is ideally placed for interrogating the position of Jews in the British literary imagination. In the 1960s the full facts of the Holocaust were beginning to come to light and, after the Suez crisis of 1956 and the Six Day War in 1967, questions surrounding the legitimacy of Israel – and by implication, Judaism's place in the modern world and imaginary – were highly topical (as Quin's letter to Sward at the start of this section identifies). For example, Tony Benn's 1970 response to Enoch Powell's 1968 'rivers of blood' speech consciously evoked the Holocaust. Benn's wording – 'the flag of racialism that has been hoisted in Wolverhampton [Powell's constituency] is beginning to look like the one that fluttered 25 years ago over Dachau and Belsen' – is, for Kushner, evidence of gross misappropriation.[68]

This kind of misrepresentation was exacerbated by a pervasive, casualised prejudice against Jews at this time in British culture, as Muriel Spark's story 'The Gentile Jewesses' (1963) evidences when a character claims that to admit Jewish heritage would be 'bad for business'. The narrator adds: 'she would have been amazed at any suggestion that this attitude was a weak or wrong one'.[69] Spark's story critiques British attitudes of a pervasive anti-Jewish prejudice concurrent with a refusal to admit that anti-Semitism is perhaps deeply bound up with British liberalism. According to Cheyette, 'the history of modern and contemporary anti-Semitism [is in fact] part of the history and culture of the liberal nation state'.[70] In different ways, Benn's speech and Spark's story connect a supposedly increased liberalism with a simultaneous perpetuation of anti-/allosemitism and of Jewish stereotypes. Quin provides a generative and complex response to this context via her deconstruction of the woman's ambivalent desire for the Jewish man. And, as my readings throughout this chapter have shown, Quin's writing of, for example, the female gaze, static sex scenes and ambiguous, transgressive desires in *Passages* cumulatively call into question what kinds of sexual and cultural freedoms were and were not possible in the supposedly liberal 1960s era of the book.

## Precisely Caught Experience

As the woman and man travel ever onwards, the Mediterranean setting of *Passages* – like the engagement with the question of Jewishness – locates it in a specific geographical landscape and a particular historical and political moment. Throughout their journey, the woman and man see people who 'must be' government agents lurking outside their hotel, guards and police who 'must be' bribed, officials who try to obstruct their search. The man says: 'I think we are still being watched. He stood back from the window. There's a man on the corner—been there all morning I think he must be a Government agent or security police—do you recognise him?' (66). As he puts it in his journal: 'political situation here is intolerable. There's no hope unless a revolution starts. Bloodshed under clear skies. Such a climate brings murder/war crimes easily' (31). This threat of violence is expressed throughout the narrative by the rumours of shootings and torture. The woman imagines 'screams. Line of men against the wall, blindfolded, they fell forward, sideways, back' (9), and there are stories such as 'they took six men and shot them—tied rocks to their feet and threw their bodies into the water' (17–18) and of prisoners who have been 'beaten with truncheons on the face and head', and 'taken to the terraced roof of the building for "special treatment"' (74). In this climate, the search for the brother, who 'might have' belonged to 'the Party' (6), unsurprisingly results in a series of interrogations by police, ministers, soldiers and officers, described via tense and detailed scenes. In one example, the woman and man find 'Our papers are not in order' (6). The woman's narrative attends to the noises of 'babble' and the rustling of 'numerous papers' (6) to minutiae such as 'Sweat trickled', 'A button had fallen off' (6) and 'A scar on the interpreter's hand' (7), as time ekes out before their 'missing papers have been found' (7). This surveillance in *Passages* not only complicates and enhances the extent to which this is a narrative concerned with forms of looking and the gaze; it also adds a further dimension of intensity to the experience of travelling across an unknown and unfamiliar landscape.

While the political situation captured in the examples above locates the journey of *Passages* in Europe, its setting is at once both specific and ambiguous. Although *Passages* is set in a Mediterranean country, the presence of the phrase 'Rain walked designing its own shadow' (7) (the phrase discussed in my Introduction) connects it to the setting of Quin's mid-1960s New Mexico letters and the story 'Never Trust a Man Who Bathes with His Fingernails'. What is common across the writing of these – as opposed to the writer's more familiar English settings of *Berg* and *Three* – is that, as I have argued in both my Introduction and the discussion of the woman's sections of *Passages* above, the intensity of encountering new and unfamiliar settings causes Quin's writing to stutter and vibrate in its attempts to capture such experiences. And the *Times Literary Supplement* review praised *Passages* for the book's combination of experimental forms and structures with, particularly in the woman's sections, lucid sensory impressions. For that reader, the 'juxtaposition of precisely caught experiences' together with 'the confused overall shape of the story' are mimetic, because they 'suggest exactly the reactions of the traveller whose senses acquire a new responsiveness to detail, to particular sounds, faces, physical impressions', 'expressed with lucidity and directness'.[71]

This is a significant observation about the effect of the woman's sections of *Passages* in particular, in which the experimental forms and techniques of the book are absolutely essential for communicating the specific experiences of the journey. Though it is a book very much concerned with the woman and man's fantasies and desires, the phenomenological world that they travel through is vividly drawn. This is especially striking at the start, with the noise of 'cicadas, wind colliding with trees' and 'shadows of cypresses' (1), the 'Olives dried in the sun', the 'halva' and 'small cups of black coffee, thick, sweet' (2). Here, the vivid prose of the woman's sections does primarily seem to respond to precise features of the unfamiliar landscape. Out of a train window, she observes: 'valleys grown wider, deeper, where rivers continually change their position. Bases of the hills bent back towards the course of the river. Lights, signs from cities, villages, towns I know only from maps, brochures. Long empty stations. Tracks criss-crossed' (3). This communicates what is seen in transit, from the window of the train. The prose is responsive to and evocative of its surroundings, and the resulting accumulation of minutiae mimics the wide-eyed gaze and observations of a traveller. As throughout Quin's writing in these sections of the book, expressions of sensory experience are enhanced by unusual phrasing and patterning of language, such as 'Bases of the hills bent back'.

*Passages* ends with a 'distance behind and ahead' to 'begin another journey'. But this journey is provisional and uncertain:

*Saturday*
So let us begin another journey. Change the setting. Everything is changing, the country, the climate. There is no compromise now. No country we can return to. She still has her obsession to follow through and her fantasies to live out. For myself there is less of an argument. I am for the moment committed to this moment. This train. The distance behind and ahead. And the sea that soon perhaps we will cross (108)

As Barber identifies, in *Passages*: 'the metaphor of the journey is made over into the very substance and form of the book itself'.[72] In the momentum of its journeying content and form, *Passages* moves through and resists divergent narrative modes and structures: the forms are in flux – 'Everything is changing' – and the journey is incomplete – 'the sea that perhaps soon we will cross'. The continuous stream of the woman's prose shifts between first, second and third person with a similar mobility to the fluctuating perspective in *Berg*. In these sections of *Passages*, however, Quin has abandoned conventional paragraphing for a technique where the woman's free indirect narrative is always 'moving onward',[73] separated into passages of text by line breaks and gaps on the page which often seem arbitrary and happen mid-sentence. This combination of enjambement with fragmentation creates a continuous yet episodic and shifting movement 'from one place or point to another'. As the woman and man travel ever onwards in search of her brother, so the forms of narrative in *Passages* are always in transit across and through different passages of text. And as I have shown, to read the man's sections of *Passages* the eye must sidestep to and fro across, as well as 'onwards' and down, the page. This structure is 'controlled' and seems 'exaggerated', like a passaging horse which Quin, as an experienced horsewoman, would have well appreciated.[74]

In this way, as with the possible connections between marginalia and diary entries in the man's sections, the suggestiveness of the book's title, together with the points of convergence and overlap between the woman's and man's narratives, seem to connect disparate ideas or sections and forms of text, but what exactly the purpose or meaning of the connection is remains uncertain.[75] Jesse Kohn's response to *Passages* captures the sense in which 'the now sundered synchronicities I only vaguely sense' between the woman and man's sections, as between the different parts of the man's journal, creates the movement of 'an incoherence teased by coherence'.[76] As Bennett puts it in her 'Introduction', 'once you start to unravel its layers and combinations, its possible meanings seem endless, like a beautiful ancient puzzle'.[77] Like the geometry of 'three' in *Three*, then, multiple meanings of 'passage/s' both constitute and complicate the reading of *Passages* to disrupt, confuse and refuse the possibility of a coherent master narrative or of closure: as my analyses of Quin's texts throughout this book suggest, her writing is just not interested in such structures (nor, in response, is my reading of her work). Instead, *Passages* focuses on a woman and man's ceaseless action of passaging across and onward, in the search for a missing brother who may or may not be dead. As I have shown, this momentum happens in the vibrating syntagma at word level as well as through and across the experimental and 'improvised' structures of 'forms forming themselves' (27) of the woman and man's sections. These shifting and precarious forms of writing enable Quin to explore possibilities of the female gaze and ambivalent, unstable forms of desire.

## Notes

1. Quin, *Passages* (Sheffield: And Other Stories, 2021), p. 1. Subsequent references to *Passages* in this chapter are in parenthesis in the text. *Passages* is dedicated to Quin's own lost (half) brother: 'For Ian – in Memory'.
2. These ongoing oppositions – 'there's no chance. There's every chance at all' – is reminiscent of Beckett's ambivalent 'I can't go on. I'll go on' which Peter Boxall describes as 'at once a poetics of exhaustion, and a poetics of persistence'. *Since Beckett: Contemporary Writing in the Wake of Modernism* (London and New York: Continuum, 2009), p. 1.
3. In her recent discussion of *Passages* Hannah Van Hove has thought illuminatingly about the narrative's split forms in relation to R. D. Laing's notion of the divided self. '"The moving towards words & then from them"', see in particular pp. 106–10.
4. Bennett, 'Introduction' to *Passages*, pp. vii–viii.
5. This phrasing in the man's journal exactly repeats the observation included early on in the woman's narrative: 'she makes love with men younger than herself', p. 5.
6. This scene is later also echoed in the marginalia of the man's diary sections in *Passages*, which describes a 'frescoe' where two girl acrobats grapple with a bull. One is 'about to perform a backwards somersault' and the other 'stretches out her hands as if to catch the flying figure', p. 106.
7. In de Sade's writing, which Quin seems to invoke here, sex props add to the sense of distance: they 'have the power to change [the person] into a <u>thing</u>, and that is precisely what he wants, to remove himself by becoming an object'. Simone de Beauvoir, *Must We Burn de Sade?* trans. Annette Michelson (London: Peter Neville, 1953), p. 40.
8. Respectively: Quin, letter to Sward, September 1966 and Quin, letter to Sward, 17 October 1966, Robert Sward Papers, Series 1.1, box 8.
9. Helen Burke, 'People Wandering', *The Irish Press*, 8 April 1969.
10. Quin had not only read Anaïs Nin's work, but she was in direct correspondence with her. Quin, letter to Robert Sward, 10 August 1966, Robert Sward Papers, Series 1.1, box 8.
11. Stevick, 'Voices in the Head', p. 234. The potential eroticism of the everyday phenomenological world is something Quin articulates in response to Dunn's question, 'Do you find things erotic?' She replies,

'Yes, I think so, inasmuch that the other day for instance there was someone poking their finger in a sort of round ashtray, putting their finger, jabbing it in and out.' *Talking to Women*, p. 203.
12. Carter, *The Sadeian Woman: An Exercise in Cultural History* (London: Virago, 2000), respectively pp. 9, 16 and 5–6.
13. Dunn, *Talking to Women*, p. 203.
14. Mary Ann Doane, *The Desire to Desire: The Woman's Film of the 1940s* (Bloomington and Indianapolis: Indiana University Press, 1987), p. 1.
15. Doane, *The Desire to Desire*, p. 2.
16. Ibid. p. 5.
17. John Berger, *Ways of Seeing* (London: The British Broadcasting Corporation and Penguin, 1972), pp. 46–7.
18. As Van Hove rightly notes in her discussion of this same passage of text, it can be read as reflecting on the associative processes of memory and on the writing process of *Passages* itself. See '"The moving towards words & then from them"', pp. 98–9.
19. Bruce Morrissette, 'International Aspects of the "Nouveau Roman" Author(s)', *Contemporary Literature*, 11:2 (Spring 1970), pp. 155–68.
20. Ibid. p. 163.
21. Quin had, by this time read John Cage's *Silence: Lectures and Writings* (1961). Quin, letter to Sward, 25 April 1967, Robert Sward Papers, Series 1.1, box 9.
22. Quin, letter to Sward, 21 September 1966, Robert Sward Papers, Series 1.1, box 8.
23. Elsewhere I have offered a fuller reading of this example from *Passages* to consider how one of Quin's source texts – Leonardo Da Vinci's *Notebooks* – echoes within this extract to enhance and complicate the chain of associations. See Williams, 'Ann Quin: "infuriating" Experiments?', in *British Avant-Garde Fiction of the 1960s*, ed. Kaye Mitchell and Nonia Williams (Edinburgh: Edinburgh University Press, 2019), pp. 151–3.
24. Roland Barthes, 'The Metaphor of the Eye', trans. J. A. Underwood, afterword to Georges Bataille, *Story of the Eye*, trans. Joachim Neugroschal (London: Penguin, 2001), p. 119.
25. Barthes, 'The Metaphor of the Eye', pp. 127, 123.
26. Ibid. p. 125.
27. Ibid.
28. Ibid. pp. 125–6.
29. Ahmed, *The Cultural Politics of Emotion*, p. 11.
30. Ibid. p. 83.
31. Deleuze, 'He Stuttered', *Essays Critical and Clinical*, p. 109.
32. Although she had disengaged with Catholicism, Quin continued to be fascinated by religion: 'Have also been reading quite a bit [. . .] a book I actually bought on Pueblo Gods + Myths. Strangely enough I had

been reading Jane Harrison's book on Greek Religion, and had been thinking how very similar the rituals, the ceremonies/respect/fear for the "underworld" was to the Indians sense of it all; anyway the book [on Pueblo religion] draws comparisons with the Greek legends, so it all seems to tie up with some of my own conclusions.' Quin, letter to Robert Sward, 17 February 1967, Robert Sward Papers, Series 1.1, box 9.

33. In terms of unacknowledged sources or echoes (such as to Da Vinci on birds, note 23 above) this phrase is also perhaps a reference to the famous Pindar line 'Oh my soul, exhaust the limits of the possible'.
34. Dulan Barber, 'The Human Sorceress', unpublished manuscript, Carol Burns Private Collection of Papers, p. 3.
35. Nye, 'Against the Barbarians'.
36. White, *Reading the Graphic Surface*, p. 97. In his critique of Brian McHale's assertion that columns of text interrupt the fictional world, White says McHale fails to consider 'the normalising impulse that attempts to assimilate what does not initially fit into an established pattern', p. 18.
37. Barthes, 'The Struggle with the Angel', *Image, Music, Text*, trans. Stephen Heath (London: Fontana, 1977), p. 131; see analysis pp. 129–31.
38. Jane Harrison, *Prolegomena to the Study of Greek Religion* (Cambridge: Cambridge University Press, 1903), p. 201. In the relief under discussion – a photograph of which is included in Harrison's book – the third siren throws herself to her death in despair at the fortitude of Odysseus.
39. The cut-up dream here is a mixture of the Medusa dream and another dream narrated on pp. 88–9 which tells a similar story of fantasised sex with a girl, this time beautiful, after the man has got rid of the two hideous guardians.
40. The focus on eyes here fittingly coincides with Quin's interest in the female gaze across the book, as well as with the parallels between *Passages* and *Story of the Eye*.
41. Derrida connects Medusa with the 'ruse' of the oblique gaze, where she represents the trait of an artistic structure that can only be looked at obliquely (as indeed are Quin's passages of text here); see *Memoirs of the Blind*, pp. 73 and 87.
42. Although Quin had long been practising the cut-up technique in letters to the Burnses, this is the first time it appears in her fiction directly labelled as such. It is a prevalent method in *Tripticks*, as I discuss below.
43. Barthes, 'The Struggle with the Angel', p. 132. Barthes' description of such an effect as oblique is particularly relevant given the oblique nature of the reading experience here – as exemplified by Medusa – as well as Quin's elsewhere oblique approach, as I discuss in my Introduction.
44. Harrison, 'Introduction' to the *Prolegomena*, p. vii.

45. Bowlby, *Freudian Mythologies*, p. 90.
46. Quin, letter to Robert Sward, August 10 1966, Robert Sward Papers, Series 1.1, box 8.
47. Bowlby, *Freudian Mythologies*, p. 9.
48. Ibid. p. 8. Bowlby also discusses the metamorphosis of mythic stories in terms of a 'stereotype' plate, whereby meaning changes and continues at the same time (like the syntagma), p. 217.
49. Quin too played this role: 'At fourteen I met my half brother for the first time and fell desperately in love with him; he died five years later and I saw myself as Antigone.' 'Leaving School – XI', p. 17.
50. Judith Butler, *Antigone's Claim: Kinship between Life and Death* (New York and Chichester: Columbia University Press, 2000), pp. 46–52.
51. In her introduction to *Passages*, Bennett notes that Quin's engagement with myth in this book is situated in the context of female experience, p. viii.
52. Quin, letter to Robert Sward, 25 July 1967, Robert Sward Papers, Series 1.1, box 9.
53. The Eichmann trial is surely what is being referred to in the report of the trial of a camp adjutant and his relationship with the commandant on pp. 58–60 of *Three*. For example, '"Did you know that there were gas-chambers?"/ "Yes. But I had no occasion to speak about them"/ "Never to your Commandant?"/ "He was a strange unapproachable man. I avoided asking him questions"', p. 59. For more on the Eichmann trial, see Hannah Arendt, *Eichmann in Jerusalem; A Report on the Banality of Evil* (London: Faber & Faber, 1963).
54. Quin, letter to Carol Burns, 22 August 1962.
55. Charles Dickens's *Oliver Twist* (1838) and George Du Maurier's *Trilby* (1894) are obvious nineteenth-century examples here, as well as George Eliot's *Daniel Deronda* (1876), which Quin had read. More contemporaneous examples are Iris Murdoch's *A Severed Head* (1961), Brigid Brophy's *Flesh* (1962) and Betty Miller's *Farewell Leicester Square* (1941).
56. For a fuller outline of the origins of this stereotype in English literature, see Marilyn Reizbaum's 'Max Nordau and the Generation of Jewish Muscle', in *The Image of the Jew in European Liberal Culture 1789–1914*, ed. Bryan Cheyette and Nadia Valman (Portland, OR and London: Vallentine Mitchell, 2004), pp. 130–5.
57. For more on this, see Lyndsey Stonebridge, 'The "Dark Background of Difference": Love and the Refugee in Iris Murdoch', *The Judicial Imagination: Writing after Nuremberg* (Edinburgh: Edinburgh University Press, 2011), pp. 141–65.
58. Brian Cheyette, 'English anti-Semitism: A Counter-Narrative', *Textual Practice*, 25:1 (2011), p. 23.
59. Ibid. pp. 22–3. Cheyette locates within English culture what he calls 'more troubling forms of anti-Semitism (post-1967) which [have] yet to

receive scholarly attention', p. 27. Given this, the representation of the Jew in Quin's 1969 *Passages* seems of particular import and interest.
60. Zygmunt Bauman, 'Allosemitism: Premodern, Modern, Postmodern', in *The Image of the Jew in European Liberal Culture 1789–1914*, ed. Bryan Cheyette and Nadia Valman (Portland, OR and London: Vallentine Mitchell, 2004), p. 143.
61. Ibid.
62. Barber, 'The Human Sorceress', p. 5.
63. Quin too, at this time, had a Jewish lover – Sward – whose cultural lineage was a main source of attraction: 'I remember you saying that someone Jewish would be the most suitable for me!!' Quin, letter to Carol Burns, 17 March 1967. Quin and Sward included a section entitled 'The Jewish Question' in their piece 'Living in the Present'. *The Unmapped Country: Stories & Fragments*, pp. 72–6, see p. 74.
64. Elsewhere he asks: 'What have I in common with Jews? I have hardly anything in common with myself', p. 25, as well as the already cited 'She says I talk Hebrew in my sleep, yet I only know a few words in that language', p. 33.
65. Jean-Paul Sartre, *Anti-Semite and Jew*, trans. George J. Becker (New York: Schocken Books, 1973). Sartre puts it more strongly than this: 'it is the anti-Semite who creates the Jew', p. 143.
66. This is especially the case when it is positioned as opposite Hellenistic and supposedly 'free' thought, which Quin also does in *Passages*. For more on this idea, see Gillian Rose, 'New Jerusalem Old Athens: The Holy Middle', *The Broken Middle: Out of Our Ancient Society* (Oxford: Blackwell, 1992), pp. 277–96, see especially pp. 282–3.
67. Cheyette, 'English anti-Semitism', p. 24.
68. Kushner, 'The Holocaust and Pressure Politics', in *Philosemitism, Antisemitism and 'The Jews'*, ed. Tony Kushner and Nadia Valman (Farnham and Burlington, VT: Ashgate, 2004), p. 252. Kushner criticises Benn for appropriating a Jewish tragedy for the purposes of political rhetoric and catalogues several ways in which the speech was erroneous.
69. Muriel Spark, 'The Gentile Jewesses', *The Stories of Muriel Spark* (London: The Bodley Head, 1985), p. 272.
70. Cheyette, 'English anti-Semitism', p. 24.
71. Unsigned review, 'Lovers', *Times Literary Supplement*, 3 April 1969.
72. Barber, 'The Human Sorceress', pp. 1–2.
73. '*Passage*. The action of going or moving onward, across, or past; movement from one place or point to another, or over or through a space or medium; transit. To move sideways in riding, the horse making controlled and exaggerated stepping movements. Also in extended use: to move from side to side or to and fro'. Selected definitions from *Oxford English Dictionary* online, available at https://www.oed.com/search?searchType=dictionary&q=passage&_searchBtn=Search (accessed 20 February 2022).

74. 'I wonder how much riding horses gave me my rhythms with my own writing?!!', Quin, letter to Robert Sward, 4 October 1966, Robert Sward Papers, Series 1.1, box 8. Of Quin's horse riding, Paddy Kitchen says: 'She rode as she wrote, naturally and with splendour'. 'Catherine Wheel: Recollections of Ann Quin', p.53.
75. With a narrative structured upon the proliferation of divergent echoes of its title, Hassam suggests that *Passages* is similar to but predates the technique used by Robbe-Grillet in *Topology of a Phantom City* (1976). *Writing and Reality*, pp. 96–7.
76. Jesse Kohn, 'PAS SAGES', *Music & Literature No. 7* (2016), p. 163.
77. Bennett, 'Introduction' to *Passages*, p. viii.

Vignette

# Moving onwards

> The knowledge that soon she would cross the border to a country, his country America, where once more she would feel a stranger.
> And England?
> How distant it seemed now. Yet in moments a longing.
> But for what?
> She had no sense of belonging there either. A vague feeling of 'roots'. A certain kind of identity. The freedom of knowing her way around. But the greyness. Oh that grey, grey thing creeping from the sky, smoke, buildings, into the pores of skin. Grey faces. No she could not go back to that.
>
> Quin, 'Eyes that Watch Behind the Wind', p. 111

Quin spent much of her short writing life restless, leaving England for Europe and America whenever finances allowed, crossing borders and moving onwards in search of new experiences while also seeking the space she needed to be able to write. During the early 1960s, she had travelled to Bantry in Ireland, to Italy, Paris, Amsterdam and Scotland. In the summer of 1964, Quin journeyed across Italy and the Ionian Sea, initially to Parga, and then on to Athens, Corfu, Ithaca and Kolymos, hoping to make it to Istanbul but being prevented by riots. A postcard to John Calder from this time has a photograph of statues of 'Olympia. Centaur seizing a Lapithan girl' on the front, and on the back, scribbled in black felt-tip, 'S.O.S. £.s.d. needed – desperate. Istanbul riots. Please forward to: c/o L. Matheovdaki, 4, Seremeti, Corfu, Greece'.[1] The postcard depicting classical Greece and Quin's words describing tumultuous political circumstances and pressing financial need are striking for how they connect with and communicate her fluctuating movements caught between the desire for excitement, for life to be 'EXPERIENCE in caps period', and the desire for flight.[2] 'I have very much two extremes', she said to Nell Dunn, to sometimes be the life and soul of the party but then a desperate need for stability and seclusion, for the 'peace and stillness' to write, as well as an ongoing emotional and here again material precariousness.³

In late spring 1965 she sailed to New York to take up her Harkness Fellowship. Quin did not enjoy this first trip to America. She felt increasingly frenetic and conflicted, and hated what she called this 'whale's mouth of a city, where people paddle—swim up sidewalks that are fallen ladders'.⁴ 'Oh these Yankee Apple Icecream people', she wrote to John Calder, 'with their lives like gobbled gum with the teeth marks showing! They even have a schedule (skedule!) for suffering. Aie.'⁵ But at the end of that year Quin returned to America, and this time liked it more, spending time in the Bahamas and San Francisco – in a 'crazy yellow house on a barge, just outside Sausalito, which is across from the Golden Gate bridge, and is really lovely – I guess it's the nearest to my idea of living in a tower! Anyway it gives me that sense of stillness which I find necessary to do any writing'.⁶ She went on to the Lawrence Ranch near San Christobal, New Mexico – 'a lovely lovely place' – and settled for the next year or so nearby in Placitas: 'Mountains. Mesas. Space. Ah Space'.⁷ This time in America in the mid-1960s was a productive one, the real heart of Quin's writing career. She was energised by the adventure and stimulation of being in a completely new landscape, and by her experimentations with psychedelic drugs and the short story form – she wrote to Marion Boyars that she was writing stories 'at a fantastic rate' and that their 'curved shape' was 'new, exciting'.⁸ Her enjoyment of the short form is no surprise. Quin saw herself as a poet writing in novelistic form, and during this period her writing was inspired by intense friendships with American poets such as Robert Creeley, Robert Sward and Larry Goodell.⁹

But the mid- to late 1960s was also a period of disruption and upheaval for Quin. Letters from the time show her vacillating between self-assurance and vulnerability in both work and love life. In 1967 she lived with Sward in Iowa for a while before they returned together to London for a few months. By the time they travelled to Mexico in spring 1968, it had become clear he would not divorce his wife. Devastated, Quin returned to Placitas, before retreating to the McDowell Artists' Colony in New Hampshire. During the subsequent writing of *Tripticks*, which had begun as a short story co-written with Sward, Quin felt deeply unsure of her ability to write about America and lost confidence in the book: 'Decided to more or less abandon Tripticks, that was a presumption on my part to think that I could write about this country in that way – and frankly it seemed a device.'¹⁰

## Notes

1. Quin, postcard to Calder, received 28 July 1964, Calder and Boyars manuscripts, Lilly Library Collection, Series II, box 52, folder 2.
2. Quin, 'Ghostworm', p. 133.
3. Quin in Dunn, *Talking to Women*, pp. 199, 185.
4. Quin, letter to Carol Burns, 14 May 1965.
5. Quin, letter to Calder, 19 February 1966, Calder and Boyars manuscripts, Series II, box 52, folder 2. During this first trip to America Quin met and become intimate with the British artist John Carter.
6. Quin, letter to Marion Boyars, 6 November 1965, Calder and Boyars manuscripts, Series II, box 52, folder 2.
7. Respectively Quin, letter to Carol Burns, 4 June 1965 and Quin, letter to Carol Burns, 20 June 1966.
8. Quin, letter to Marion Boyars, cited in Jennifer Hodgson's 'Introduction' to *The Unmapped Country: Stories & Fragments*, p. 11. Most of the stories and pieces included in this recent collection are from this period between 1966 and 1969.
9. For a wonderfully attentive reading of connections and miscommunications between Creeley and Quin via their published works and correspondence, see Clarke, '"S" and "M": The Last and Lost Letters Between Ann Quin and Robert Creeley'.
10. Quin, letter to Marion Boyars, 11 September 1968, Calder and Boyars manuscripts, Series II, box 52, folder 3. And *Tripticks* was criticised for a supposed hackneyed parodying of American culture in several of its press reviews; see *The Irish Press*, 10 June 1972; *The Times Literary Supplement*, 5 May 1972; *Time Out*, 26 May 1972.

Chapter 4

# *Tripticks*: Impoverished Style as Cultural Critique

## A Surface of Screens

> We look at the present through a rear view mirror. We march backwards into the future.[1]

> Days were nights. Dreams were reality. Reality seen through a rear-view mirror.[2]

Like *Passages*, *Tripticks* is a travel narrative. But in place of Mediterranean trains, this is a road trip across the highways of a post-Second World War, affluent, post-Beat, and verging on postmodern America; and while search predominantly motivates the former, here it is chase. This fourth book's unnamed male protagonist is pursued by his 'No. 1 X-wife and her schoolboy gigolo' (7): 'It was when hitting Highway 101 I noticed they were following' (10) – actually, as he later admits, 'who was chasing who I had forgotten' (136). The protagonist drives a Chevrolet – 'as soon as I climbed into the Chevy they began the chase again' (19) – his ex-wife and her lover follow in a Buick. As in these examples, much of *Tripticks* is viewed through the front windscreen and rear-view mirror of a car and accompanied by its protagonist's 'I' drawl. Its scenes are also seen in and through a variety of other screens, from a two-way mirror (10), to IBM computers (53), to the television – 'tube' (52) or 'boob tube' (53), and these various screens are used to scrutinise American consumer culture. Such surfaces magnify, filter and distort what the protagonist sees: 'faces, glass faces behind me, twisted into grotesque shapes by the Pacific winds' (12).

The book is a triptych of three sections: the first and third are from the protagonist's perspective and primarily consist of loosely connected streams of an often ironic first person narrative, paratactic paragraphs, lists, headlines, an interview, and illustrations; the middle section takes the form of subtitled letters to the protagonist from various other characters including his ex-wife and parents. Together, these sections create a confusing and increasingly anxious text where, like *Berg*, it is not quite clear what is fantasised and what takes place outside the protagonist's mind. Of all Quin's oeuvre *Tripticks* has been the least discussed. It is also the most overtly formally 'experimental' – not least because of the inclusion of Carol Annand's pop art illustrations – and the resulting mixed form text is ambiguous, cacophonous and allusive. While in *Three* and *Passages* the reader negotiates between texts and perspectives that are visually differentiated on the page, and which take distinct forms, in *Tripticks* source texts are ubiquitous, and most are inextricable and indistinguishable from the protagonist's narrative voice.

The frenetic pace and rhythm created by the narrative forms and playful, rhythmic patter of *Tripticks* complement and communicate the automobile-driven momentum of its content. Cars, as symbols of American prosperity, call to mind the supposed connection between car travel and (consumerist) freedom – between the individual 'free spirit' and the commercial system she buys into.[3] In *Ways of Seeing*, Berger points out that the density and speed of visual messages, and more specifically of publicity images, means that they belong to 'the moment': 'We see it as we turn a page, as we turn a corner, as a vehicle passes us.'[4] Berger insightfully explains how, while it is usually we who pass the image, we get the impression that publicity images pass us – in doing so he draws attention to the experience of passivity in relation to such images, which seem literally active as well as acting upon us. *Tripticks* dramatises and exposes similar thinking about images, in terms of the pace and effects created by the continual change and shift of narrative modes in response to which there is little space for processing or reflection as they pass by the reader.[5] The result is a text of surfaces which resists the readerly desire for interpretation, depth or meaning: shifting surfaces in which, as the protagonist realises at the end of *Tripticks*, he can, at best, only ever access a moment-to-moment truth or understanding. In this, the book depicts an American culture not of depth and meaning, but of constantly negotiated and changing truths. The reading effect of such a text seems anticipated by Quin as early as *Berg*: 'You looking for comprehension. Apprehension only in the curve of the road, the winding crescents.'[6]

The undifferentiated stream of images experienced thorough the windscreen on the road in *Tripticks* is paralleled by those on the television in various motel rooms. This was the 'age of television' in America and, at this time, 'the most popular TV shows revealed a nostalgia for a simpler, rural or small-town way of life'.[7] Quin's narrative is aware and dismissive of such a trend when the protagonist declares: 'Burn Down Peyton Place, and inhale deeply stretched time with red eyes' (8).[8] This critique engages with the problem of a situation where – as Theodor Adorno and Max Horkheimer put it – television, film and radio no longer bother to pretend to be art, as if their being big business alone can justify 'the rubbish they deliberately produce': Adorno and Horkheimer claim that this kind of 'culture industry' inevitably leads to the 'impoverishment of aesthetic matter'.[9] A similar form of critique of American TV is expressed in the wry injunction to 'inhale deeply stretched time with red eyes': watching too much television will make our eyes sore and red, our vision (or ability to see) blurred and impaired. Looking at the television screen has the power to distort and extend time, just as the rear-view mirror – according to the quotations which open this chapter – might seem to reverse its direction. Both forms of screen manipulate the experience of time by creating a fragmented but inescapable momentum. In *Tripticks*, not only does the eye look at what is on the television screen, it inhales and absorbs its insidious content. Television is ubiquitous and diffuse; it is in the very air the protagonist breathes, an enjoyable drug with a doping, levelling effect:

> I lay on the under-sized Queen bed and watched the tube. The everywhere check, if you push-me pull-you, all wired for a trance in the wilderness. It will be there through good and bad in the empty hours, just when you need it. Sounds made visible, a missile's white clicking teeth, a dolphin's voice-prints pick arsonist and Nasser on phone. The sound 'ga' helps make a conviction. A mental patient relaxes. 'Ah' says the President, the big-sky man hemmed in 'every man his own furnace'. Hottest prospect is a fat male genius says a post-graduate historian. The issue is as old as freedom, 'In my day we all had faces'. Mere millionaires don't count now. Monsters of Moonport, the biggest discovery since Columbus. The frenzy of youth manipulated by the viewers' communication that puzzles, excites and involves. Worth a risk, change the channel with real foes on every side looking for a wedge, while cavorting cops aim low, clicking shutters, cut and faint. Ban the Germ Mediterranean style towards the doomsday bug. No withering seal limbs, upside-down biology. We can see you on 15 Caribbean islands caught in the crossfire. (52–3) (Layout as per Quin's original text)

The numbing comfort of television is available everywhere and will be there, so it claims, 'through good and bad in the empty hours, just when you need it', 'all wired for a trance in the wilderness'. As with Berger's description of publicity images, the protagonist's trance here is not energising or creative, but passive; he lies on the bed with the stream of images passing before his eyes. Television offers 'Sounds made visible' with content ranging from missiles to dolphins to the President, represented in terms of a cut-up mixture of quotations and clichés. The rapid, list-like, free-association of the prose communicates the speed of the stream of sounded and visible images. It also ironises the lack of distinction television culture makes between the serious and the banal, for how can the meaningless sound 'ga' express a conviction about anything? This kind of lack of differentiation recalls Robert von Hallberg's claim in his assessment of American culture that 'anything goes with anything else, so evened out are expectations now'.[10]

The irony above – directed towards, for example, the big-sky man, the fat male genius and the 'real foes' being fought off by cavorting cops – is aware of such 'evened out' expectations. In this, Quin uses the inclusive nature of television to not only expose mainstream American culture, but to show how the counter-culture movement – the 'frenzy of youth' – which apparently rejected the mainstream, was in fact being 'manipulated' and subsumed into it too. Joan Didion makes similar claims in *Slouching Towards Bethlehem*, which chronicles the counter-cultural movement in Haight-Ashbury in late 1960s San Francisco. She describes disorder and dysfunction, and claims that while this movement supposedly scorned the 'soulless materialism' of American culture, it was in fact 'less in rebellion against society than ignorant of it, able only to feed back certain of its most publicised self-doubts, *Vietnam, Saran-Wrap, diet pills, the Bomb*'. It is this passive mimicry she most despairs of.[11] The passage above activates and critiques a similar impulse by regurgitating some of the counter-culture's well-known criticisms – the missile/bomb, the landing on (and claiming of) the moon, the conflict of Caribbean crossfire (Cuba). The implication in both Quin's and Didion's texts is that the 'frenzy of youth' is not able to offer much more than a surface critique because of how it has also already been co-opted by mainstream American culture.[12]

Not only is the protagonist's road trip punctuated by repeated television watching in motel rooms, but the book's fast-paced episodic narrative form is also reminiscent of the experience of watching commercials. Marshall McLuhan and Quentin Fiore remind us that the structure of adverts provides an essential insight into the medium of television, because adverts have no time for narrative or plot.[13] So too

*Tripticks*. The protagonist's screen-focused gaze is bombarded with messages about what to buy: 'Why not see for yourself a different big scene (for a nominal extra charge) that whirls you as if you were on a carousel' (24). The ventriloquy of this kind of comment, which both articulates and mimics the language of adverts, has a double effect; it contains a cynical joke about the power of advertising and at the same time seems caught up in its whirl.[14] Zambreno's reading of *Berg*, entitled 'The Ventriloquist', picks up on the polyvocity and layering of Quin's writing, with its inclusion of and fascination with 'the bleating of voices from advertisements'.[15] And according to Bowlby, the connection between screen and purchase is endemic in consumer culture: in the act of watching television and cinema screens even the pleasure of 'just looking' is something already paid for.[16] In *Tripticks*, depictions of the protagonist's viewing perpetuate, exaggerate and question such a connection via a narrative form which imitates the experience of being bombarded by advertising to ironise a consumerist culture supposedly founded on choice: 'An unprecedented freedom, but a freedom only to switch channels' (127).[17] With such witty asides, and with the book's shifting surface of screens, Quin both mimics and interrogates the consumerism of late 1960s America.

## Critiques of Counter-Culture

Throughout *Tripticks*, the depictions of drugs and drug-taking also call the ideas and motives of the counter-culture into question and show how these activities too had already been absorbed into mainstream capitalist culture. Quin's inclusion of drugs came from experience, and the short story version 'Tripticks', co-written with Sward, won *Ambit*'s 1968 writers-on-drugs competition.[18] Her partly joking letter to the editors, which accompanied the story, claims:

> This is written under my usual combination of nicotine, caffein [*sic*] and of course, the birth pill I take – Orthonovin 2.
> 
> I should like to emphasize however that although I have never written under the influence of Pot, Peyote, Acid, Hash, etc., I am absolutely certain that having taken these, especially Peyote and LSD, they did actually open out a much wider possibility for my writing afterwards – like I think the time thing is important, i.e.: it might have taken me ten perhaps longer years to have reached the stage in writing I am at the moment, so I would like you not to disregard this aspect which I feel so strongly about.[19]

While Quin denies writing the story under the direct influence of mind-expanding drugs, she claims that taking such drugs, 'especially Peyote and LSD', had influenced and progressed her writing. That this link between drugs and the creative process was made while writing *Tripticks* is unsurprising. Not only does its protagonist talk about and take drugs, but it is set in America, where the writer herself took Peyote and LSD in the mid-1960s. The idea that psychedelic drug-taking was inspirational and expansive for creativity, as well as being a spiritual experience, had of course already been written about in Aldous Huxley's *The Doors of Perception* (1954). And in Quin-era America this idea had been turned into a sometime fame and money spinner by Timothy Leary, who founded the 'League for Spiritual Discovery' in 1966.[20] January 1967 had seen the 'Gathering of the Tribes for the First Human Be-In' in San Francisco and the ensuing fall-out of the youth movement.[21] Connections between drugs, the search for spirituality, the open road and the counter-culture movement were also already being dramatised in mainstream culture: *Hair* opened on Broadway in 1968, and *Easy Rider* came out in 1969. According to Jay Stevens in *Storming Heaven: LSD and the American Dream*, 'consumer choice, in the grand American tradition, had come to the private revolution'.[22]

*Tripticks* ironises this situation and calls it into question with remarks such as 'Pot and pop-pills are morally right' (17), which interrogates the youth movement's claims about the connection between drugs and religious experience at the same time as inverting and parodying mainstream culture's censuring of drug-taking as morally wrong. The 'evened out' narrative of *Tripticks* shows not only how television, advertising and the road trip are part of mainstream American culture, but how the ideas of drug-taking libertarianism and the counter-culture had been consumed by it too. For Eli Zaretsky, the so-called counter-cultural move away from the cult of the materialist individual in fact – especially in terms of its drug-induced spiritualism and hippie style – remained immersed in the same self-admiration and commodification it professed to escape.[23] In *Tripticks*, Quin parodies this kind of position, for instance when the protagonist remembers his ex-wife's drug-taking and her saying:

> Let's have a party, let's have a fix. I just don't feature getting strung out, I just don't dig it. Like there's no need for it, no need at all. You got a habit, you like your habit, it makes you feel so good, so very very good, you gotta feed your habit, you gotta be good to your habit, it's gonna be good to you. But you don't be good to your habit, then it's gonna turn on you and be mean, real mean.

It's gonna make you hurt, it's gonna give you such awful pain. And man, I don't like pain, no kind of pain. That's why I got a habit in the first place. You know that commercial we watch I always get a bang out of it. You know the one with a bunch of women doing yoga, and this babe starts laying it on another babe about how good this yoghourt is for you. The second babe takes another mouthful. She swallows this stuff and closes her eyes. Then she says something that always makes me break up. She says 'Now this is inner peace.' And every time I see that commercial I say, 'yeah, inner peace,' and I think about my habit. (133–4) (Layout as per Quin's original text)

The mimicry of youth culture is clear here – the ex-wife just does not 'dig' getting 'strung out' 'man', and Quin's narrative is funny for its humorous ventriloquism of a certain type of speech. The advert links the supposed goodness of yoga and 'yoghourt', and enables the ex-wife to think of her drug-taking as connected with inner peace and sustenance and framed in terms of consumer culture. The connections made in the passage above, between a drugged-up counter-culture and the adoption of practices such as yoga, expose a merging between the desire for spiritual experience and increasing commodification. In 'Anticipating the Spiritual Legacy of the 1960s', Franca Bellarisi considers this context in relation to colonialism and exploitation.[24] She argues this is evident in the Beats' championing of Buddhism or The Beatles' widely publicised stay in an ashram in Rishikesh in 1968, which she discusses as examples of appropriation rather than genuine engagement with spiritual practices. For Bellarisi, any avenues 'likely to help the individual transcend the barriers of the socially and linguistically conditioned self' were tried out, be it drugs or Buddhist meditation, as if the effects would be the same and both would cleanse the 'doors of perception'. As a result, she argues, the western individual assumed that both eastern spiritual practices and mind-enhancing drugs were equally on the market and there to be consumed.[25] What perhaps began as a genuine belief in the spiritual and creative potential of psychedelics became an obsession with drug-taking as a purchasable end in itself. As Theodore Roszak puts it in his consideration of youth counter-culture, the movement ended up 'proclaiming that personal salvation and the social revolution can be packed into a capsule'.[26]

Quin's representations of drug-taking in *Tripticks* ironise not only its commodification, but also the idea that psychedelics bring 'inner peace'. Many drug-taking experiences in the book are ambiguous, expressing angst more than peace, and the protagonist quips that 'To cope with neuroses and nuisances there was a centre offering help after bad trips' (45). When he finds some photographs of his then wife in 'what looked like some black mass orgy' (59), she immediately arranges for a black mass to be held, led by a 'sleepy-eyed, scraggle-bearded' man, Nightripper: 'it was rumoured he was also called Mystic Murderer'. This figure cynically reinscribes the connection between drugs and spiritual quest in reductively consumerist terms: '"Most black magic", he drawled "is a hustle to get fast money"' (59). The protagonist's nightmarish drug experience follows:

> The scene resembled a Bosch vision of hell. Some of the women were staring, some were unusually happy, some were sick, others were screaming, and some said the walls were moving. These days if one escapes being hijacked in an airplane, mugged in the street, or sniped at by a man gone berserk, one apparently still runs the risk of getting accidentally zonked by the hors d'oeuvres at a friendly neighbourhood cocktail party. As soon as I thought this I began hallucinating, and ultimately freaked out, overturning the altar, calling Nightripper my motherfucking father. Apparently everyone soon left, except the girl, who my wife asked to stay, hoping between them they could bring me through. I remember there was a point when I didn't want to come down, but remain on an edge that appeared to touch upon a very thin line between life and death, and such power! I felt I was capable of anything, by merely putting my hand out things would fall or rise. I was Satan with God as my servant. (62) (Layout as per Quin's original text)[27]

Drug-taking and religion are aligned here, though not in terms of spiritual enlightenment – the protagonist overturns the altar, and the scene is described as resembling 'a Bosch vision of hell'.[28] This drug experience, where some of 'the women' are 'sick' and 'screaming' and the protagonist is 'hallucinating', 'freaked out' and 'upon a very thin line between life and death', seems to directly contrast with the 'inner peace' which doesn't 'feature getting strung out' in the yoga and 'yoghourt' extract above. At the same time, the tone of the narrative delivery here – 'one apparently still runs the risk of getting accidentally zonked by the hors d'oeuvres at a friendly neighbourhood cocktail party' and 'such power!' – similarly includes this more intense scene within the narrative's parodic stance. Such a tone, together with the episodic form of *Tripticks*, evens out drug-taking scenes of both bliss and nightmare to further show how this aspect of the so-called counter-culture had, along with everything else, already been absorbed into America's mainstream consumerism.

## Cut-up Words and Pictures

According to Alan Burns, Quin generated *Tripticks* almost 'entirely through cut-up'.[29] In his analysis of William Burroughs's use of the cut-up, Nathan Moore assesses how, while the technique seems to be the result of control, it is actually about freedom from control in terms of both content and method.[30] The cut-up creates distinct effects which, while they do not have coherent meaning as such, by being freed from the principal systems and structures of meaning have 'a particular evocativeness' which, Moore points out, is not that of 'structural relations but singular intensities' – very much a quality of Quin's writing here as elsewhere.[31] With this, the cut-up resists the illusion of cause-and-effect relationships that narrative usually creates or implies. It also reminds us that this writing is not generated by an author, but by 'itself', and dramatises the fact that 'All writing is cut-up, already composite, hybrid, impure, unstable.'[32] It is a technique which cuts words free from their sense and allows them to function outside of, and almost pre-emptively of, their ordinary usage, and to create new meanings. Cut-up language is caught up in a continual process of becoming which escapes the tyranny of a fixed 'meaning' bound up with the symbolic order of the dominant culture.

Quin uses the cut-up not only in a similar way to Burroughs – to cut words free from their ordinary usage and interrogate American culture – but also to question the technique itself. While the cut-up suggests generative freedom, the inevitable acts of selection and editing that take place require (artistic) control. In *Tripticks*, Quin mobilises this double sense of the cut-up, and the particular effects of this can be usefully thought about in relation to Berger's discussion of Francis Bacon, which considers what the painter called 'involuntary marks' on the canvas.[33] According to Bacon, these are chance elements of composition which enable his paintings to be more deeply suggestive. The problem is, as Berger points out, these involuntary marks are mixed in with the consciously painted, so it is often impossible to distinguish which of the marks are the 'accidental'.[34] The apparently random and yet always necessarily selective cut-up technique of Quin's writing in *Tripticks* creates a similarly ambiguous and unstable effect: it is impossible to tell which elements of the writing are cut-up, accidental collage, and which are consciously created narrative. This double sense of the cut-up is then further reinforced and challenged by the book's combination of writing and illustration.

Not only do Carol Annand's pictures enhance the pulp fiction feel of the written narrative – stories of sexualised women and shadowy men, dodgy motels and suspenseful close-ups, an unknown pursuant always over your shoulder – they also echo and extend the written narrative's wider thinking about television and the visual image. When talking about her process in an interview with Alan Burns, the illustrator says:

> I tried to make a visual narrative run parallel with Ann's narrative. I used the same Cut-up technique she used. I drew from commercial sources, clichéd images from Time magazine, American adverts and so on; sex images of suspenders and things, and pretzels and high-heeled shoes. The trouble is we didn't start the work together. The book was worked out as a literary text and I came in right at the end, after it had been agreed with the publishers. The ideal is to start together so that together you discover what you are doing, and you are continually swoping [sic] information, so that the whole thing is built up as one.
> Burns: So you end up not with an illustrated text but an integrated text?
> Annand: Yes. For example, because I came in late the type had been worked out and I was not allowed to break it up. The nearest I could get to an integrated book was to run small drawings along the bottom of the pages.[35]

For Annand, *Tripticks* is illustrated but not integrated, because although she used similar techniques and sources to Quin, the illustrations were not commissioned or added until the layout of the typescript had already been set. Alan Burns's *Dreamerika* (also 1972) is an example of an integrated illustrated text – its photographs, illustrations and cartoons were composed at the same time as the writing.[36] In *Tripticks*, while some of the images seem to directly respond to, extend and 'illustrate' the written narrative, with others there is no discernible connection between visual and written material: yet in both cases Annand's non-integrated images complement, participate in and generate the overall effects of *Tripticks* because of its inclusive 'evened out' approach in which randomness and dissonance is key. Sometimes there are clear connections between Annand's images and Quin's writing – the protagonist is described as wearing a Brooks Brothers' shirt (7) and one is drawn (11); the 'twisted' faces in the glass (12) have already appeared in illustration (11); the comment that 'your ex-wife chipped in' (118) in a narrative about marriage is flanked by a drawing of a bride and groom poised to cut a cake where instead there is a huge plate of chips labelled 'French Fries' (119).

Other connections between the writing and illustrations are more indirect. The protagonist claims that when his No. 1 X-wife's father was younger he was 'a dead ringer for Shirley Temple' (73); the following transcript for an interview with 'Shirley' is illustrated and Annand herself comments on the juxtaposition, or even collision, of the 'lesbian scene alongside the computerised face of Shirley Temple'. For Burns, Annand's 'treatment of Shirley Temple exactly gets her ambiguous innocence. The way she's extremely knowing and sophisticated, yet that sophisticated surface is just a surface: a sly comment very much in tune with Ann's book'.[37] While the image of Temple's face is clearly directly connected with the written text, the lesbian scenes are not, and their significance is unclear. In this the dissonance of the drawings coincide with and perform the written narrative's techniques: they do not primarily 'illustrate' or explain the content or meaning but instead enhance, extend and perpetuate the tension created by the polyphonic and polyvocal forms and structures of the writing.[38]

When discussing Donald Barthelme's illustrated text *Brain Damage* (1970), Brian McHale explains how it is possible for drawings to visibly and emphatically 'bring worlds of discourse, visual and verbal, into collision', and the illustrations in *Tripticks* have a similar effect.[39] While McLuhan and Fiore celebrate the discoveries made possible by the imaginative juxtaposition and collision of seemingly disparate forms in *The Medium is the Massage*, McHale asks the shrewd question of how, in practice, we might actually read such (what he calls) split and 'schizoid' texts.[40] Is it only possible to read first one and then the other, or constantly back-and-forth, or might we be able to read the visual and verbal simultaneously? he asks, concluding that while some texts approximate simultaneity, in the end the reality of our reading experience means this is just not possible.[41] In *Passages*, Quin uses the cut-up technique alongside fragmented and parallel text layouts to create dream narratives, to challenge and fragment the reading direction, and to create and insist upon multiple and open-ended readings. In response, as I have suggested in 'Mobilising Mythologies' above, the reader must improvise a reading approach. With *Tripticks*, the reader must develop a further approach to navigate different, and often clashing and confusing, forms of textual materials and techniques. For Hilary White, in both 'Tripticks' and *Tripticks* Quin specifically employs the cut-up for the kind of surface it creates, one which lacks causality, depth and explanation and is able to portray 'a reality which often seems nonsensical or irreal'.[42] White's reading gets at how in these texts the cut-up particularly communicates the 'lack of agency' of Quin's fragmented protagonist as he contends with a system that evades understanding.[43] Annand's illustrations in *Tripticks* extend this kind of effect. The resulting tension, more often than cohesion, of cut-up visual and verbal images is effective for communicating the protagonist's confused and hectic road trip across America during which he is bombarded by a stream of images and ideas, and for both creating and ironising the often nonsensical and almost impenetrable surface of cultural claims and messages.

## A Cacophony of Clichés

> You can't get blood out of a turnip so stop thinking you are nursing a hot potato. (139)

Throughout *Tripticks*, the mimicry, splicing, cut-up and reformation of the clichés of mainstream culture are used to parodic effect to make this the most obviously and consciously politicised of Quin's books.[44] These mixed-up proverbs and clichés make for the uncanny sense that we have heard or seen it all before. Words are replaced – for example turnip for stone above – and swapped, puns and jokes are created by absurd juxtapositions. The result is a double sense in which the narration is at once both overly familiar and completely unfamiliar, the reader unsure of how to place themselves in relation to the seemingly ubiquitous, almost autonomous linguistic surface. Like the book's screens, this surface deliberately frustrates a search for meaning or depth. It proliferates in a sort of free association as opposed to sense structure in terms of sound, rhyme and syncopated rhythm – an effect that at least partly arises from Quin's cut-up technique of producing the narrative. This creates a stream of narrative tics, an example of which I quote at length here to give a fuller sense of the effects:

> Eyes that fall away to 282 feet below sea level. I am hunted by bear, mountain lion, elk and deer. Duck, pheasant, rabbit, dove and quail. He at first feels a little like George Custer at Little Big Horn. The enemy is all around and awesome. The road ahead is going to be difficult there will be some nervous Nellies and some will become frustrated and bothered and break ranks under the strain, and there will be blood, irony, dwarfs and dragons, skyrockets fired to celebrate orgasm's efficiency. Suicide in a scented Sodom. Soul on acid. Hero angelic, domestic and cosmic on a journey with God on my side and the Brownie Troop.

Meanwhile I eat a toasted cheese hamburger, and dwell on five days of unconfined feasts of roasted pig. A miracle for a man who has nothing to lose. True your family adventures may not match those of ancient Greece, but you're equipped to make history and why shouldn't you be, we've worked hard to make it that way, we took no short cuts, spared no expense, watched no clock. If you come filled with dreams it may happen that your dream changes about every 15 minutes. The most is yet to come. 3,000 miles of strawberry ice cream. Lips are frenchfries teasing cole slaw fingers. My belly a Golden Poppy and the Motto is I Have Yet To Find It. Or as posted to my 3 X-wives. Ranked according to value
vehicle
food
allied products
fabricated metal
machinery
stone
clay
glass
lumber and apparel. (8–9) (Layout as per Quin's original text)

References to America's colonising history with 'George Custer at Little Big Horn' and 'you're equipped to make history' are mixed together with an onslaught of cut-up clichés and echoes of clichés, as well as a list that mimics a record of exports or expenses. Despite a mainly first person narrative perspective, these words do not even pretend to be the protagonist's or Quin's own; they are borrowed and parodied from a wide variety of literary, historical and media texts. This produces dissonance and conflicting messages: 'The enemy is all around and awesome' and 'the road ahead is going to be difficult', but there is 'nothing to lose' and 'The most is yet to come'. The result parodies and criticises American culture: a country that claims God and Brownie Troops on its side, one that believes it is and has been equipped to make history. These are the words of the 'American Dream', which, while it 'may not match those of ancient Greece', is nevertheless righteous about its ability to be the best, the most – often in material terms.[45]

This parodic reiteration means that the prose seems to make sense because much of it is familiar; at the same time, it is difficult to interpret and possibly even meaningless: 'there will be blood, irony, dwarfs and dragons, skyrockets fired to celebrate orgasm's efficiency'. Here, Quin's technique mobilises the very words of the culture being criticised in order to express that critique, and the cacophonous cut-up of the language creates 'non-sense erected as flow, [a] polyvocity that returns to haunt all relations', to use Deleuze and Guattari's suggestive and useful articulation here.[46] In *Tripticks*, the recycling flow of polyvocity is created by a network of free association and the resulting momentum is acknowledged in 'your dream changes about every 15 minutes'. As with the depiction of television, there is a sense here that everything is up for grabs, that all has been levelled and given equal value. And like Quin's writing of adverts, an enjoyment of what is on offer infects the enjoyment of technique here: the narrative simultaneously revels in and makes fun of this culture of excess made up of 3,000 miles of ice cream and unconfined feasts of roasted pig.

This tension between enjoyment and criticism, pleasure and anxiety runs throughout the book. In this, Quin's writing in *Tripticks* is, to use Fredric Jameson's words, 'fascinated precisely by this whole "degraded" landscape of schlock and kitsch, of TV scenes and *Reader's Digest* culture, of advertising and motels, of the late show and the grade-B Hollywood film'.[47] I'd like to think for a minute here about Vladimir Nabokov's *Lolita* (1955), another road book that evidences a similarly ambivalent take on American culture, because of how its techniques and form create very different effects to those in *Tripticks*.[48] In her analysis of *Lolita*, Bowlby points out that while its supposed oppositions between Europe and America, high culture and consumerism, and literary and 'trashy' novels seem to perpetuate notions of original and fake, the book in fact challenges and resists such assumptions.[49] What drives this book on 'from one motel to the next' is the way its language actually resists Humbert's snobbery by being incorporated into Lolita's mass-cultural consumerist American world. According to Bowlby, the language of consumption is powerful enough to 'take over the poetic force of the book as though against the grain of the narrator's own intentions'.[50] The resulting narrative simultaneously expresses enjoyment and disapproval, and largely does so through the tension between the different perspectives of its two protagonists. But while also evidencing some enjoyment of the language of consumption and mainstream culture, rather than taking on a poetic force, Quin's prose in *Tripticks* is deliberately flattened and incessant. In the extract above, clichés and cut-ups dominate the narrative, and the resulting prose is without distinguishable style or character. It is often impossible to differentiate between where the words of the protagonist are penned by Quin and where they have been created by cut-up – here the accidental brushstrokes cannot be distinguished from the deliberate.

With this, not only does the narrative in *Tripticks* mimic or impersonate what its protagonist describes, it expresses and becomes what is described: degraded, debased, clichéd and boring. For instance:

> Special continuous loop tape switches track automatically for uninterrupted listening pleasure as you operate simple push-button on-and-off controls with one hand exclusive. But don't forget to practise Eniasm daily APRPBWPRAA (Affirmative Prayers Release Powers By Which Positive Results Are Accomplished). Take all your bills lay them out on the bed and then ask God what to do about them ask Him for a definite plan for eliminating comfortable fat matrons in opulent costumes feelin' smellin' knowin' the corridors of the heart. (35) (Layout as per Quin's original text)

This prose is a combination of electrical appliance instruction with a satire of religious practices and belief that culminates in a preposterously long acronym. The narrative voice has no identifiable subject except for the second person addressee of the exhortations – 'you'. This long-winded and vacuous speech is indicative of how the words here are defined by an absence of meaning, where their signifying properties are debased and devalued rather than taking on poetic force; these words are not merely descriptive but performative. In his germane discussion of David Foster Wallace, James Wood claims that the 'risky tautology' of such prose is that it shows a willingness to mangle and debase itself for the sake of its project.[51] Wallace's method pushes parody to full immersion by employing the technique of an unidentified narration that is ugly and unpleasant to read. The resulting pain of the experience is the intended result: the writing is effective precisely because it is experiential, not descriptive. In this way, Wood claims, Wallace's fiction 'prosecutes an intense argument about the decomposition of language in America' through a method that degrades and discomposes his own style, 'in the interests of making us live through this linguistic America with him'.[52] In my reading of *Tripticks*, Quin utilises the precarious strategy of impoverished prose to similar effect and for similar purposes of cultural and linguistic critique.

### Serious Irony

The deliberately boring, clichéd and non-sensical performance of imperfect imitation and reiteration above is an insightful example of how irony is at work in *Tripticks*.[53] By invoking not-quite-right utterances of a dominant cultural system again and again, the narrative scrutinises, dismembers and exposes the empty words and cultural impoverishment of that system. In a discussion of the ironic helpful for thinking further about *Tripticks*, Denise Riley articulates the relationship between irony and reiteration as positioned 'between dullness and provocation', petrifaction and newness.[54] Reading this doubleness demands 'careful stupidity'; an act of miscomprehension that stops its ears to the content of what is being reiterated and instead becomes fascinated by the word made thing.[55] Because of its excessive reiteration, the very ugliness and boredom that registers linguistic degradation is also what transforms it into something vital and active.[56] Sianne Ngai's ideas are also useful for thinking about Quin's technique here, in terms of her notion 'stuplimity', which describes the coexistence of shock and boredom – or as she puts it, the sublime and stupidity – which can be experienced when reading avant-garde texts.[57] Ngai insists on the political content of this discursive exhaustion: the tedium of aesthetic effect facilitates linguistic and philosophical questions about what it means for the individual to be linguistically and aesthetically overpowered by a large-scale cultural system.[58]

As with Riley's understanding of the specific, political purposes of irony, Quin's ironic parodying of American culture and counter-culture has serious intent.[59] This is strikingly revealed in the narrative's awareness of its own doubleness, where the mimicry and satire do not stand outside but are rather part of the world they critique. It is also evident in the cut-up, where the narrative always speaks with other voices and materials that come directly from – and which participate in – the culture being critiqued. Given the ironic and critical effects of imitation and the reiteration of cliché in *Tripticks*, it is notable that the narrative is largely generated through cut-up, a technique which both creates excessive reiteration and interrogates ideas of freedom and control. In its resulting double sense, *Tripticks* diagnoses a cultural problem at the same time as being caught up in its effects – an ambivalence that is similarly present in Quin's writing of the female gaze and the woman's desire for the Jewish man in *Passages*. In *Tripticks*, this doubleness takes the paradoxical form of pleasure in the consumerist world of surfaces at the same time as anxiety about what is lost in this. Put another way, there is a tension between the polyvocity that seems to be all that there is, and a residual desire to think beyond and break through this surface, a desire for authentic engagement with the world that remains despite a culture which denies it. *Tripticks* displays a confused and contradictory allegiance to the world of materialism and surfaces at the same time as expressing a search for meaning and depth beyond this: it moves beyond criticism and parody of consumerism into an ironic mode that simultaneously both enjoys and rejects it. This irony is at once playful and knowing, anxious and nostalgic. The paradoxical effect of such irony is what Alan Wilde, in his taxonomy of twentieth-century ironic modes, terms 'disjunctive': nostalgic and anxious for the possibility of authenticity at the same time as realising this might no longer be possible.[60] Wilde's thinking about irony, and his notion of the disjunctive mode, are useful for explaining how in *Tripticks* Quin's writing is coterminous with a sense of its own belatedness: this is not a post-modern text however much it might seem to be in terms of its focus on surfaces and parody.[61] Its irony is not the post-modernist ironic mode of assent; instead the narrative's road trip charts the degradation but not complete dissolution of the search for meaning.

The years of the book's gestation were an important period for cultural critique (especially of a disjunctive mode) – as confirmed by a range of presciently coincident and relevant texts. Key examples of these are R. D. Laing's *The Politics of Experience and The Bird of Paradise* (1967); McLuhan and Fiore's *The Medium is the Massage* (1967); Roszak's *The Making of a Counter Culture* (1969); Berger's *Ways of Seeing* (1972); Deleuze and Guattari's *Anti-Oedipus: Capitalism and Schizophrenia* (1972); Barthes' *Mythologies*, 1957 (translated into English, 1972). These are all concerned with similar questions to those being asked in *Tripticks*: of the relationship between the individual and the system as well as the relationship between surface and depth – in this *Tripticks* is the book of Quin's which most clearly thinks alongside contemporaneous cultural theories. In 'Thinking and Moral Considerations', for example, Hannah Arendt argues that at this point in time the question of depth had become particularly problematic because it was seen to be outdated, belonging to a philosophy or metaphysics that had 'fallen into disrepute'.[62] In late 1960s America the very concept of 'truth' had become problematic (as it has again now). This was a context – and here Arendt makes specific reference to the Vietnam War – where 'the facts' were agreed upon by consensus rather than by their being objectively true. The pursuit of truth or depth had become almost wholly sacrificed for surface: 'image-making had become global policy' so much so that the stream of images became the reality and as a result the relationship with history was being broken.[63]

*Tripticks* engages with precisely this question: it is both enthralled by and deeply despairing of globalised image-making, especially in the context of something like the Vietnam War. This is evident in a description of the Apollo moon landing:

> Two of our kind stand with their own four feet on the moon. Two earthlings representing both sexes (though they are men) all races (though they are pinkish-white beneath their white space suits) and all nations (though they are from the United States, as you might infer from the patches on their sleeves). How far, after all, is the moon from the earth? Precisely the same distance as Vietnam – across the living room. (127) (Layout as per Quin's original text)

The book's disjunctive ironic mode is evident here: the 'global' surface image that the narrative ventriloquises and declares is undermined by the qualifications or 'truths' about America's treatment of women, people of colour and people from different countries, given in parenthesis. The narrative is simultaneously part of what is happening – 'our kind' – and alienated from it – 'earthlings'. The result is funny and knowing, but it also exposes how television, as a media form representing dominant cultural values, distorts and flattens the news, to deny diversity and make everything seem equally important; so that everything from the moon to the Vietnamese war against colonialism is seen at precisely the same distance – 'across the living room'. With this, the narrative exposes how problematic the notion of truth had become in 1960s America, at the same time as expressing a desire for truth and seriousness.

Similarly, despite the critique of the commodification of spirituality in *Tripticks*, the narrative remains caught up in the question of – and wish for – some kind of authenticity: its disjunctive ironic mode suggests a nostalgia for meaning and seriousness at the same time as a suspicion that this hope might finally be denied. In my reading, the book is ultimately unable to shake off its predilection for spiritual contemplation-towards-revelation that the homophone of *Tripticks* suggests. While Didion is suspicious of the late 1960s turn to religion, seeing its urge as a dangerous 'itch for the transcendental, for purification. Right there you've got the ways that romanticism historically ends up in trouble, lends itself to authoritarianism',[64] Roszak alternatively sees this urge as a vital rejection of technocracy, as a powerful and important force in the movement away from a prejudice against religion. In his reading, the counter-culture's defection from sceptical, secular intellectuality is 'remarkable'.[65] As with the letter of Quin's that I discuss in my Introduction, which expresses a desire for 'the magic usage of things', Roszak longs for a 'magical vision of life'.[66] In *Tripticks*, then, despite the narrative's shifting surfaces, and despite

Quin's own rejection of Catholicism and the book's scepticism of hippie appropriation, a residual interest in spirituality and search for meaning persists; this tentative and precarious desire is most clearly expressed in the book's serious irony and its silent scream.

## The Silent Scream

The final scene of *Tripticks* takes place in a church. After its protagonist has, shivering and scared, 'Ghost-wormed' (191)[67] his way in there to seek shelter, he sits feeling uneasy and cautious, wondering whether he has escaped the figure of 'the Inquisition' (190) who pursues him. While he knows he can only ever acquire a 'moment-for-moment-truth', can only approach reality 'from an angle somewhat off-centre', this does not stop his desire to expose 'false and ideological constructs about the world and [let] reality emerge as it really is' (191). As with the book's serious irony, here a desire for depth, for 'reality as it really is', remains. This wish seems ultimately denied by the book's final paragraph:

> Sitting there brooding, I discovered a breathing space, but a space before the scream inside me was working itself loose. A scream that came from a long series of emotional changes. Fear for safety and sanity, helplessness, frustration, and a desperate need to break out into a stream of verbal images. The pulpit could become an extension of my voice, my skin, my dreams. Leaning over the wood, staring at the spluttering candles, the slanting eyes of the statues all around me, their shadows like kachina gods dancing in the walls of the earth. Earth moving out into the world. I opened my mouth, but no words. Only the words of others I saw, like ads, texts, psalms, from those who had attempted to persuade me into their systems. A power I did not want to possess. The Inquisition. (191–2) (Layout as per Quin's original text)

The endless chatter of the book ends with silence, with a wordless, soundless scream. Sitting there brooding, breathing, breaking down, the protagonist opens his mouth, but voices nothing. This scream, the narrative claims, has been working its way up inside him for some time; it comes from 'a desperate need to break out into a stream of verbal images'. What break out instead are visions of the insistent words of others, spoken in the powerful languages of commerce and religion. These are not the 'voices in the head' of *Berg* but are external and all around. And rather than sounding or hearing these words, the protagonist *sees* them.

Tripticks: Impoverished Style as Cultural Critique    137

Carol Annand, *Tripticks*, p. 192.

This act of looking figures and dramatises the reading experience as well as foreshadowing the book's close: after the words of the final paragraph are the six 'silent' drawn images above, which work to contrast and extend the protagonist's final experience. In one way, these minimal line drawings of empty internal and external locations disperse the fear and tension of the words; in another, they enhance the polarisation between frantic speech and silent scream; between a dramatic and dynamic space, and the desire for stillness. For while the protagonist looks for solace and comfort in a spiritual space, this is not what he finds. Instead, his fear and desperate desire for verbalisation are answered by the awful realisation that articulation might finally not be possible. Even the supposed safe haven of the religious building has been absorbed into the machinations and endless verbiage of the dominant cultural system – 'ads, texts, psalms'.[68] This final scene in the church with 'shadows like kachina gods dancing in the walls of the earth' connects with ideas of religion and spirituality elsewhere in the narrative to suggest that these might not be able to reconnect the protagonist to a more genuine, or more meaningful, self-expression. In this, the protagonist ultimately seems denied his desire for meaning, stuck between the persuasive strength of an all-powerful consumerist culture and the terrors of an inquisition. The book's ending asks what lies outside or beyond this system, this linguistic surface, and fears it might not know.

At the same time, the silent scream presences the narrative's disjunctive nostalgia for seriousness or depth. This scream is a significant image in Quin's writing; it appears again in 'Ghostworm' (also set in America and written at a similar time): 'She entered a subway, silently screaming in the Inferno'; and in 'Eyes that Watch Behind the Wind': 'Screaming silently / in a space she had so nearly found'; in Ruth's silent scream during the marital rape scene in *Three* as I have discussed, and in *The Unmapped Country*, as I discuss in the next chapter.[69] The dreadful irony of these silent, screaming mouths calls to mind iconic screams in paintings by Edvard Munch and Francis Bacon. Quin's screams have specific similarities with each: they express the anxiety of the former and interrogate the act of looking of the latter. As Jameson reminds us, what Munch's scream particularly foregrounds and instantiates is the 'atrocious solitude and anxiety' that the absent scream would have expressed.[70] This absence of both the scream and its expression is heightened by the 'gestural content' of the painting, which, for Jameson – whose aim is to show the redundancy of modernist angst – 'already underscores its own failure' because of the incompatibility between the aurality of screaming, and the silent medium of painting.[71] He sees this failure as proof that the affect of such anxiety is no longer appropriate in a post-modern world where, he claims, the alienation or degradation of the subject has been replaced by its dissolution and fragmentation.[72]

In my reading, the scream at the end of *Tripticks* expresses nostalgia for such angst and affect. It comes 'from a long series of emotional changes. Fear for safety and sanity, helplessness, frustration, and a desperate need' (191). Here, at the end of Quin's last complete book, the otherwise ceaseless reiteration of clichés and voicing of unease is silenced. The protagonist opens his mouth to express horror at the situation, but voices nothing, 'no words' come out. He cannot express his inarticulate pain. His desire to expose false ideologies and speak something more meaningful and real, however partial that articulation may have been, is denied. There is a paradoxical fear that the scream of the individual might no longer be possible at the same time as the belief that it might yet be recuperated or recreated. The writing contains a similar problem of gestural content to Munch's painting: 'I opened my mouth, but no words. Only the words of others I saw.' Communication is both possible, in the writing, and not possible, in his inability to voice the words. The disjunction here is deliberate: it describes the reading experience as much as the protagonist's by assuming the reading process is a silent one which involves *seeing* the words (of others) rather than voicing them aloud. At the same time, the insistent 'I' and 'my' voice of the protagonist throughout the book marks his final failure to voice not as dissolution, but rather as degradation of the subject. Despite his morphing and blurred 'many names. Many faces' (7) and many voices, this subject remains – 'I somehow exhibited a remarkable adaptation to the peculiar surroundings, resisting burial under the constantly shifting roles' (132).

Like Bacon's screaming pope and triptych paintings, several aspects of the soundless scream at the end of *Tripticks* purposely foreground sight. In his discussion of cultural experience in *Playing and Reality* (1971), Winnicott considers the meaning and importance of Bacon's distorted faces. He concludes that Bacon's painting of these faces is bound up with a desire to be seen and connects this with a desire for understanding by postulating both developmental and historical processes which depend on being seen.[73] This observation is useful for thinking about the ending of *Tripticks*, where the protagonist sees 'the words of others' and is seen by 'eyes of the statues all around me'. Unlike the female gaze in *Passages*, which connects looking to gender and desire, or Quin's engagement with visual culture in *Three* and *Tripticks*, what the protagonist sees at the end here are words. His dreadful anxiety – the 'Fear for safety and sanity', of being found by the figure of 'the Inquisition' – and his feelings of being watched by the statues connect this scene with Berger's discussion of Bacon's triptych paintings in his piece 'Francis Bacon and Walt Disney' (1972). Berger reminds us that the seeming isolation of each of the images is undermined by their always being watched by a spectatior or indeed by the other paintings of the three. Moreover, the triptych form, where each figure is isolated in his own canvas and yet visible to the others, means these figures are always both simultaneously alone and completely without privacy.[74] This anguished loneliness is distinct from the anxiety displayed in Munch's painting, because here the 'worst has already happened'.[75] For Berger the poignancy of Bacon's screaming figures lies in their ignorance of this fact. The poignancy of Quin's protagonist, while he is similarly both isolated and watched, is not so much to do with his ignorance as a feeling of insignificance in the face of the endless words which ignore and deny him.

More specifically, Lyndsey Stonebridge considers the importance of looking in relation to Bacon's paintings in their post-Second World War context and in connection with the Eichmann trial. Looking, she proposes, is never balanced, passive or neutral; instead, it is always implicated and participatory, an activity with inalienable moral content.[76] Bacon's particular presentation of gaping and disintegrating figures doubly foregrounds this quality of looking – the painted figures are in glass boxes as well as the paintings being framed and literally behind glass. The glass in and over these paintings means that not only is the viewer reflected in the glass frame being looked at and through, but it is also as if the viewer is projected into the paintings themselves. The protagonist in *Tripticks* is similarly projected into and participates in the world of the words he looks at (as does the reader). His act of looking at the end of the book is intimately bound up with the agonised nothing that comes out of his mouth.

The ethical import of the scene and its nostalgia for depth and meaning are reinforced by the melodrama and visual extravagance of the candlelit church pulpit and the final, exaggerated fear of 'the Inquisition'. This melodrama, together with the signification of the scream, alerts the reader to a deposit of 'moral seriousness' (to use Nye's phrase) in *Tripticks* that the meaningless patter and parody of its narrative surface seem to deny. Drawing on Peter Brooks's claim that melodrama is the principal mode for 'uncovering, demonstrating, and making operative the essential moral universe in a post-sacred era' for my concluding words here,[77] in this final scene there is a clear resonance with both Wilde's assertion that the ironic mode actively participates in history, and Arendt's claim that this was an era when philosophy and metaphysics had 'fallen into disrepute'. Irony and melodrama may appear as flippancy, but in fact both have qualities which render them able to penetrate beyond the world of surfaces, and to reach towards meaningfulness. On the one hand, melodrama is clearly role play; on the other, it dramatises and expresses the fact that something is always lost in attempts to signify, capture and perform something meaningful.

My readings in this chapter have shown how the precarious allegiance to both depth and surface in *Tripticks* – evident as I have suggested in the book's disjunctive irony and silent scream, and in its clichéd and impoverished, parodic prose – expresses a complex and immersive cultural critique. As with all of Quin's books, the title holds clues which in turn guide, confuse and extend the reading experience: its trip is a drug experience as well as a road journey across America;[78] verbal tics and tricks abound in a cut-up narrative created from the words of others. Through these trips and tics, and in both its homophone and structural allusion to triptychs, *Tripticks* foregrounds, ironises and interrogates the act of looking at images as a vital part of its residual desire for meaning and to see beyond the surface of things.

## Notes

1. Marshall McLuhan and Quentin Fiore, *The Medium is the Massage* (San Francisco: Hardwired, 1967), p. 75.
2. Quin, *Tripticks* (Chicago: Dalkey Archive Press, 2002), p. 139. Subsequent references to *Tripticks* are in parenthesis in the text. The 'retro-visor' is also a motif for visual and verbal play in Christine Brooke-Rose's *Thru*, as Glyn White points out in *Reading the Graphic Surface*, p. 128. Brooke-Rose's book begins: 'through the driving-mirror four eyes stare back', *Thru* (London: Hamish Hamilton, 1975), p. 1.
3. The road theme and unstoppable verbiage of *Tripticks* recalls Jack Kerouac's *On the Road* (1957), although more likely as criticism than homage. Quin had written: 'simply hating 'On the Road' – what a lot of sentimental rubbish and so tedious how it goes on and on in this phoney pseudo 'isn't life crazy but it's life man' sort of fashion'. Letter to Carol Burns, 17 August 1961.
4. Berger, *Ways of Seeing*, pp. 129–30.
5. Theodor Adorno and Max Horkheimer claim that in response to the flow of images on a screen 'sustained thought is out of the question if the spectator is not to miss the relentless rush of facts'. *Dialectic of Enlightenment*, trans. John Cumming (London and New York: Verso, 1997), p. 127.
6. Quin, *Berg*, p. 24.
7. David Farber and Beth Bailey, *The Columbia Guide to America in the 1960s* (New York: Columbia University Press, 2001), p. 57.
8. *Peyton Place*: a bestselling book as well as prime-time small town soap opera, which aired in the mid- to late 1960s.

9. Adorno and Horkheimer, *Dialectic of Enlightenment*, pp. 121, 124. For Robert von Hallberg, the fate of American culture hung in the balance, 'so powerful was the sense that television would abruptly change national taste and sensibility, as it surely did. The idea of national taste is now almost anachronistic.' *American Poetry and Culture 1945–1980* (Cambridge, MA and London: Harvard University Press, 1985), p. 194.
10. Hallberg, *American Poetry and Culture*, p. 190.
11. Joan Didion, *Slouching Towards Bethlehem* (Farrar, Straus and Giroux: New York, 1968), p. 123.
12. Dick Hebdige provides a more positive appraisal of youth culture when he identifies American hippie culture as a 'decisive break' with its parent culture. *Subculture: The Meaning of Style* (London and New York: Routledge, 1979), p. 121. For another defence of youth counter-culture, see Theodore Roszak, *The Making of a Counter Culture: Reflections on the Technocratic Society and Its Youthful Opposition* (London: Faber & Faber, 1970).
13. McLuhan and Fiore, *The Medium is the Massage*, pp. 92, 126.
14. Adorno and Horkheimer declare this kind of ambivalence as the success of advertising in the culture industry: consumers feel compelled to buy and use its products even though they see through them. *Dialectic of Enlightenment*, p. 167.
15. Zambreno, 'The Ventriloquist', p. 145. *Tripticks* is not directly discussed by Zambreno, however, or by any of the pieces in this issue's section on Quin.
16. Rachel Bowlby, *Just Looking* (London and New York: Methuen, 1985), pp. 1–6.
17. For Adorno and Horkheimer, in a culture of economic coercion the 'freedom' to choose an ideology is only in fact the freedom to choose what is always the same. *Dialectic of Enlightenment*, p. 167. See also Berger, *Ways of Seeing*, p. 131.
18. The story is a broadly similar but less developed version of the first forty or so pages of the book. Many phrases are exactly the same, although, for example, names are given to characters in the short version that are subsequently anonymised. See Quin, 'Tripticks', *The Unmapped Country: Stories & Fragments*, pp. 77–94.
19. Quin, letter to the editors, *Ambit*, 35, 1968, p. 42. J. G. Ballard was one of these editors. He comments: 'when *Ambit* launched a competition for the best fiction or poetry written under the influence of drugs, Lord Goodman, an intimate of Prime Minister Harold Wilson, raised the threat of prosecution. In fact, we were equally interested in the effects of legal drugs – tranquilizers, antihistamines, even baby aspirin. The competition, and the 40-pound prize which I offered, was won by the bookist Ann Quin.' *The Atrocity Exhibition* (London: Flamingo, 2001), pp. 145–6.

20. Timothy Leary's role in the counter-culture movement is discussed at length throughout Jay Stevens's *Storming Heaven: LSD and the American Dream* (London: Heinemann, 1988), and is condemned in Roszak's chapter 'The Counterfeit Infinity: The Use and Abuse of Psychedelic Experience', *The Making of a Counter Culture*, pp. 155–77.
21. See the chapters 'Slouching Towards Bethlehem' and 'Starving, Hysterical, Naked' in Stevens, *Storming Heaven*, pp. 91–121.
22. Ibid. p. 347.
23. Eli Zaretsky, *Secrets of the Soul: A Social and Cultural History of Psychoanalysis* (New York: Vintage, 2005), pp. 327–8. See also Bowlby, *Just Looking*, p. 29.
24. Franca Bellarisi, 'Anticipating the Spiritual Legacy of the 1960s: "Beatness" and "Beat Buddhism"', in *In and Around the Sixties*, ed. Mirella Billi and Nicholas Brownlees (Viterbo, Italy: Sette Città, 2003), pp. 19–44.
25. Bellarisi, 'Anticipating the Spiritual Legacy of the 1960s', pp. 24, 26.
26. Roszak, *The Making of a Counter Culture*, p. 177.
27. The phrasing at the end of this extract is reiterated in Quin's unpublished story 'Matters of the Heart', where the narrator recalls: 'an acid trip, and that same feeling that I don't want to come down, as if I am on the edge of a revelation, a very thin line between life and death', unpublished manuscript, Carol Burns Private Collection of Papers, p. 9.
28. Hieronymus Bosch used the triptych form not only for spiritual contemplation but for dreadful warning. Quin saw his paintings when travelling in Italy: 'saw the Bosch paintings – fantastic colour and tones (so used to just glimpsing reproductions!)'. Letter to Carol Burns, 24 July 1962.
29. Alan Burns claims: 'I know she wrote the book entirely through cut-up'. 'Blending Words with Pictures', *Books and Bookmen*, 17:10 (July 1972), n.p. According to Hall in 'The Mighty Quin', 'the end product relies heavily on cut-ups from "Time", "Life", television commercials and Yankee sex and criminology pulp', p. 8.
30. Nathan Moore, 'Nova Law: William S. Burroughs and the Logic of Control', *Law and Literature*, 19:3 (Fall 2007), pp. 435–70. In 1963 Quin had quipped 'call me Ann Boroughs' – the misspelling nicely implying Burroughs himself, the pastiche aspect of cut-up composition and Quin's own act of 'borrowing' that technique. Letter to Carol Burns, 29 January 1963.
31. Moore, 'Nova Law', p. 439.
32. Ibid. p. 437. Although he is not mentioned in Moore's discussion, this understanding of texts of course calls to mind Barthes' 'The Death of the Author', *Image, Music, Text*, pp. 142–8.
33. Quin had been 'furious and saddened' to miss the 1962 Bacon exhibition. Letter to Carol Burns, 5 July 1962. After the 1963 Bacon/Moore

exhibition she wrote: 'I could have happily stayed there all day.' Letter to Carol Burns, July 1963.
34. Berger, *About Looking* (London: Writers and Readers Publishing Cooperative, 1980), pp. 112–13.
35. Burns, 'Blending Words with Pictures'.
36. See also McLuhan and Fiore, *The Medium is the Massage*, where the multidirectional and integrated text directly dramatises the claim that linear narrative is no longer possible and that we must develop a new way of reading.
37. Burns, 'Blending Words with Pictures'.
38. In his discussion of Alasdair Gray's 1981 *Lanark: A Life in Four Books*, White points out that the illustrations do not 'straightforwardly depict the content of the prose'. Instead, they are 'narrative "continued" by other means, which challenges the reader to synthesise the additional content'. *Reading the Graphic Surface*, respectively pp. 184, 192.
39. Brian McHale, *Postmodernist Fiction* (London and New York: Routledge, 2001), p. 190.
40. Ibid. I considered a similar question about reading direction and process when discussing *Passages*: the inclusion of pictorial illustrations in *Tripticks* further complicates this.
41. Ibid. pp. 190–3.
42. Hilary White, '"Turning her over in the flat of my dreams": Visuality, Cut-up and Irreality in the Work of Ann Quin', *Women: A Cultural Review, (Re)turning to Ann Quin*, 33:1 (2022), pp. 114–30, p. 128. Of all Quin's texts, 'Tripticks' and *Tripticks* have been the least discussed by scholars and White's discussion of 'Tripticks' offers an illuminating extended reading of Quin's use of the cut-up to create a dreamlike and dislocated sense of reality.
43. White, '"Turning her over in the flat of my dreams"', p. 116.
44. Hall calls it her 'first political work', in 'The Mighty Quin', p. 8.
45. While many welcomed the material abundance that post-war economic prosperity made possible, some scorned – as Quin's narrative seems to here – the 'soulless materialism of America's consumer society' which ranked everything according to material value. Farber and Bailey, *The Columbia Guide to America in the 1960s*, p. 55.
46. Gilles Deleuze and Félix Guattari, *Anti-Oedipus: Capitalism and Schizophrenia*, trans. Robert Hurley, Mark Seem and Helen Lane (London: Continuum, 2011), p. 144.
47. Fredric Jameson, *Postmodernism, or, The Cultural Logic of Late Capitalism* (Durham, NC: Duke University Press, 1991), p. 2.
48. Burns says of *Tripticks*: 'there's all sorts of undigested literary matter floating about, and personal influences like Creeley and Nabokov and me', 'Blending Words with Pictures'. Quin had both read the book and seen the film version of *Lolita*: despite reservations, she thought it 'A very funny film tho' and worth seeing'. Letter to Carol Burns, 4 January 1963.

49. Bowlby, *Shopping with Freud* (London and New York: Routledge, 1993), see pp. 56–64. See also Berger, *Ways of Seeing*, pp. 21–4.
50. Bowlby, *Shopping with Freud*, p. 65.
51. James Wood, *How Fiction Works* (London: Jonathan Cape, 2008), p. 27.
52. Ibid.
53. Elsewhere in Quin's writing – for example with the phrase 'rain walks designing its own shadow' – I have suggested that reiteration is used as a mode of reaching towards the intensity of experience; see my Introduction to this book. In *Tripticks* Quin uses reiteration for a specific ironic purpose, to reveal the emptiness of certain kinds of signification.
54. Denise Riley, *The Words of Selves: Identification, Solidarity, Irony* (Stanford, CA: Stanford University Press, 2000), p. 157.
55. Ibid.
56. Ibid. p. 159.
57. Sianne Ngai, *Ugly Feelings* (Cambridge, MA and London: Harvard University Press, 2005), p. 2. Ngai's analysis of her main examples, Gertrude Stein and Beckett, is careful to make the distinction between the reader's stupefaction when confronted by a thick or muddy text and the text's own 'stupidity'. Quin was reading Stein while writing *Tripticks*. Letter to Carol Burns, 6 September 1968.
58. Ngai, *Ugly Feelings*, pp. 265–78. See also Barthes' claims about the 'mythologies' of consumer culture in his essay 'Myth Today', *Mythologies*, trans. Annette Lavers (London: Vintage, 2000), pp. 109–59.
59. Riley explains how, while it may appear as disengagement, irony is in fact an expression of deep engagement. 'Echo, Irony and the Political', *The Words of Selves*, pp. 146–84. Nye's appraisal of *Tripticks* in 'Against the Barbarians' praises the 'deposit of seriousness in the text' which he opposes to the parody: 'a species of frenetic satire that will allow little to occur to the narrator [. . .] without grimaces on the part of the author'. While I disagree with Nye's patronising dismissal of Quin's parody, I agree with his perception of seriousness in *Tripticks*.
60. Alan Wilde, *Horizons of Assent: Modernism, Post-modernism, and the Ironic Imagination* (London: Johns Hopkins University Press, 1981), p. 3. In Wilde's notion of disjunctive irony, the world appears disconnected and fragmented but aesthetic closure may yet be possible.
61. In their discussion of *Tripticks*, Brian Evenson and Joanna Howard similarly place it 'on the cusp of postmodern', in 'Ann Quin', *Review of Contemporary Fiction*, 23:2 (Summer 2003), p. 71. For Jordan, 'The experimentalists' [and she includes Quin in this group] weakness – their belatedness, repetitiveness, submissiveness – might also be read as stubborn dissention'. *Oblique Strategies*, p. 3.
62. Arendt, 'Thinking and Moral Considerations', *Responsibility and Judgement* (New York: Schocken Books, 2003), p. 161.

63. Arendt, 'Lying in Politics', *Crises of the Republic* (Harmondsworth: Penguin, 1973), p. 20. For further discussion of Arendt's thinking here, see Cathy Caruth's 'Lying and History', in *Thinking in Dark Times: Hannah Arendt on Ethics and Politics*, ed. Roger Berkowitz, Jeffrey Katz and Thomas Keenan (New York: Fordham University Press, 2010), pp. 79–94.
64. Didion, *Slouching Towards Bethlehem*, p. 120.
65. Roszak, *The Making of a Counter Culture*, p. 141.
66. Ibid. p. 257.
67. This 'verb' is surely a reference to the story 'Ghostworm' (1968), *The Unmapped Country: Stories & Fragments*, pp. 125–50.
68. Barthes talks about the anonymous ideology and systemic distortion in which everything is steeped, and which overlays everyday and individual life with the codes and conventions of those in power. See in particular his discussion in 'Myth Today', *Mythologies*, pp. 116–30.
69. Quin, 'Ghostworm' and 'Eyes that Watch Behind the Wind', *The Unmapped Country: Stories & Fragments*, respectively pp. 147, 117.
70. Jameson, *Postmodernism*, p. 16.
71. Ibid.
72. Ibid. pp. 13–18. The move from the anguish of a coherent individual to anguish about the very possibility of a coherent individual at all recalls Brian McHale's description of the shift in the 'dominant' from modernism to post-modernism being from epistemological to ontological crisis. *Postmodernist Fiction*, pp. 9–10.
73. Donald Winnicott, *Playing and Reality* (London: Tavistock Publications, 1971), p. 114.
74. Berger, *About Looking*, p. 114. That Berger is discussing Bacon's triptychs is, of course, of particular relevance given the title of Quin's book here.
75. Ibid.
76. Lyndsey Stonebridge, 'The Perpetrator Occult: Francis Bacon Paints Adolf Eichmann', *Holocaust Studies: A Journal of Culture and History*, 17:2 (Summer/Autumn 2012), pp. 101–20. Quin herself had expressed an awareness of the moral content of Bacon's paintings: 'A photo, Michael had up on his wall, haunts me, of a baby born after Hiroshima. It looked so unreal, one couldn't really believe such a thing possible, same reaction as one has, perhaps, to Francis Bacon's paintings.' Quin, letter to Carol Burns, 28 September 1962.
77. Brooks, *The Melodramatic Imagination* (New Haven, CT: Yale University Press, 1995), p. 15.
78. Hall notes that 'Tripticks [...] is a US name for an AA motor route'. 'The Mighty Quin', p. 8.

Vignette

# Breakdown, breakthrough

On 27 November 1969 the ICA (Institute of Contemporary Arts) hosted a 'Writers Reading' event.[1] Quin was nervous about reading from and exposing what she saw as the weaknesses of *Passages*. So rather than reading from that book she sat wordless on stage, attempting ESP (extrasensory perception) with the aim of communicating universal love.[2] This caused considerable unrest as well as some hostility among the audience. Bowing to the pressure to speak, Quin answered some questions and gave a reading, but rather than her own words she read from John Cage: *Silence* replacing silence. This wasn't enough to salvage the performance and the audience were unimpressed. Quin responded differently. She smiled as she came down from the stage and described the experience as a breakthrough not breakdown.

Afterwards, Quin did have a series of breakdowns and periods of psychosis during which her mental health was highly precarious and her behaviour and delusions increasingly dangerous and unpredictable. These began when she caught the boat to Holland with John Carter, her then lover, to see in the 1970 New Year. On the journey over, Quin remained on the freezing deck refusing to eat, experiencing visions of Cleopatra's barge with her father on it. When they arrived in Amsterdam, Carter had to stop her running out onto the river, which was only thinly covered in ice. Quin was given sedatives and admitted into a psychiatric hospital. Once out and having returned to London, she became anxious that she was at the centre of a conspiracy and escaped with an Arts Council grant to Denmark, Norway and then Sweden. There, she was found in a snowdrift in a delusional state and was again hospitalised. Refusing to eat or sleep, she found herself force fed and given electroconvulsive therapy. This was a distressing and desperate period for Quin, an awful time of blankness that she described as much worse than the breakdowns, which she sometimes found to be energising and inspiring. The institutionalisation and brutal electric shock therapy 'treatments' completely – and completely unsurprisingly – suppressed her creativity; she said to Carol Burns that she felt as if both her angels and her demons were gone.

Quin recovered from this low period and returned to writing, but finances were again desperate after she was turned down for further Arts Council grants. In search of a new direction and escape from the grind of secretarial work, she enrolled at Hillcroft Women's College – 'a Residential College, established in 1920, for women between 20 and 45+, who have missed out educationally in their teens'[3] – and returned to formal education as a mature student for the academic year 1972–3. She studied psychology, sociology and English literature:

> having a whole year in which to have some systematic study, and participate in seminars, tutorials, and attend lectures, and discuss what I was reading with other people, seemed to me ideal; a way-out of the rut I felt I had got myself into.[4]

Hillcroft provided a secure and stimulating environment that brought Quin respite. Her piece 'Second Chance' describes this as one of the few relatively happy and stable times of her later life: 'we all seem to get on very well indeed'.[5] Studying and writing essays brought mental stimulation and a sense of progress. In February 1973, she wrote an essay on George Eliot's *Middlemarch* and suffragism; at the same time, she reread *Daniel Deronda*, and began working on *The Unmapped Country* and 'Matters of the Heart'. Her approach to assignments was unconventional, but Quin did well at Hillcroft and began applying to university that spring. She wrote to Boyars:

> went to East Anglia and hated it, such a desolate 'Brave new world' kind of place, felt I couldn't stick it out there for 3 years, so even if they do offer me a place I shall refuse! Sussex, on the other hand, is a super place.[6]

In the end Sussex refused her a place and East Anglia made an offer. So, had things been different, had she not swum too far out to sea that August bank holiday, in the autumn of 1973 Quin would have gone on to study for a Creative Writing degree there under Angus Wilson.

## Notes

1. The 'Writers Reading' 'collective' included Paul Ableman, Alan Burns, Carol Burns, Barry Cole, Eva Figes, B. S. Johnson, Jeff Nuttall, Ann Quin, Alan Sillitoe and Stefan Themerson. Although diverse, this group were united by 'a profound interest in prose as a form of expression and not simply as a medium for story-telling'. Alan Burns and B. S. Johnson, Introduction to *Writers Reading* pamphlet (London: J & P Weldon, 1969), p. 1.
2. Burns recalls: 'she did her Quin thing, that is to say that she came onto the stage and looked at people, she wouldn't say a goddam word! She just stared, she either implied or she actually stated that we sort of "think communicate". Bryan Johnson was "furious with her"'. Jonathan Coe, *Like a Fiery Elephant: The Story of B. S. Johnson* (London: Picador, 2004), p. 405.
3. Quin, 'Second Chance', *The Guardian*, August 1973.
4. Ibid.
5. Ibid.
6. Quin, letter to Boyars, 10 April 1973. Calder and Boyars manuscripts, Series II, box 52, folder 4.

Chapter 5

# *The Unmapped Country:*
# Unravelling Stereotypes of Madness

## Writing the Mind

In his critique of *Tripticks*, Robert Nye had written: 'It can still be hoped that Miss Quin will chuck the box of tricks away and sit down one day to write a whole book in which observation of the heart's affections is allowed to predominate and inform.'[1] This gendered and patronising review, and the distinction between a so-called box of tricks and the 'observation of the heart's affections', which he saw as her writing's main strength, nevertheless stung Quin into response. She wrote to Boyars: 'Am also well into another book – another journey of discovery/ rediscovery and taking Robert Nye's criticism seriously: writing/ dealing with "matters of the heart".'[2] But rather than narrating the 'heart's affections', what both the unfinished and unpublished short story 'Matters of the Heart' and incomplete book *The Unmapped Country* narrate are their protagonists' experiences of madness and subsequent incarceration in psychiatric hospitals.[3] After the Mediterranean train journey quest of *Passages* and chase of the American road trip in *Tripticks*, *The Unmapped Country* is Quin's final search narrative, a largely interior one into the landscapes of the mind and psychiatric institution. In *The Unmapped Country* Sandra is asked by a psychiatrist to 'Tell me about the journey you took',[4] and in 'Matters of the Heart' Linda says, 'This is, I suppose, the first stage on the real journey.'[5]

The title of *The Unmapped Country* is inspired by a particular moment in *Daniel Deronda* which considers the possibility of writing the elusive and perhaps even unknowable 'unmapped country' of the psyche:[6]

But that movement of mind which led her to keep the necklace, [. . .] was more peculiar, and what would be called less reasonable. It came from that streak of superstition in her which attached itself both to her confidence and her terror – [. . .] It was something vague and yet mastering, which impelled her to take this action about the necklace. There is a great deal of unmapped country within us which would have to be taken into account in an explanation of our gusts and storms.[7]

Gwendolen Harleth, Eliot's complex female protagonist, feels compelled to keep 'the necklace' she had previously attempted to pawn, a necklace she rightly suspects Daniel Deronda of recovering on her behalf. When she is impelled by 'something vague and yet mastering' not to try to rid herself of the necklace a second time, Eliot's third person narrator seems to know what makes her act in this way – 'it came from that streak of superstition in her which attached itself to both her confidence and her terror' – whereas Gwendolen herself does not. As elsewhere in the novel, here her confusion about Deronda and the necklace is used to suggest a larger uncertainty and unknowability within Gwendolen herself. This 'unmapped country' within her, the text suggests, can in turn tell us about an unknown within people in the world outside the text, something 'within [all of] us' that 'would have to be taken into account in an explanation of our gusts and storms'. In this characteristic move from particular to universal experience, Eliot's narrator seems simultaneously situated within and outside of the world of the text, able to speak to and of both. It is this kind of authoritative position that MacCabe interprets as Eliot's metanarrative – 'that language which tells us what is *really* happening'.[8]

Yet here as elsewhere in her writing, Eliot's narrator is not the transparent and unwritten window on reality MacCabe claims it to be. Gwendolen's 'movement of mind', the narrator tells us, is 'more peculiar, and what would be called less reasonable'. This 'what would be called' troubles the narrator's position. It 'would be called less reasonable', but by whom? The narrator does not claim such a judgement for themselves, and there is the suggestion that what is 'reasonable' may not always offer an adequate articulation of 'peculiar' experience. Neither the language of reason, nor the narrator, can quite pin down 'that movement of mind', can quite explain or articulate it. As with the unknowability of the 'unmapped country', this moment in the passage demonstrates a troubling of the authority of the narrator as much as an enactment of it – in Eliot's writing here, as with much of Quin's, particularly *Berg*, we see the window as much as looking through it. Though in some ways the narrator can read, understand and articulate things that Gwendolen herself cannot, its position is nevertheless also revealed to be uncertain and limited. In this, the passage suggests the difficulty of finding a narrative position from which to write the mind.

This moment in *Daniel Deronda* was particularly suggestive for Quin's attempt to write madness. *The Unmapped Country* also engages with madness in terms of its own historical and cultural moment. The unmapped country of the mind had been to some extent 'mapped out' by earlier twentieth-century psychoanalysis; in the 1960s and 1970s the idea that madness was something in need of a further or different mapping preoccupied the fields of psychiatry and anti-psychiatry.[9] Writing in 1978, Shoshana Felman refers to the 'well known' fact that madness was the 'crucial question in the current cultural scene', with people keen to promote their '"madness"' goods as the latest thing in order to publicize [their] avant-gardism'.[10] This 'fashion' for madness – as well as the challenge it presented to narrative representation – had already been explored in fiction of the 1960s, for example Ken Kesey's *One Flew Over the Cuckoo's Nest* (1961), Jennifer Dawson's *The Ha-Ha* (1961) and Sylvia Plath's *The Bell Jar* (1963). Dawson's mad protagonist can never find the right words when speaking, for example, and Plath's is a budding writer whose illness renders her unable to read or write.

Felman's *Writing and Madness* takes this question of language and articulation further to ask whether and how it might be possible to know or write madness at all given that this will also always necessarily be in the language of 'reason, which masters and represses madness' and therefore always works to exclude and deny it.[11] In this, she makes a distinction between the attempt to write 'about' madness, at a distance from the experience, and writing 'of' it: how, Felman asks, might this latter even be possible? A similar focus on the potential failure and limitations of the language of reason is, in my reading, present in Eliot's suggestion that Gwendolen's 'movement of mind . . . was more peculiar, and what would be called less reasonable'. There, the 'reasonable' prose of the third person narrator can only gesture towards but not fully explain or know the psyche. If we follow Felman and accept that peculiar or 'unreasonable' experience refuses meaningful articulation, Eliot's claim that the 'unmapped country' must be taken into account in an *explanation* of 'our gusts and storms' can be taken further to ask how or whether a text – or language – might explain, know or express madness at all. With Felman's thinking as my primary critical frame, in this chapter I argue that Quin is similarly engaged in probing the (im)possibilities of writing madness and more specifically, in subverting and unravelling its clichés.

## A Failure of Articulation

For Giles Gordon, who included the first chapter of *The Unmapped Country* in the collection *Beyond the Words* – the title of which was taken from Quin's phrase 'spaces between words' (167) – this was an example of her writing at its most lucid and perceptive. He wrote: 'Judging by the opening chapter printed here, it could have been her most considerable work.'[12] *The Unmapped Country* consists of two chapters of an unfinished book. The first chapter narrates its protagonist Sandra's experience of madness and incarceration in a psychiatric hospital and in this it engages with the particular question of the possibility of writing madness within an institutional context. It charts the course of one of Sandra's days via short sections that communicate the scheduled minutiae of her day in the form of free indirect third person past tense narrative, journal entries and transcripts of dialogues. She converses with psychiatrists and fellow patients, writes in and reads old entries in her diary, and attends a group therapy session and ward party; she spends time walking and drawing shapes in snow in the hospital grounds, as well as several times trying (and not being allowed) to go to sleep; she is also visited by her lover Clive, a man who wants to leave as soon as he has arrived, but not before she has performed her 'duty' and taken 'him in her mouth' (173). At the end of the day, and the chapter, she is finally allowed sleep. It ends with 'The pendulum swung back' (192). The second chapter is a shorter, less complete text, which takes the form of a continuous, mostly first person present tense perspective (with slippages into third person) expressing Sandra's experiences of visions prior to incarceration.

*The Unmapped Country* opens with a description of Sandra's morning session with one of the hospital psychiatrists:

> 'Good morning and how are we today?'
> 'Bloody rotten if you must know.'
> 'Why is that – tell me more?'
> Silence. Patient confronted psychiatrist. Woman and man. She looked at the thin hair he had carefully placed over his yellow husk. Thin lips, almost no lips. Thick hands, bunches of spiders on his knuckles. He wrote or doodled, leaning forward, back.

'I don't like your madness.'
'What do you mean by that, Sandra?'
Pen poised, ready to stab yet another record. She could not see his eyes, the light bounced, spiralled in his spectacles. Black tentacles crept from his nostrils. In the distance a woman screamed. (159)

This opening is written from a third person perspective which closely sympathises with the protagonist. In it, the patient/psychiatrist opposition is not only stated –'Patient confronted psychiatrist' – it is exacerbated by the dehumanising, revolting description of the almost lipless, yellow husked, pen stabbing and eyeless doctor. This description is in staccato, reduced to fragments of close-up detail: the result is both observationally specific and evocative, but also sent up, exaggerated and villain-esque. The strangeness of the details – the 'bunches of spiders on his knuckles,' the 'black tentacles' which creep from his nostrils – undermines the sense in which the clarity of the prose could imply an objective or 'transparent' record of the meeting. The nature of the description and effect of the exaggeration calls into question whose perspective the narrative is focalised from, whether Sandra's or the narrator's. Here as across the first chapter of *The Unmapped Country*, Quin employs an ambivalent and destabilising free indirect style. What results is an ambiguous description, one which knows that the notion of the 'evil' doctor and mad 'victim' are already encoded and mapped out. The passage plays out (and begins to challenge) stereotypical power oppositions – sane/mad, doctor/patient, man/woman, human/animal, villain/victim – while at the same time subverting and undoing them: the patronising 'how are we today' is cut down by the 'bloody rotten' answer. In this, the writing does not so much describe the scene as perform, unravel and interrogate already overly encoded and stereotyped ideas.

Sandra, under attack from the doctor's questioning, offers mutinous silence and terse, tightly controlled answers in return, despite the horror of having to listen to another woman scream. In contrast with this inarticulate and agonised sound heard 'in the distance,' Sandra's protests are perfectly comprehensible and lucid: they are also ludic, irreverent and playful; she says it is the doctor's madness she does not like. His response is to ask what she means, which admits her speech could indeed have meaning in spite of her supposed 'madness'. This question is central to my reading of *The Unmapped Country* in this chapter: in what ways it might be possible for language and writing to *mean* madness? Sandra's lucid-ludic response is a technique which indicates the wider double sense of Quin's precarious writing in this text, as well as elsewhere in her writing, where what seems to be in one register often carries within it, and implies, the sense of another. This produces a narrative perspective that continually undermines and undoes itself: the possibility of writing meaningfully 'about' Sandra's madness, from the outside, is challenged at the very same time as it is performed.

Sandra's discussion with the doctor shows her command of language while at the same time questioning the meaningfulness of this language as well as of their exchange. Elsewhere, the narrative questions the possibility of articulating madness:

> If speech at all then it was the spaces between words, and the echoes the words left, or what might really be meant under the surface. She knew, had known. No longer knew. Only remembered. In the recollection, pictures, words, visions, thoughts, images built themselves into citadels, gigantic towers that toppled with the weight of it all; the top heavier than the foundations. Last events came first, the beginning at the end, or suddenly reversed, or slid into panels midway. Had ECT done that – damn them? (167)

For Derrida, any attempt to speak about madness will always fail because 'madness is what by essence cannot be said'.[13] When Sandra attempts to articulate her experience above, all that remains are 'the spaces between words, and the echoes the words left'. The passage indicates that madness has broken her relationship with language to the point that she no longer knows but only remembers what words might mean or meant, or how they might speak and relate to experience. She has lost the ability to put words in orderly – and ordinary – coherence and a space has opened up, between her experience and language, so that speech is always just out of reach. There is also a sense in which this particular failure of articulation – the lacunae of rational or ordinary speech – may be precisely what reaches towards 'what might really be meant under the surface'. Yet this possibility seems always denied and in deferral. Causality is deconstructed – 'last events came first, the beginning at the end, or suddenly reversed, or slid into panels midway'. While the passage implies this severance and obliteration may have been caused by ECT, Derrida's assertion that the attempt to articulate madness is always in deferral – always an act of amnesia – suggests that such effects could be bound up with experiences of mental illness.[14]

The amnesia of Sandra's relationship with language in the passage above, then, engages with the vexed wider question of writing (or speaking) about madness at all. The ambivalence of the narrative perspective, where it is not always possible to tell which words are the narrator's and which Sandra's, is particularly important here. The instability of its free indirect slippage is used by Quin to show that attempts to articulate madness, to know or write about it in the external 'language of reason' of the third person narrative perspective, will always fail. As Quin's text here demonstrates, the crucial challenge is how to write about madness when, as Felman points out, 'to talk *about* madness is always, in fact, to deny it'.[15] Throughout the first chapter of *The Unmapped Country*, the institutional aspect of Sandra's context is reinforced by the presence of the third person voice, which, despite its closeness to and sometimes blurring with her perspective, is nevertheless one that primarily attempts to describe madness from without, and therefore to deny it: Quin's writing here exposes such an attempt as an 'illusion of reason'.[16] In the extract above, we might read the failure as being Sandra's own when what is being expressed is a failure of articulation itself.

## Activating Stereotypes

One way that Quin's writing explores this failure of articulation in *The Unmapped Country* is by mobilising stereotypes of madness:

> The Red Queen breathing through the tunnel. Her face at the bottom of the lavatory, grinned up. Flush her away. Sandra sat for some time in the lavatory, the only place she could be by herself and not be distracted, and go back over the journey; even so their voices interrupted 'It's all in the head you must realise that – in the head in the head inthehead inthehead inthehead...' and she saw the doctor's faceless presence behind his desk, like the painting 'Le Principe du Plaisir,' by Magritte, except the figure in the painting was infinitely better, more pleasing. Then there was the Red Queen's face; even when dead her mother, no doubt, would be watching her. And Clive – what of Clive? Frightened of his own madness; seeing her actions, reactions as interpretation of what he considered a madness just round the corner for himself. (163)

This description of madness places Sandra's experience in the context of Lewis Carroll's 'Red Queen'. Elaine Showalter claims that for women writers representing madness, 'Alice's journey through the looking glass is a more apt analogy than Ophelia's decline'.[17] When Sandra sees the face of her mother, referred to throughout *The Unmapped Country* as the Red Queen, grinning up from the bottom of the toilet, the vision clearly knows and refers to this intertext. Sandra's vision of the 'faceless presence' of the doctor in this scene is described in terms of René Magritte's *Le Principe du Plaisir*. That painting's title, which can be translated as 'The Pleasure Principle', of course refers to Freud whose psychoanalytic theories sought to map the mind, and it depicts a doctor's face obliterated by a shining light representing the 'light of reason', which works in Quin's text above to question the usefulness of reasonable language and Enlightenment thinking to explain or articulate the experience of madness. This reference to Magritte's image both reiterates – 'the light bounced, spiralled in his spectacles' – and contrasts with the detail of the description and behaviour of the psychiatrist at the beginning of the chapter: together, both images work to question the status and reasonableness of these doctors.

As in that opening conversation, the slippage here interrogates and undoes assumed oppositions between reason/madness, clarity/confusion, knowledge/ignorance. A similar challenge is revealed by the instances of free indirect style. While the quotation marks around the 'it's all in the head' speech of 'their voices' suggests a third person narrative position, in places the perspective is more ambiguous and unidentified: for example, it seems to inhabit Sandra's first person viewpoint, with 'And Clive – what of Clive?' collapsing third person distance. Such ambivalence is taken further in the second chapter of *The Unmapped Country*, which is narrated in a confused prose where the distinction between what happens in- and outside of Sandra's head is at times almost completely elided through the slippage between first and third person pronouns – an elision reminiscent of *Berg*, or the woman's sections of *Passages*, although the nature of Sandra's experience is more surreal, and the fantasised even harder to separate from 'reality'.

In the first chapter of *The Unmapped Country*, the depiction of madness is complicated by how narrative sympathy with Sandra's experience contrasts with a resentment of and resistance to her fellow patients, with scenes where the perspective seems to be horrified by and alienated from them:

> Someone changed the television channel. Screams of protest.
> 'Well you weren't watching anyway just natter natter natter.'
> 'That's not fair we were watching.'
> 'No you fucking wasn't.'
> 'No need for that.'
>    Silence. A picture came on of a table laden with food.
> 'Looks nice doesn't it?'
> 'Not poisoned like it is in here.'

> They leaned forward and watched the picture intently.
> They leaned back and swallowed their saliva; carried on chattering, nose picking, knitting; fingers plucked at buttons, cigarettes, fingers at fingers, a battle of insects. (183)

The anonymising and distancing effects of 'someone' and 'they' here is reinforced by the disembodied and depersonalised speech of the squabbling patients. 'They' have been so reduced by the institution (which they think feeds them 'poisoned' food) that they are left with nothing to argue about and invest in but the television – the ubiquitous drug of *Tripticks*. The listing technique above demonstrates the dehumanising effects of an institutional experience which leaves people salivating, chattering, nose picking, reduced to 'insects'. But such a description also seems to condemn them with its own disgust: their frantic, plucking fingers and the knitting are ordinary activities made strange, frightening and ridiculous. In this way, at the same time as criticising what is done to the patients, here again, as with the Red Queen, the narrative voice remains at a distance from them. This double effect, which both sympathises with and is removed from these patients, works to further complicate the question of how or whether madness might be written. The wider cast of characters above provide a familiar 'known' sense of the chaos and bedlam of archetypal mad people, but it is precisely because of this that the narrative seems unable to know or sympathise with them. In this scene, the narrative perspective remains outside a seemingly inaccessible, unreasonable and alien experience, and resorts to cliché.

The writing of madness in *The Unmapped Country* is called into question by the ambivalence of its representation of these other patients, who are depicted as more stereotypically 'mad' than Sandra who, even when hallucinating her mother as the Red Queen grinning up at her from the bottom of a toilet, seems to remain lucid and ironically aware. Other patient behaviours represented by Quin range from unnamed characters who scream, are drugged, whimper, rant and rave, to the apparently nonplussed, one of whom tries on post-lobotomy wigs: 'Well I got this lobotomy op coming up and they shave the head you see – nice isn't it – they designed it specially so it would look like my own hair' (178). The variety of representation here, as well as the shifts between serious and darkly humorous tones, and between stereotype and sympathy, rethinks contradictions in the way those who are apparently mad have been perceived and represented in literature and art – from grotesquely bestial to visionary seer.[18]

The simultaneous horror and humour of the strangely normalised chatter about lobotomy surgery and the backdrop of screams and gurgles do not represent the psychiatric hospital as a place of refuge from the outside world, but one where the mad person is confined, reduced, misinterpreted, and acted upon with drugs, electroconvulsive therapy and surgery: the patients here are powerless and at the mercy of the institution and its systems.[19] Although Quin's narrator is not an omniscient third person, D. A. Miller's discussion of the wider 'institution' of such a narrator is useful for thinking about the representation of institutionalisation in *The Unmapped Country*. Miller claims that even when third person texts contain a censure of discipline and the institution, they in fact exercise policing powers of their own and the narrator is the key representative of textual institutionalism, specifically the language of reason.[20] In this, even a supposedly sympathetic third person narrator is also always an agent of an apparently rational interpretative frame. This kind of position can be seen in *Daniel Deronda*, for example, where the narrator questions the limits of its knowledge at the same time as ultimately claiming an understanding of Gwendolen that she does not have herself. In Quin's text, on the other hand, the uncertain free indirect narrative perspective calls the 'institutions' of third person narrator and psychiatric hospital into question, a narratorial position and space that, in *The Unmapped Country*, both depict and activate stereotypes of madness.

### A Paranoid Reading of Signs

For Felman, 'Madness is, before all else, an intuition about the functioning of the symbol, a blind and total faith in the revelation of a sign.'[21] In *The Unmapped Country*, the protagonist's name, (Cas)Sandra, alerts Quin's reader that this will be a text concerned with the reading of signs. In different versions of Greek mythology, Cassandra is alternately able to speak or hear the future (even, in some versions, to hear the language of animals), and foresees, but is powerless to stop, her own demise. Quin's second chapter of *The Unmapped Country*, set before Sandra is hospitalised, is mostly narrated from her perspective and focuses on how she experiences the world. The style, form and tone of the writing in this chapter is quite different to the first.[22] In it, Sandra hallucinates a world full of signs and clues where she interprets ordinary and everyday things as telling her what will happen or what she should do – and she has total faith in the function and meaning of these signs. With this, Sandra's madness is significantly bound up with the way she reads the world. Of the actual activity of reading, she says, 'It takes me a long time to read now, a paragraph holds so much significance, and everything links up' (203), and her reading of the world is similarly slowed and saturated – in this, to use Felman's words, Sandra's madness may be described as 'an intoxicating reading' of word and world.[23] So while the first chapter of *The Unmapped Country* shows reason's failure to write madness, the second insists on madness as a reading of signs.

In *Daniel Deronda*, Gwendolen's instinct is that the necklace is somehow an important thing-become-sign of the future. She recognises the rescuings of the necklace as portents, signifiers of things to come if only she were able to read them. Both Eliot and Quin's texts are interested in foreshadowing and signification, and both are aware that interpretation is based on clues but question how and who is able to interpret these. Gwendolen is unable to read them properly and Sandra is mad, and in this second chapter her madness is written in terms of attempts to read the world around her and of signs that feel significant and coercive even though their meaning is unclear. Both Sandra's experiences and Quin's writing here express and come up against an 'irreducible resistance to interpretation'.[24] Quin is always working with the energy of such resistance, in the shifting pronouns and narrative perspectives across her oeuvre, for instance, and the suggestive titles of *Passages* and *Tripticks* which seem to guide but also frustrate the reader's interpretation – in this chapter of *The Unmapped Country*, such a quality comes to the fore: both the writing's form and its subject matter resist interpretation, and the significance or meaning of the apparent clues and signs is irreducibly opaque.

The confused present tense narrative is told in a mixture of third and first person; this latter is not necessarily synonymous with Sandra, although the chapter is mainly focalised from her perspective. It opens with an unidentified non-human first person perspective, 'I am a bird hovering, searching for human shape, from the vapours of the air, space, I settle into the waters of the womb and dream ancestral dreams', who then 'climb[s] up enamel cliffs and step[s] into the shape of a woman I no longer know, or is it that I know her only too well?' (193). Despite the strangeness of this opening, the situation of the ensuing narrative then seems fairly mundane: Sandra waits, in both anxiety and anticipation, for Clive's return from work. When he arrives asking 'What did she do with herself all day, was she better?' the apparent 'normality' of the scenario is ironised, disrupted and refused as Sandra reads his behaviour in terms of 'fugitive visions': red lights in the flats opposite that act as a warning, her attempts 'to draw out the Knight, with the help of the North star' when Clive slumps on the sofa, and 'the spectre of his Grandfather [who] refuses the warmth' (194). Sandra seems to exist in a wholly over-determined world, one where her behaviour and next step are always informed and directed by the signs she reads around her: 'I have to go back into the past of this existence; the interpretation lies before me here and now' (196). In this, the writing in this second chapter of *The Unmapped Country* is a kind of maddened performance of 'intoxicating' reading, where all objects signify more than themselves and bear great symbolic importance – 'Two blue cars parked outside this house, a sign that it is all right' (198). Sandra interprets Clive's speech and behaviour in this way. For instance, his criticism – 'You're not going in for all that cranky vegetarian stuff are you Sandra?' – is followed by – 'His grandfather prongs a turnip. Other spectres come and go' (194). And, when Clive admits he doesn't mind vegetables really, the narrative continues: 'But listen to what he is really saying, gestures belie what is being said; hand clutches throat. The faces round the walls are in conspiracy' (195).

Such experiences intensify when Sandra leaves the flat and the precarious vulnerability of her situation become clear: the world outside is overwhelmingly full of signs and visions. Some, such as the blue cars parked outside the house and the belief that the pulse in her wrist 'twitches in time with the vibration of the stars' (196), are benevolent and allow her a feeling of communion with the world similar to the one described in *Berg*. Others – the park that 'used to be a shelter from the concrete and steel, it is now another inferno teeming with serpents' (200), the belief that her radio is being tapped – are frightening and alienating. Such anxieties push Sandra into stealing an outfit for disguise and fleeing in such a panic that she gets lost. The chapter ends with Sandra wanting to call on one of the 'Underground movement' – the people she believes are protecting her – for help, but fearing that even these might 'pretend they didn't know, couldn't help, pretend I was some mad woman and call the police' (207).

Throughout the chapter, Sandra also sees or hallucinates agents of control everywhere – the police, Russian spies and members of the underground movement – in what can be read as Quin's conscious acknowledgement of paranoia as a stereotype of both madness and the cold war:

> I move like a blind person. But the signs are there. As long as I keep within the Controlled Zone I will be safe, outside of that it is enemy territory. The traffic lights are for me all the way. My right side gives me the route to take. But it is all very difficult to learn. A pain goes through my left side, I have taken the wrong turning. I am out of the controlled zone. Two Russian spies are waiting on the corner, just like in a corny film, hiding behind newspapers. The traffic speeds up, then slows down so I can run across the road and into the park. (199)

Sandra is 'a blind person', unable to see rationally though at the same able to see signs which communicate a different 'truth' of things. These signs lead her – 'traffic lights are for me' 'right side gives me the route to take' – through a safe, controlled zone. But reading such signs is difficult and she takes a wrong turning – 'pain goes through my left side'. These dramatic, physical responses to the right or wrong reading of signs communicate a visceral and embodied experience of madness. At the same time, the experience is written as if seen on a screen where spies 'are waiting on the corner, just like in a corny film, hiding behind newspapers'.[25] This 'just like in a corny film' makes the scene seem distanced and unreal, as well as ironic and clichéd; it adds to the stereotyping of doctors and patients in the first chapter. In this way, stereotypes of madness also frame Sandra's experiences in the scene above.

More specifically, the paranoia of her madness here is written in terms of the cold war – the spies who watch Sandra are Russian.[26] Elsewhere Sandra thinks there is a 'Russian woman agent' (202) following her. Similar cold war paranoia pervades 'Matters of the Heart', especially after Linda has had a breakdown: 'A large grinning chap from Red China in the Restaurant car watched me. And there's a large Russian woman occupying the seat opposite mine.'[27] It is also no coincidence that the pervading agent of oppression in both narratives, 'the Red Queen' – who will, Sandra thinks, be watching her 'even when dead' (163) – is also a 'Red' agent, simultaneously a figure of the cold war and a madness stereotype. Adam Piette makes the point that the cold war manifested as a 'paranoid plotline' in many Anglo-American texts at this time.[28] This paranoia, according to Piette, tapped into the longing for a direct link between private fantasies and the military-industrial complex running the world. He calls this 'the most powerful of dreams: that the big world of the cold war has an entranced relationship with the [individual] citizen's unconscious'.[29] Similarly, while Quin's strange second chapter of *The Unmapped Country* immerses the reader in Sandra's unconscious experiences of madness – revealed at the chapter's start where she is 'the shape of a woman I no longer know', in her 'total faith in the revelation of a sign', and in the dramatic irony of the idea that she could 'pretend I was some mad woman' – her paranoid reading of signs can at the same time be read as engaging with the text's 'big world of the cold war' context.

## Visions of God

The insistent vision of God's face across Quin's writing is a further and wonderfully complex and suggestive stereotype of madness and/or religious experience.[30] R. D. Laing reinterpreted psychiatric patients' previously pathologised claims to seeing – or even being – God by claiming that 'madness' (and specifically schizophrenia) might be better thought of as a mode of insight and prophecy, of religious vision and spiritual quest. The visions of God's face in *The Unmapped Country* can be read as both invoking and unravelling such a claim.[31] It is sent up, for example, in the behaviour of one of Sandra's fellow patients, Annie Carr (in what is surely a reference to Mary Barnes, who smeared shit as self-expression during her widely publicised 'therapy' with Laing and Joseph Berke), who shouts 'May the blessed Virgin shit on you – shit shit shit' (162).[32] Another patient, Thomas, believes he is 'Judas Iscariot reincarnated'; that 'God is Mrs Carr, and my young friend Bob is Jesus Christ' (161). As above, in response his God Annie Carr's speech is profane: 'you cunt you bloody fucking cunt' (162); at the lunch table she exposes herself – 'Annie Carr shouted, pushing out her left breast, dipping it in the gravy' – and then tears off her nightdress 'and on all fours gave herself to the linoleum' (165). Annie's behaviour poses no challenge to Thomas's belief, showing the strength of his delusional worldview, and this provides a further questioning of representations and perceptions of 'madness'.

Yet the apparent irony and critique of romanticised stereotypes of madness as spiritual quest present in such examples is complicated by the insistent vision of God's face that recurs throughout Quin's writing and thinking. In *Berg*, Berg says 'But I don't believe in God, and how boring heaven must be just looking at His face', while his mother's words respond, 'there's nothing more beautiful nothing more wonderful than looking upon God's face'.[33] In her diary in 'Matters of the Heart', Linda records: 'I saw the face of God – just like a Blake picture, snowy white hair and beard, in His face every conceivable landscape: valleys, mountains, lakes, rivers, oceans, trees;

the whole universe in fact.'[34] The image is also present in chapter two of *The Unmapped Country*: 'Staring at the white wall I see a face appear. White against white. Soon valleys, mountains, forests, rivers, lakes and many oceans appear in the face, in the white hair and long beard. The eyes contain day and night, and in their depths stella spaces. Each strand of hair is luminous. I know it is God's face' (198). Quin's own experience of this vision seemed, she said, 'so much more purposeful than anything I could ever write'.[35] She continues:

> It's very difficult to talk about, but I just knew it couldn't be anything else. There was every possible landscape in the face: valleys, trees, mountains, hills. It was composed of every landscape, and it looked like a picture from Blake, with snowy white hair and a long white beard. It was important to my work because I have found it difficult to believe in writing since.[36]

This experience is difficult to talk about – both hard to put into words and embarrassing to admit – but 'I just knew it couldn't be anything else'. This 'knowledge' is not logical or reasonable and is in fact counter to those things; nevertheless, it seems (and feels) irrefutable. This is an experience on the edge of madness, for religious beliefs, experiences and visions have the strange status of being both indicators of madness and of reasonable, 'sane' faith. Like madness, a vision of God understood as religious experience is also an experience at the very edge of what it is possible to communicate. And for Quin, this crisis of knowledge and understanding is necessarily also a crisis of writing: 'I have found it difficult to believe in writing since.'

The slippage between Quin's vision and its echoes across *The Unmapped Country* and 'Matters of the Heart' is an example of reiteration at work in such a way that it begins to hiccup and unravel, to make strange and trouble meaning. The rewriting of the vision is explicitly grounded in the romanticism of Blake – who by the 1960s had become an 'icon of campus revolution', and rather misread and clichéd[37] – at the same time as refusing it. The vision is exposed to a ridicule the writer seems to anticipate in the interview above, when Sandra attempts to depict it during a painting therapy session:

> In a grain of sand the whole universe – something like that, Blake put. He had visions. A God who laughed, belched, snored and picked His nose. Her God had been straight out of Blake, long snowy beard and snowy locks, and in His face every conceivable landscape.
> 'That's a funny face Sandra.'
> 'It's God.'
> 'Looks like a lump of shit to me.' A patient said, making up her face with paint brushes. (172)

The reference to Blake's poetic visions seems undermined by the claim that his God was one that 'laughed, belched, snored and picked His nose', much like the 'nose picking' mad patients in the television-watching extract above. The capitalised 'His' here is juxtaposed in between 'picked' and 'nose' to ironic effect: it simultaneously denies and seems to bow to religious conventions of respect. Further, the assertion that 'Her God had been straight out of Blake, long snowy beard and snowy locks, and in His face every conceivable landscape' is at odds and deliberately jars with the preceding description. And when Sandra's representation of this laughing, snoring, belching, nose-picking God is likened to a 'lump of shit', not only is this comment transgressively funny, it is also a moment of verbal instability and slippage – from face to faeces. While this faeces serves to deface the face of God – just as the patient who describes Sandra's picture as 'a lump of shit' makes up her face with paint, which in turn recalls Mary Barnes's painting with shit – it also signifies an absurdly ambivalent and blurry meaning, a maddened language.[38] Here, not only is the reiteration of variations of the beauteous and flowing image of God disrupted by 'His' bad habits, which disrupts and defamiliarises the repetition, but, at the very level of the language itself, the face (of God) represses and denies, yet also always already carries within it, the faeces.

### Unknitting Iterations of Madness

> [T]o give madness a voice, to restore its language: a language of madness and not about it.[39]

One way Quin's writing might *mean* madness – might give it a voice, restore its language – is by knowingly invoking and ironising, and therefore calling attention to and unravelling, some of its stereotypes. Here I develop my reading of God's face to consider in more detail how reiteration and cliché work to create maddened effects. In my reading of the effects of Quin's emphatic and excessive detail, this aspect of *The Unmapped Country* slips from a writing about madness to a writing *of* it: the madness is not separated from a language that speaks about it but comes from within. In such moments the question of perspective is undone, and language is activated into an excess it cannot know or explain. The prose seems to break free from narrative control, into 'a madness that is acted out in language, but whose role no speaking subject can assume':[40]

> Those who were not chattering, stalked the room, or fluttered on chairs, made stabbing movements with knitting needles, reams of coloured wool spilled onto the floor, dribbled yellow and red between flapping arms, someone croaked, another barked. A mouth opened, closed, opened again, no sound came. But eventually a howl did emerge. Doors opened, and in rushed the keepers. The howl continued. People turned their heads, froze in contorted positions, as the keepers bent over a young girl struggling on the floor; her head curiously twisted; the white of her eyes showed through dark feathers, damp with sweat. The howl changed to a gurgle, the gurgle to gasps, as the body writhed in the net of arms. And like a huge octopus the group moved slowly out of the room. The girl's shoe remained, on its side. Someone kicked it across the floor. The knitting needles pierced the air, click click click, and bodies took up their preceding positions, and went through the motions of survival of the fittest. (186–7)

The sound at the centre of this passage is the howl of the 'young girl': this recalls the distant woman's scream that Sandra hears at the start of the book – as well as the silent scream at the end of *Tripticks* and screams elsewhere in Quin's writing. Here, while initially 'A mouth opened, closed, opened again, no sound came', 'eventually a howl did emerge'. This sound of protest is soon reduced to a gurgle and then gasps as the girl's writhing body is subdued by the 'net of arms' of the 'keepers'. There is deliberate poignancy in the girl's abandoned shoe kicked across the floor after she has been taken from the room. In this scene the girl is reduced to a howling beast, the image of an archetypal mad person. In this, her madness both seems to reinforce the opposition of madness and reason, and at the same time, as with the characters Annie Carr and Thomas, her madness emerges as a familiar 'role to be played'.[41] The howl signifies her disconnection from the policing and institutional language of reason, as well as her powerlessness: the doctors (or 'keepers') are the oppressors of the scene who take her away. The girl's howl is also a sign of the condition that has led to her incarceration: a condition which is itself a label assigned from the outside and in the words of other, more 'reasonable' people for, as Felman reminds us, 'the term madness is [always] borrowed from the language of others'.[42] Such a reading extends my discussion of *The Unmapped Country* so far in this chapter, which claims that Quin's prose exposes the inevitable failure of attempts to write *about* madness, because such writing will always work to stereotype and exclude it.

I propose – and this is my key claim here – that when we look more carefully, what is also at work in the extract above is precisely a language *of* madness. The writing is punctuated – its surface pierced – by repeating, stuttering onomatopoeic 't's and 'k's, which perform the violence not only of the knitting but of the illness and of the keepers' restraint of the girl, as well as acting to instantiate the concrete meanings of the words. These sounds repeat those in the extract cited earlier: 'chattering, nose picking, knitting; fingers plucked at buttons, cigarettes, fingers at fingers, a battle of insects' (183). The briefer evocation of sounds there are repeated, exaggerated and proliferated in this longer piece, where sustained consonance makes the language strange and unwieldy, and denies transparency: this, the knotted pattern of the texture insists, is certainly not unwritten narration. Instead, the patterning of the language – a glossomania in terms of sound, movement and rhythm rather than sense – deliberately performs and instantiates the madness it writes.[43] In this way the writing stutters in terms of sound patterns, but also meaning patterns, and this strains the passage to create a sense of becoming; this is description becoming something else. As Deleuze observes – and as I have discussed in the Introduction to this book and in the chapter on *Passages* – stuttering often comes about as part of an attempt to capture unfamiliar experiences in such a way that language is activated into new meanings.[44]

But even more than this, the performance of the language here spills over and out of control: 'reams of coloured wool spilled onto the floor, dribbled yellow and red between flapping arms, someone croaked, another barked'. With this, the text unravels just as the knitting does, dramatising and infecting Quin's writing process as it juxtaposes and interweaves sound and sense connections to create a knotty and tangled surface. Knitting is knotting with gaps; it produces a tangled order out of reams of wool. This is an ideal metaphor for writing which spills over with meaning; indeed it had already been used as such by Quin herself in Ruth's knitting in *Three*,[45] as well as by one of Quin's key influences, Virginia Woolf, in *To the Lighthouse*.[46] Elsewhere, knotting had been used as a metaphor for the patterning of madness and psychological binds: in *Knots* (1970), Laing claims that language is able to reveal such experiences – ones that cannot be articulated in the language of reason – through word patterns such as 'knots, tangles, fankles, impasses, disjunctions, whirligigs, binds'.[47] In these examples, as well as in *The Unmapped Country* here, the images of knitting and knotting both invade the text and are the text – in Quin's writing madness is generated at the point where the text, writing about itself, tangles up, knots and unravels.

The flow of the spilling and dribbling of this undoing directly contrasts with the overwhelming quantity of jerky and unpleasant movement – stalked, fluttered, stabbing, flapping, writhed, kicked – and sound – chattering, croaked, barked, howl, click – throughout the extract. In particular, the sound of the 'click' reverberates with prose elsewhere, for example, 'The nurse clicked her teeth, and took mental note of the patient's words' (164). Not only is the onomatopoeia of the 'ck' and 't' here similarly threatening, but the repetition into a different context – from the click of the nurse's disapproval to the 'click click click' of knitting needles piercing the air – is strange and insistent. Such descriptions are unstable and unsettling. Rather than making a claim to representation, this excess creates a maddened effect: knitting has a common-sense, mundane reality in the world outside the text, but an insistent, threatening and unstable one within it. This ambivalence unsettles the reader's perception of how to receive the text: does language remain under the control of a third person narrator here? How does the equivocation of the words affect meaning and interpretation? Are there places where the accelerating repetition of sounds, effects and intertexts means that the writing is no longer about madness but also somehow performative of it?

In my reading, this ambivalent effect, where the writing is both a free indirect narrative description of Sandra's experience and 'writing-gone-mad' – in terms of its knitting of exaggerated signification and knotted profusion of detail – is the most persuasive way that *The Unmapped Country* manages at once to be both about and of madness. This becomes clearer if we also consider the effect of the bird metaphor. The flapping, fluttering patients are as if birds in the 'parrot house' (186) with the staff as keepers. Throughout Quin's writing, birds take on an over-signified, hallucinatory quality. In *The Unmapped Country*, for example, the 'gigantic bird [which] wheeled, then plummeted down' (160), the gulls that Sandra sees 'circle the ship's mast' (160) and the gulls that 'circled above the grey buildings' (179) in the first chapter are echoed in the ambiguous opening of the second: 'I am a bird hovering, searching for human shape' (193). These birds not only recall the gulls in *Berg*, but also the definitions of 'gull' alongside a reference to 'gullibility' and the description of birds flying in formation in *Passages*, an image which in turn itself reverberates with and recalls Leonardo's description of birds' flight.[48] More specifically, Sandra's distancing from language is described in terms of birds: 'Once she had understood the language of birds, now no longer, it took her all her time to understand her own language' (167). This echoes the connections made between madness and the 'language of birds' elsewhere in Quin's writing, for example in 'Ghostworm'; 'She had wanted to understand the language of birds. They spoke now get out getoutgetoutget.'[49] In turn, these surely reference Septimus's hallucinations of birds talking to him in Greek in Woolf's *Mrs Dalloway*.[50] In this way, Sandra's claim to have once understood the language of birds both describes an experience of madness and at the same time, through the very insistence of the imagery, activates and makes strange familiar signs of madness by sending out part-repeated ripples of already over-encoded images and ideas.

In this, chains of signification move across Quin's writing here and beyond to emphatically perform a sense of 'hallucinatory inflation'.[51] This inflation comes precisely because the images and signs in *The Unmapped Country* echo and hallucinate, and are in a sense relentlessly pursued by, a literary inheritance of madness, not only of Kesey, Plath and Dawson, but also Woolf, and beyond that back to Eliot's gusts and storms of the 'unmapped country' of the psyche.[52] Here, then, the madness of Quin's text is in part created by an obsessive internalisation and activation of others' representations of madness and mental unease. This generates not only the seemingly banal and clichéd aspects of the writing, the sense in which we have 'heard it all before' – for example, the wider cast of characters or Sandra's conversation with the psychiatrist at the start of the text – but also provides the necessary cultural repository out of which Quin's writing is able to signify and activate madness through the very profusion of its reference and reiteration. Riley claims Echo as initiator of the ironic, who 'fingers strangeness simply through listening to what [the narrative] hears being reiterated'.[53] For irony to grip, she claims, unease as well as boredom alerts us to the fact that something sounds as if it is in the wrong register. And Quin's writing of madness here, as with the use of irony in *Tripticks*, knows and activates this aspect of reiteration; as I have demonstrated, the writing is punctuated by phrases that are funny and knowingly clichéd at the same time as creating an oppressive and troubled effect. In this way, in *The Unmapped Country*, the boredom that registers cliché also transforms the words into something vital and active, for 'reiteration produces more than inert copies'.[54]

So, ironically, it may in part be the very the excess of repetition and stereotype in *The Unmapped Country*, the fact that it comes after and knows other writing about madness, which enables it to move beyond description (or explanation) and towards an expression or activation of it. Put another way, the glossomania of the reiterating and over-determined forms and qualities of Quin's writing elsewhere – its lack of space and lacuna – finds its most convincing expression here. Although *The Unmapped Country* expresses a failure to articulate madness, it is also precisely the seeming exteriority of the rippling echoes of intertexts – both of others and Quin's own – that make this writing so strange. Like Felman's argument in *Writing and Madness*, *The Unmapped Country* insists on madness as a literary thing. In this, Quin's final, unfinished book can be read as example of 'literature's particular way of speaking' madness, which precisely consists in its unsettling the boundary 'between psychosis and stereotype'.[55] The form of the writing, exemplified in the passage above, brings madness into a state of coming out in the language: it 'is not the *origin* of [the] writing, the *cause* of meaning, but an *effect*' of the excessive repetition.[56] In this way, I suggest, the ironic, unstable and unruly proliferation of echoes in *The Unmapped Country* created by Quin's unknitting and unravelling of iterations of madness work to evoke 'madness *inside of* thought', inside of writing, in such a way that it might begin to activate a form of madness at the level of language itself.[57]

## Notes

1. Nye, 'Against the Barbarians'.
2. Quin, letter to Boyars, 16 January 1973. Calder and Boyars manuscripts, Series II, box 52, folder 4.
3. I use the term 'madness' as it is the one Quin herself uses in *The Unmapped Country*. It is also, as Charley Baker, Paul Crawford, B. J. Brown, Maurice Lipsedge and Roland Carter point out, the term which best includes and represents the social, personal and cultural contexts of the 1960s/1970s. *Madness in Post-1945 British and American Fiction* (Basingstoke and New York: Palgrave Macmillan, 2012), p. 3.
4. Quin, *The Unmapped Country*, in *The Unmapped Country: Stories & Fragments*, pp. 159–208, p. 160. Subsequent references to *The Unmapped Country* in this chapter are in parenthesis in the text.
5. Quin, 'Matters of the Heart' (1973), unpublished manuscript, Carol Burns Private Collection of Papers, p. 16.
6. Chapters from *The Unmapped Country* were first published in *Matrix* 6 (London: City Literary Institute, October 1974), and Gordon, *Beyond the Words: Eleven Writers in Search of a New Fiction*. *Daniel Deronda* is given as the inspiration for *The Unmapped Country* in *Matrix* 6, p. 15.
7. George Eliot, *Daniel Deronda* (Oxford: Oxford University Press, 1984), p. 235.

8. MacCabe, *James Joyce and the Revolution of the Word*, p. 24.
9. Laing became one of the most prominent and famous figures of this zeitgeist after the publication of, for example, the widely read *The Divided Self* (1960) and *The Politics of Experience and The Bird of Paradise* (1967). Laing's popularity is discussed by Jenny Diski in *The Sixties* (2009).
10. Shoshana Felman, *Writing and Madness*, trans. Shoshana Felman, Martha Noel Evans and Brian Massumi (Palo Alto, CA: Stanford University Press, 2003), pp. 12, 13.
11. Felman, *Writing and Madness*, p. 41.
12. Gordon, 'Introduction', *Beyond the Words*, p. 11.
13. Jacques Derrida, *Writing and Difference*, trans. Alan Bass (London: Routledge, 1995), p. 43.
14. Deleuze describes the violent effects of madness on language as 'less a question of recovering meaning than of destroying the word'. *The Logic of Sense*, trans. Mark Lester (London: Althone Press, 1990), p. 88.
15. Felman, *Writing and Madness*, p. 252, my italics.
16. Ibid. p. 36.
17. Elaine Showalter, *The Female Malady: Women, Madness and English Culture, 1830–1980* (London: Virago, 1987), p. 211.
18. Similar debates abound in wider critical discussion of madness: for example, Derrida's critique of Foucault's attachment to the 'concept of madness as unreason'. *Writing and Difference*, p. 38. Louis Sass refutes the 'ubiquitous image of madness as irrationality', arguing instead for an interpretation of madness (and specifically schizophrenia) as reason *in extremis*. *Madness and Modernism*, p. 2.
19. In 1961 Erving Goffman called the asylum a place in which the person's self 'is systematically, if often unintentionally, mortified'. *Asylums* (Harmondsworth: Penguin, 1970), p. 24.
20. D. A. Miller, *The Novel and the Police* (Berkeley, CA and London: University of California Press, 1988), p. 23.
21. Felman, *Writing and Madness*, p. 71.
22. Gordon dismissed this second chapter as 'apocalyptic and wishy-washy' and did not include it in *Beyond the Words*.
23. Felman, *Writing and Madness*, p. 64.
24. Ibid. p. 254.
25. This recalls the stereotypes of agents in *Passages* as well as the stereotyping of mainstream culture in *Tripticks* – here there is a similar sense of fascination and critique.
26. In Hall, 'The Mighty Quin', Quin says she believes that 'The Russians [are] interested in her', p. 8.
27. Quin, 'Matters of the Heart', p. 14. Both *The Unmapped Country* and 'Matters of the Heart' are pervaded by images of snow and whiteness, the archetypal post-nuclear holocaust image. The desire for white

blankness is also notably one that Jenny Diski connects with mental breakdown in *Skating towards Antarctica* (1998).
28. Adam Piette, *The Literary Cold War: 1945 to Vietnam* (Edinburgh: Edinburgh University Press, 2009), p. 11.
29. Piette, *The Literary Cold War*, p. 3.
30. For Felman, madness is 'the illusion of being able to salvage something from time, the belief in the possibility of eternity... in God'. *Writing and Madness*, p. 84.
31. See R. D. Laing, *The Politics of Experience and The Bird of Paradise* (Harmondsworth: Penguin, 1967). For Laing, 'if God does not exist, everything is permitted', p. 114. See also Quin, 'Matters of the Heart': 'if, as Dostoievsky [sic] puts it, there is no God then everything is permitted', p. 26.
32. Mary Barnes' experience is narrated by Mary Barnes and Joseph Berke in the extraordinary *Mary Barnes: Two Accounts of a Journey through Madness* (London: MacGibbon and Kee, 1971).
33. Quin, *Berg*, p. 133.
34. Quin, 'Matters of the Heart', p. 11.
35. Hall, 'The Mighty Quin', p. 8.
36. Ibid.
37. Victor Sage, 'The Greater Tragedy Imposed on the Small: Art, Anachrony and the perils of Bohemia in Rebecca West's *The Fountain Overflows*', in *British Fiction After Modernism*, ed. Marina MacKay and Lyndsey Stonebridge (Basingstoke and New York: Palgrave Macmillan, 2007), p. 169.
38. John Wilkinson identifies this kind of verbal slippage – his examples are 'jewelry [sic] and jewry/Boers and De Beers' – as an example of 'automization', where the appearance of the word itself becomes the focus. 'Too-Close Reading', *The Lyric Touch: Essays on the Poetry of Excess* (Cambridge: Salt Publishing, 2007), p. 159. Automisation is one of the forms of 'schizophrenic' language that Wilkinson takes from Sass, *Madness and Modernism*, pp. 178–80.
39. Wilkinson, *The Lyric Touch*, p. 14.
40. Felman, *Writing and Madness*, p. 252.
41. Ibid. p. 82.
42. Ibid. p. 80.
43. For an extended discussion of the nausea, alienation, sense of meaninglessness created by 'glossomania' and excessive reiteration, see Sass, 'Languages of Inwardness', *Madness and Modernism*, pp. 174–209.
44. Deleuze, 'He Stuttered', p. 110.
45. Quin, *Three*, pp. 50–1.
46. Throughout 'The Window', Mrs Ramsay knits a 'heather-mixture stocking, with its criss-cross of steel needles at the mouth of it' for the lighthouse keeper's little boy. Woolf, *To the Lighthouse* (London: Wordsworth Classics, 2002), p. 19. The action stands as metaphor for

the interwoven patterning of Mrs Ramsay's thoughts as well as the constructedness of the prose. The repetition of this trope in *The Unmapped Country*, then, not only enacts these same aspects of the metaphor but also interweaves references to Woolf, that, given Quin's close familiarity with and admiration of her work, are surely deliberate.
47. R. D. Laing, *Knots* (New York: Random House, 1970), preface, n.p. Throughout the book Laing generates patterns of neuroses and psychoses through partial and ambivalent repetition.
48. Quin, *Passages*, pp. 29, 12.
49. Quin, 'Ghostworm,' p. 126.
50. 'A sparrow perched on the railing opposite chirped Septimus, Septimus, four or five times over and went on, drawing its notes out, to sing freshly and piercingly in Greek words how there is no crime and, joined by another sparrow, they sang in voices prolonged and piercing in Greek words.'. Virginia Woolf, *Mrs Dalloway* (London: Penguin, 2000), p. 26. As the notes to the text confirm, Woolf herself had 'imagined she heard the birds singing in Greek', p. 218.
51. Felman, *Writing and Madness*, p. 67.
52. There is perhaps even a further echo, with Allen Ginsberg's writing of madness in his 1956 *Howl* in the howling of the girl in *The Unmapped Country*.
53. Riley, *The Words of Selves*, p. 157.
54. Ibid. p. 159.
55. Felman, *Writing and Madness*, p. 253.
56. Ibid. p. 98.
57. Ibid. p. 48.

# Afterword: Where Next?

This book has offered the fullest appraisal of Quin's writing and life to date. I have argued that the precarious writing of Ann Quin is striking precisely because of its unstable shifting between, on the one hand, aesthetic and literary purposes, questions and techniques that aim to transgress, test out and mobilise the possibilities of experimental prose and, on the other, its engagement with and destabilising of the wider social, cultural and political questions of the 1960s and 1970s. This is clear in, for example, how the tactile aesthetics of clothes and make-up in *Berg* are used to depict a shabby seaside setting and performances of gender and desire; how the ambiguous collage of journal forms in *Three* reveal the text's subversion of marriage and class, as well as enabling its consideration of sexual violence; how the disrupted sequencing of the woman's sections in *Passages* reconsider sexuality in the era of free love, and how the fragmented sections of the man's journal question the woman's ambivalent desire and British attitudes to Jewishness; the critique of both the counter-culture and consumer culture via impoverished style, cliché and the cut-up in *Tripticks*; and the activation of stereotypes and unravelling of cliché to engage with questions of madness and the cold war in *The Unmapped Country*. The short interchapters between the critical chapters have created an oblique structure pertinent and sensitive to Quin. The aim of these biographical vignettes has been to resonate with, extend and enrich the literary critical work of the main chapters and to encourage a sideways reading between life and writing, rather than to be read as if giving access to the 'person' or secret of Ann Quin.

With my primary focus on the major works, I have not had space in this book for sustained engagement with Quin's short stories, except for some analysis of 'Never Trust a Man Who Bathes with His Fingernails' and the unpublished 'Matters of the Heart'. Most of her 'stories and fragments', written across the 1960s and early 1970s, were published together for the first time in *The Unmapped Country: Stories & Fragments*. The pieces included there range from the dark and vividly nightmarish 'Nude and Seascape' and confusing cacophony of 'Ghostworm', to the vivid New Mexico landscape of 'Eyes that Watch Behind the Wind', and grotty English interiors of 'A Double Room' and 'Every Cripple Has His Own Way of Walking', to the one-sided phone call of 'Motherlogue'. Quin's delight in the possibilities of the short form was no doubt in part because writing these brought some financial relief, but also because of the aesthetic opportunities afforded by this restricted space and 'curved shape'. The short form enabled Quin to intensify the literary strategies at work in her longer texts: the poetic patterning of sound and rhythm; shifting and uncertain narrative perspectives; polyvocity; intensely drawn details and sensory experiences. Quin's shorter works make for fascinating and disturbing reading. This writing produces different kinds of defamiliarising effects to the longer texts as well as reworking similar patterns and preoccupations – the sea, violence, thwarted and possible desires, psychology and psychosis. There is currently a notable gap in terms of critical responses to her short stories and fragments, however, and this is a clear area for future development in Quin scholarship.

Reading Quin's writing is valuable not only for disrupting the story of twentieth-century British fiction, but also, as my readings and analyses throughout this book have demonstrated, for establishing her importance as one of the pre-eminent female experimental writers of her era. Her writing's precarious ambivalence of both/and, enabled by its sheer range of experimental forms and techniques, creates a poetics of possibility that still feels startling, fresh and challenging when read today. This is how and why Quin's writing compellingly appeals to and resonates with contemporary writers and readers. In order to think about the effects and relevance of this, my sideways reading methods – and the paratactic structure of this book – have embraced the necessarily participatory and reiterative aspects of encountering this vivid, fragile, bold and extraordinary oeuvre.

# Bibliography

Adorno, Theodor and Horkheimer, Max, *Dialectic of Enlightenment*, trans. John Cumming (London and New York: Verso, 1997).
Ahmed, Sara, *The Cultural Politics of Emotion* (Edinburgh: Edinburgh University Press, 2004).
Arendt, Hannah, *Crises of the Republic* (Harmondsworth: Penguin, 1973).
Arendt, Hannah, *Eichmann in Jerusalem: A Report on the Banality of Evil* (London: Faber & Faber, 1963).
Arendt, Hannah, *Responsibility and Judgement* (New York: Schocken Books, 2003).
Baker, Charley, Crawford, Paul, Brown, B. J., Lipsedge, Maurice and Carter, Roland (eds), *Madness in Post-1945 British and American Fiction* (Basingstoke and New York: Palgrave Macmillan, 2012).
Ballard, J. G., *The Atrocity Exhibition* (London: Flamingo, 2001).
Barber, Dulan, 'Afterword' to *Berg* (London: Quartet Books, 1977).
Barber, Dulan, 'The Human Sorceress', unpublished manuscript, Carol Burns Private Collection of Papers.
Barnes, Mary and Berke, Joseph, *Mary Barnes: Two Accounts of a Journey through Madness* (London: MacGibbon and Kee, 1971).
Barthes, Roland, *A Lover's Discourse*, trans. Richard Howard (London: Penguin, 1990).
Barthes, Roland, *Image, Music, Text*, trans. Stephen Heath (London: Fontana, 1977).
Barthes, Roland, *Mythologies*, trans. Annette Lavers (London: Vintage, 2000).
Barthes, Roland, 'The Metaphor of the Eye', trans. J. A. Underwood, afterword to Georges Bataille, *Story of the Eye*, trans. Joachim Neugroschal (London: Penguin, 2001).
Bauman, Zygmunt, 'Allosemitism: Premodern, Modern, Postmodern', in *The Image of the Jew in European Liberal Culture 1789–1914*, ed. Bryan Cheyette and Nadia Valman (Portland, OR and London: Vallentine Mitchell, 2004).

Beauvoir, Simone de, *Must We Burn de Sade?*, trans. Annette Michelson (London: Peter Neville, 1953).
Bellarisi, Franca, 'Anticipating the Spiritual Legacy of the 1960s: "Beatness" and "Beat Buddhism"', in *In and Around the Sixties*, ed. Mirella Billi and Nicholas Brownlees (Viterbo, Italy: Sette Città, 2003), pp. 19–44.
Benjamin, Walter, *Illuminations*, trans. Harry Zorn (London: Pimlico, 1999).
Bennett, Claire-Louise, *Checkout 19* (London: Jonathan Cape, 2021).
Bennett, Claire-Louise, 'Introduction' to *Passages* (Sheffield: And Other Stories, 2021), pp. v–ix.
Berger, John, *About Looking* (London: Writers and Readers Publishing Cooperative, 1980).
Berger, John, *Ways of Seeing* (London: The British Broadcasting Corporation and Penguin, 1972).
Berne, Eric, *Games People Play* (London: Penguin, 1964).
Bowlby, Rachel, *Freudian Mythologies: Greek Tragedy and Modern Identities* (Oxford: Oxford University Press, 2007).
Bowlby, Rachel, *Just Looking* (London and New York: Methuen, 1985).
Bowlby, Rachel, *Shopping with Freud* (London and New York: Routledge, 1993).
Boxall, Peter, *Since Beckett: Contemporary Writing in the Wake of Modernism* (London and New York: Continuum, 2009).
Bronfen, Elisabeth, *Over Her Dead Body: Death, Femininity and the Aesthetic* (Manchester: Manchester University Press, 1990).
Brooke-Rose, Christine, *Thru* (London: Hamish Hamilton, 1975).
Brooks, Peter, *Reading for the Plot: Design and Intention in Narrative* (Cambridge, MA and London: Harvard University Press, 1984).
Brooks, Peter, *The Melodramatic Imagination* (New Haven, CT: Yale University Press, 1995).
Bruce, Sylvia, review of *Three*, unpublished manuscript, Carol Burns Private Collection of Papers.
Burke, Helen, 'People Wandering', *The Irish Press*, 8 April 1969, n.p.
Burns, Alan, 'Blending Words with Pictures', *Books and Bookmen*, 17:10 (July 1972), n.p.
Burns, Alan and Johnson, B. S., 'Introduction', *Writers Reading* pamphlet (London: J & P Weldon, 1969).
Burns, Carol, Piece in memory of Ann Quin, Carol Burns Private Collection of Papers.
Butler, Alice, 'Ann Quin's Nighttime Ink: A Postscript', MA dissertation, The Royal College of Art, London, 2013, available at http://www.alicebutler.org.uk/wp-content/uploads/2016/03/Butler_AnnQuin_Book.pdf (accessed 18 November 2022).
Butler, Judith, *Antigone's Claim: Kinship between Life and Death* (New York and Chichester: Columbia University Press, 2000).
Carter, Angela, *Nothing Sacred: Selected Writings* (London: Virago, 1992).

Carter, Angela, *The Sadeian Woman: An Exercise in Cultural History* (London: Virago, 2000).

Caruth, Cathy, 'Lying and History', in *Thinking in Dark Times: Hannah Arendt on Ethics and Politics*, ed. Roger Berkowitz, Jeffrey Katz and Thomas Keenan (New York: Fordham University Press, 2010), pp. 79–94.

Cheyette, Bryan, 'English Anti-Semitism: A Counter-Narrative', *Textual Practice*, 25:1, (2011).

Clarke, Chris, '"S" and "M": The Last and Lost Letters Between Ann Quin and Robert Creeley', *Women: A Cultural Review*, special issue: *(Re)turning to Ann Quin*, 33:1 (2022), pp. 33–51.

Coe, Jonathan, *Like a Fiery Elephant: The Story of B. S. Johnson* (London: Picador, 2004).

Cohen, Joshua, 'Introduction' to *Three* (Sheffield: And Other Stories, 2020), pp. v–x.

Cohen, Stanley, *Folk Devils and Moral Panics: The Creation of Mods and Rockers* (Oxford and New York: Basil Blackwell, 1987).

Darlington, Joe, *The Experimentalists: The Life and Times of the British Experimental Writers of the 1960s* (London: Bloomsbury Academic, 2021).

Deleuze, Gilles, *Cinema 2: The Time-Image*, trans. Hugh Tomlinson and Robert Galeta (London: Athlone Press, 1985).

Deleuze, Gilles, *Essays Critical and Clinical*, trans. Daniel Smith and Michael Greco (London and New York: Verso, 1998).

Deleuze, Gilles, *The Logic of Sense*, trans. Mark Lester (London: Athlone Press, 1990).

Deleuze, Gilles and Guattari, Félix, *Anti-Oedipus: Capitalism and Schizophrenia*, trans. Robert Hurley, Mark Seem and Helen Lane (London: Continuum, 2011).

Derrida, Jacques, *Derrida: A Critical Reader*, trans. and ed. David Wood (Oxford and Cambridge, MA: Blackwell, 1992).

Derrida, Jacques, *Memoirs of the Blind: The Self-Portrait and Other Ruins*, trans. Pascale-Anne Brault and Michael Naas (Chicago and London: The University of Chicago Press, 1993).

Derrida, Jacques, *Writing and Difference*, trans. Alan Bass (London: Routledge, 1995).

Didion, Joan, *Slouching Towards Bethlehem* (New York: Farrar, Straus and Giroux, 1968).

Diski, Jenny, *The Sixties* (Basingstoke and New York: Palgrave Macmillan, 2009).

Doane, Mary Ann, *The Desire to Desire: The Woman's Film of the 1940s* (Bloomington and Indianapolis: Indiana University Press, 1987).

Doolittle, Hilda, *Helen in Egypt* (New York: New Directions Publishing Corporation, 1974).

Dunn, Nell, *Talking to Women* (London: Silver Press, 2018).

Dutton, Danielle, 'Unpacking Ann Quin's Comic Tragedy', *Music & Literature No. 7*, (Houston, TX: Taylor Davis-Van Atta, 2016).
Eliot, George, *Daniel Deronda* (Oxford: Oxford University Press, 1984).
Ellmann, Maud, *Elizabeth Bowen: The Shadow Across the Page* (Edinburgh: Edinburgh University Press, 2003).
Evenson, Brian, 'Introduction' to *Three* (Chicago: Dalkey Archive Press, 2001).
Evenson, Brian and Howard, Joanna, 'Ann Quin', *Review of Contemporary Fiction*, 23:2 (Summer 2003).
Farber, David and Bailey, Beth, *The Columbia Guide to America in the 1960s* (New York: Columbia University Press, 2001).
Felman, Shoshana, *Writing and Madness*, trans. Shoshana Felman, Martha Noel Evans and Brian Massumi (Palo Alto, CA: Stanford University Press, 2003).
Ferris, Natalie, *Abstraction in Post-War British Literature 1945–1980* (Oxford: Oxford University Press, 2022).
Freud, Sigmund, *Beyond the Pleasure Principle and Other Writing*, trans. John Reddick (London: Penguin, 2003).
Friedman, Ellen G. and Fuchs, Miriam, *Breaking the Sequence: Women's Experimental Fiction* (Princeton, NJ: Princeton University Press, 1989).
Goffman, Erving, *Asylums* (Harmondsworth: Penguin, 1970).
Gordon, Giles, *Beyond the Words: Eleven Writers in Search of a New Fiction* (London: Hutchinson, 1975).
Gordon, Giles, 'Introduction' to *Berg* (Chicago: Dalkey Archive Press, 2001), pp. vii–xiv.
Groes, Sebastian, *British Fictions of the Sixties: The Making of the Swinging Decade* (London and New York: Bloomsbury, 2016).
Guy, Adam, 'Ann Quin on Tape: *Three*'s Auralities', *Women: A Cultural Review*, special issue: *(Re)turning to Ann Quin*, 33:1 (2022), pp. 73–92.
Guy, Adam, *The nouveau roman and Writing in Britain after Modernism* (Oxford: Oxford University Press, 2019).
Hall, John, 'The Mighty Quin', *The Guardian*, 29 April 1972, p. 8.
Hallberg, Robert von, *American Poetry and Culture 1945–1980* (Cambridge, MA and London: Harvard University Press, 1985).
Hansen, Denise Rose, 'Little Tin Openers: Ann Quin's Aesthetic of Touch', *Women: A Cultural Review*, special issue: *(Re)turning to Ann Quin*, 33:1 (2022), pp. 52–72.
Hardy, Thomas, *Tess of the D'Urbervilles* (London: Penguin, 1979).
Harrison, Jane, *Prolegomena to the Study of Greek Religion* (Cambridge: Cambridge University Press, 1903).
Hassam, Andrew, *Writing and Reality: A Study of Modern British Diary Fiction* (London and Westport, CT: Greenwood Press, 1993).
Hebdige, Dick, *Subculture: The Meaning of Style* (London and New York: Routledge, 1979).

Hodgson, Andrew, *The Post-War Experimental Novel: British and French Fiction, 1945–75* (London: Bloomsbury Academic, 2020).
Hodgson, Jennifer, 'Introduction' to *The Unmapped Country: Stories & Fragments* (Sheffield: And Other Stories, 2018), pp. 7–12.
Jacques, Juliet, 'Fundamental Uncertainties: On *Three*', *Music & Literature No. 7*, (Houston, TX: Taylor Davis-Van Atta, 2016).
Jameson, Fredric, *Postmodernism, or, The Cultural Logic of Late Capitalism* (Durham, NC: Duke University Press, 1991).
Johnson, B. S., *Aren't You Rather Young to Be Writing Your Memoirs?* (London: Hutchinson, 1973).
Jordan, Julia, *Late Modernism and the Avant-Garde British Novel: Oblique Strategies* (Oxford: Oxford University Press, 2020).
Josipovici, Gabriel, *What Ever Happened to Modernism?* (New Haven, CT and London: Yale University Press, 2010).
Kitchen, Paddy, 'Catherine Wheel: Recollections of Ann Quin', *London Magazine*, 19 June 1979, pp. 50–7.
Kohn, Jesse, 'PAS SAGES', *Music & Literature No. 7* (Houston, TX: Taylor Davis-Van Atta, 2016).
Kovacs, Andras Balint, *Screening Modernism: European Art Cinema, 1950–1980* (Chicago and London: The University of Chicago Press, 2007).
Kushner, Tony and Valman, Nadia (eds), *Philosemitism, Antisemitism and 'The Jews'* (Farnham and Burlington, VT: Ashgate, 2004).
Laing, R. D., *Knots* (New York: Random House, 1970).
Laing, R. D., *The Politics of Experience and The Bird of Paradise* (Harmondsworth: Penguin, 1967).
Levy, Deborah, 'Ann Quin and Me', *Music & Literature No. 7* (Houston, TX: Taylor Davis-Van Atta, 2016).
MacCabe, Colin, *James Joyce and the Revolution of the Word* (London and Basingstoke: Macmillan, 1978).
Mackrell, Judith, 'Ann Quin', *British Novelists since 1960, Dictionary of Literary Biography*, ed. Jay Halio (Detroit, MI: Gale Research, 1983).
McHale, Brian, *Postmodernist Fiction* (London and New York: Routledge, 2001).
McLuhan, Marshall and Fiore, Quentin, *The Medium is the Massage* (San Francisco, CA: Hardwired, 1967).
Miller, D. A., *The Novel and the Police* (Berkeley, CA and London: University of California Press, 1988).
Miller, J. Hillis, 'Derrida's Destinerrance', *MLN*, 121:4 (2006), pp. 893–910.
Mitchell, Kaye and Williams, Nonia (eds), *British Avant-Garde Fiction of the 1960s* (Edinburgh: Edinburgh University Press, 2019).
Moore, Nathan, 'Nova Law: William S. Burroughs and the Logic of Control', *Law and Literature*, 19:3 (Fall 2007), pp. 435–70.
Morley, Loraine, 'The Love Affair(s) of Ann Quin', *Hungarian Journal of English and American Studies*, 5:2 (1999), pp. 127–41.

Morrissette, Bruce, 'International Aspects of the "Nouveau Roman" Author(s)', *Contemporary Literature*, 11:2 (Spring 1970), pp. 155–68.
Murdoch, Iris, *A Severed Head* (London: Vintage Classics, 2001).
Nelson, Maggie, *The Argonauts* (London: Melville House, 2016).
Ngai, Sianne, *Ugly Feelings* (Cambridge, MA and London: Harvard University Press, 2005).
Nicholls, Peter, 'Surrealism in England', in *The Cambridge History of Twentieth Century English Literature*, ed. Laura Marcus and Peter Nicholls (Cambridge: Cambridge University Press, 2004).
Nishino, Noriko, 'Between Fluidity and Stability: Reading Ann Quin's Experimental Novels', doctoral thesis, University of Tokyo, 2021.
Nye, Robert, 'Against the Barbarians', *The Guardian*, 27 April 1972.
Osborne, Nell, '"I'm telling you to stop": Staging the Drama of Rape, Experiment and Sexual Consent in Ann Quin's *Three* and Muriel Spark's *The Driver's Seat*', *Angles*, 13 (2021), doi: 10.4000/angles.3818.
Piette, Adam, *The Literary Cold War: 1945 to Vietnam* (Edinburgh: Edinburgh University Press, 2009).
Poirier, Richard, 'Writing Off the Self', *Raritan*, Summer (1981), pp. 106–33.
Quin, Ann, 'A Double Room', *The Unmapped Country: Stories & Fragments* (Sheffield: And Other Stories, 2018), pp. 31–50.
Quin, Ann, *Berg* (Sheffield: And Other Stories, 2019).
Quin, Ann, 'Every Cripple Has His Own Way of Walking', *The Unmapped Country: Stories & Fragments* (Sheffield: And Other Stories, 2018), pp. 51–64.
Quin, Ann, 'Eyes that Watch Behind the Wind', *The Unmapped Country: Stories & Fragments* (Sheffield: And Other Stories, 2018), pp. 108–24.
Quin, Ann, 'Ghostworm', *The Unmapped Country: Stories & Fragments* (Sheffield: And Other Stories, 2018), pp. 125–50.
Quin, Ann, 'Leaving School – XI', *The Unmapped Country: Stories & Fragments* (Sheffield: And Other Stories, 2018), pp. 15–24.
Quin, Ann, letter to the editors, *Ambit*, 35 (1968).
Quin, Ann, letters and manuscripts, Carol Burns Private Collection of Papers.
Quin, Ann, letters and papers, Robert Sward Papers, Special Collections, Washington University Library, Series 1.1, boxes 8–10.
Quin, Ann, letters, postcards and papers, Calder and Boyars manuscripts, Lilly Library Collection, box 52, folders 2–4, scrapbooks 211 and 214.
Quin, Ann, 'Matters of the Heart', unpublished manuscript, Carol Burns Private Collection of Papers.
Quin, Ann, 'Never Trust a Man Who Bathes with His Fingernails', *The Unmapped Country: Stories & Fragments* (Sheffield: And Other Stories, 2018), pp. 95–107.
Quin, Ann, 'Nude and Seascape', *The Unmapped Country: Stories & Fragments* (Sheffield: And Other Stories, 2018), pp. 25–30.

Quin, Ann, 'One Day in the Life of a Writer', *The Unmapped Country: Stories & Fragments* (Sheffield: And Other Stories, 2018), pp. 209–11.
Quin, Ann, *Passages* (Sheffield: And Other Stories, 2021).
Quin, Ann, 'Second Chance', *The Guardian*, August 1973.
Quin, Ann, selected readings from *Three*, made available by Larry Goodell: https://duende.bandcamp.com/album/ann-quin-reads-from-three-1965.
Quin, Ann, *The Unmapped Country*, *The Unmapped Country: Stories & Fragments* (Sheffield: And Other Stories, 2018), pp. 159–208.
Quin, Ann, *Three* (Sheffield: And Other Stories, 2020).
Quin, Ann, *Tripticks* (Chicago: Dalkey Archive Press, 2002).
Quin, Ann, 'Tripticks', *The Unmapped Country: Stories & Fragments* (Sheffield: And Other Stories, 2018), pp. 77–94.
Quin, Ann and Sward, Robert, 'Living in the Present', *The Unmapped Country: Stories & Fragments* (Sheffield: And Other Stories, 2018), pp. 72–6.
Radford, Andrew and Van Hove, Hannah, *'Slipping through the Labels': British Experimental Women's Fiction, 1945–1975* (Cham: Palgrave Macmillan, 2021).
Reizbaum, Marilyn, 'Max Nordau and the Generation of Jewish Muscle', in *The Image of the Jew in European Liberal Culture 1789–1914*, ed. Bryan Cheyette and Nadia Valman (Portland, OR and London: Vallentine Mitchell, 2004), pp. 130–5.
Riley, Denise, *The Words of Selves: Identification, Solidarity, Irony* (Stanford, CA: Stanford University Press, 2000).
Rose, Gillian, 'New Jerusalem Old Athens: The Holy Middle', *The Broken Middle: Out of Our Ancient Society* (Oxford: Blackwell, 1992), pp. 277–96.
Roszak, Theodore, *The Making of a Counter Culture: Reflections on the Technocratic Society and Its Youthful Opposition* (London: Faber & Faber, 1970).
Rourke, Lee, 'Book of a Lifetime: *Berg*, by Ann Quin', *The Independent*, 27 August 2010.
Sage, Victor, 'The Greater Tragedy Imposed on the Small: Art, Anachrony and the Perils of Bohemia in Rebecca West's *The Fountain Overflows*', *British Fiction After Modernism*, ed. Marina MacKay and Lyndsey Stonebridge (Basingstoke and New York: Palgrave Macmillan, 2007).
Sarraute, Natalie, *The Age of Suspicion*, trans. Maria Jolas (New York: George Braziller, 1963).
Sartre, Jean-Paul, *Anti-Semite and Jew*, trans. George J. Becker (New York: Schocken Books, 1973).
Sass, Louis, *Madness and Modernism: Insanity in the Light of Modern Art, Literature, and Thought* (London and Cambridge, MA: Harvard University Press, 1994).

Schor, Naomi, 'Reading in Detail: Hegel's *Aesthetics* and the Feminine', in *Feminist Interpretations of Hegel*, ed. Patricia Jagentowicz Mills (University Park: Pennsylvania State University Press, 1996), pp. 119–47.
Sewell, Brocard, *Like Black Swans: Some People and Themes* (Padstow: Tabb House, 1982).
Showalter, Elaine, *The Female Malady: Women, Madness and English Culture, 1830–1980* (London: Virago, 1987).
Spark, Muriel, *The Driver's Seat* (London: Penguin, 2006)
Spark, Muriel, *The Stories of Muriel Spark* (London: The Bodley Head, 1985).
Stallybrass, Peter and White, Allon, *The Politics and Poetics of Transgression* (Ithaca, NY: Cornell University Press, 1986).
Stevens, Jay, *Storming Heaven: LSD and the American Dream* (London: Heinemann, 1988).
Stevick, Philip, 'Voices in the Head: Style and Consciousness in the Fiction of Ann Quin', in *Breaking the Sequence: Women's Experimental Fiction*, ed. Ellen G. Friedman and Miriam Fuchs (Princeton, NJ: Princeton University Press, 1989), pp. 231–9.
Stonebridge, Lyndsey, 'The "Dark Background of Difference": Love and the Refugee in Iris Murdoch', *The Judicial Imagination: Writing after Nuremberg* (Edinburgh: Edinburgh University Press, 2011), pp. 141–65.
Stonebridge, Lyndsey, 'The Perpetrator Occult: Francis Bacon Paints Adolf Eichmann', *Holocaust Studies: A Journal of Culture and History*, 17:2 (Summer/Autumn 2012), pp. 101–20.
Sweeney, Carole, *Vagabond Fictions: Gender and Experiment in British Women's Writing, 1945–1970* (Edinburgh: Edinburgh University Press, 2020).
Unsigned review, 'Lovers', *Times Literary Supplement*, 3 April 1969.
Van Hove, Hannah, '"The Moving Towards Words & Then from Them": Circling Passages, Circling Quin', *Women: A Cultural Review*, special issue: *(Re)turning to Ann Quin*, 33:1 (2022), pp. 93–113.
Waugh, Patricia, *Harvest of the 1960s; English Literature and Its Background 1960 to 1990* (Oxford: Oxford University Press, 1995).
White, Glyn, *Reading the Graphic Surface: The Presence of the Book in Prose Fiction* (Manchester and New York: Manchester University Press, 2005).
White, Hilary, 'The Limits of Looking: Conceptualising the Frame in Ann Quin's *Berg* and Christine Brooke-Rose's *Out*', *Angles*, 13 (2021), doi: 10.4000/angles.4398.
White, Hilary, '"Turning her over in the flat of my dreams": Visuality, Cut-up and Irreality in the Work of Ann Quin', *Women: A Cultural Review*, special issue: *(Re)turning to Ann Quin*, 33:1 (2022), pp. 114–30.
Wilde, Alan, *Horizons of Assent: Modernism, Post-modernism, and the Ironic Imagination* (London: Johns Hopkins University Press, 1981).

Wilkinson, John, 'Too-Close Reading', *The Lyric Touch: Essays on the Poetry of Excess* (Cambridge: Salt Publishing, 2007).

Williams, Nonia, 'Ann Quin: "infuriating" Experiments?', *British Avant-Garde Fiction of the 1960s*, ed. Kaye Mitchell and Nonia Williams (Edinburgh: Edinburgh University Press, 2019).

Williams, Nonia, '"LOST! HANSOME GOLE BROOCH": Broken, Lost and Forgotten Objects in Woolf, Mansfield and Stein', in *Modernist Objects*, ed. Noelle Cuny and Xavier Kalck (Clemson, SC: Clemson University Press, 2020), pp. 209–24.

Williams, Nonia, '(Re)turning to Quin: An Introduction', *Women: A Cultural Review*, special issue: *(Re)turning to Ann Quin*, 33:1 (2022), pp. 2–17.

Williams-Korteling, Nonia, '"Designing its own shadow" – Reading Ann Quin', doctoral thesis, University of East Anglia, 2013.

Willmott, R. D., 'A Bibliography of Works by and About Ann Quin', *Ealing Miscellany, Number 23* (London: Ealing College, 1982).

Wilson, Leigh, '"So thrilling and so alive and so much its own thing": Talking to Claire-Louise Bennett about Ann Quin', *Women: A Cultural Review*, special issue: *(Re)turning to Ann Quin*, 33:1 (2022), pp. 18–32.

Winnicott, Donald, *Playing and Reality* (London: Tavistock Publications, 1971).

Wood, James, *How Fiction Works* (London: Jonathan Cape, 2008).

Woolf, Virginia, *A Room of One's Own* (London: Grafton Books, 1987).

Woolf, Virginia, *Mrs Dalloway* (London: Penguin, 2000).

Woolf, Virginia, *To the Lighthouse* (London: Wordsworth Classics, 2002).

Zambreno, Kate, 'The Ventriloquist: A Brief Meditation on Ann Quin', *Music & Literature No. 7* (Houston, TX: Taylor Davis-Van Atta, 2016).

Zaretsky, Eli, *Secrets of the Soul: A Social and Cultural History of Psychoanalysis* (New York: Vintage, 2005).

# Index

Adorno, Theodor, 120
Ahmed, Sara, 38–9, 94
allosemitism, 103
Amis, Kingsley, 102–3
Amis, Martin, 102–3
And Other Stories (independent publisher), 5
Annand, Carol, 119, 127–8, 129, 137
*Anti-Semite and Jew* (Sartre), 104
anti-Semitism, 101–2, 104, 105
Apollo moon landing, 134–5
archives, 1–2, 13
Arendt, Hannah, 134, 140
art house cinema, 63–5

Bacon, Francis, 126, 138, 139–40
Ballard, J. G., 142n19
Barber, Dulan, 25, 27–8, 97, 103, 107
Barthelme, Donald, 128
Barthes, Roland, 80n13, 93–4, 97, 99, 134
Bataille, Georges, 89, 93–4
Bauman, Zygmunt, 103
Beckett, Samuel, 109n2
*Bell Jar, The* (Plath), 152
Bellarisi, Franca, 124
Benjamin, Walter, 79n9
Benn, Tony, 105
Bennett, Claire-Louise, 5, 7, 8, 19n13, 23, 52
  on *Berg*, 34, 36
  on *Passages*, 88, 108
*Berg* (Quin), 15, 23, 25–47
  auto-fictional mode, 17
  bodily awareness, 45–6

cross-dressing, 41–2
dead moth, 45
frames and perspectives, 29–33
gender and desire, 37–42
meaning/meaninglessness of existence, 2
mirrors, 45
narrative perspective, 26, 30–2, 34–5
and Oedipal story, 25–9, 68–9
patricide, 25–7
pet animals, 26, 43–4
religion, 163
setting, 25
sex scenes, 89–90
sticky details, 33–7
syntax, grammar, sentence structure, 29–30
uncertainty, poetics of, 33
ventriloquist's dummy, 26, 27
water, 52
windows as framing device, 29, 31, 32
CHARACTERS
  Aly Berg/Alistair Greb, 25–9, 30, 31, 37, 38, 39–42
  Edith, 25, 26, 30, 40–1
  Judith, 25, 26, 27, 30, 37, 38–9, 40–1, 43
  Nathaniel, 25, 26, 27, 28–9, 30, 39–40, 42, 43
Berger, John, 90, 119, 126, 134, 139–40
Bergman, Ingmar, 64, 66
'Beyond the Pleasure Principle' (Freud), 56–7

bird metaphors, 168–9
Black Mountain poets, 80n17
Blake, William, 164–5
Bosch, Hieronymus, 143n28
Bowen, Elizabeth, 13–14
Bowlby, Rachel, 28, 99, 100, 131
Boxall, Peter, 109n2
Boyars, Marion, 116, 150
*Brain Damage* (Barthelme), 128
Brighton, 36
*Brighton Rock* (Greene), 37
Bronfen, Elisabeth, 58
Brooke-Rose, Christine, 5
Brooks, Peter, 57, 140
Brophy, Brigid, 5
Bruce, Sylvia, 66
Burns, Alan, 1, 5, 20n22, 84, 126, 127
Burns, Carol, 1, 2, 28, 64, 84, 101–2
Butler, Alice, 2
Butler, Judith, 100

C (McCarthy), 5
Cage, John, 91, 147
Calder, John, 2, 115, 116
Carroll, Lewis, 156
Carter, Angela, 37–8, 90, 92
Carter, John, 147
Cheyette, Brian, 102, 104, 105
chiropody, 28
cinema
    art house cinema, 63–5
    mid-century cinema, 90
Clarke, Chris, 1, 2
classism, 7–8, 70–4
Cohen, Joshua, 5, 56, 62, 68–9, 70
Cohen, Stanley, 72–3
consumer culture, 122
counter-culture movement, 121
    critiques of, 122–5
creation as violence, 20n23
creative process, 10
Creeley, Bobbie, 84
Creeley, Robert, 2, 80n17, 84, 116
cross-dressing, 41–2
cut-up technique, 111n42, 126–31, 133

*Daniel Deronda* (Eliot), 148, 150–2, 159
    Gwendolen Harleth, 150–2, 159, 160

Dawson, Jennifer, 152
death, 79nn8 & 9
    by drowning, 52–3, 54, 55–6
death drive, 55–8
Deleuze, Gilles, 12, 95, 130–1, 134, 171n14
*Delta of Venus* (Nin), 89
Derrida, Jacques, 11, 14, 155
destinerrance, 20n28
deviancy amplification, 72
Didion, Joan, 121, 135
disgust, theory of, 94
Diski, Jenny, 171n27
Doane, Mary Ann, 90
Doolittle, Hilda (H.D.), 100
*Doors of Perception, The* (Huxley), 123
'Double Room, A' (Quin), 33, 36
*Driver's Seat, The* (Spark), 57
drugs and drug-taking, 122–5
Dunn, Nell, 85, 115–16
Dutton, Danielle, 5, 25, 30, 35, 44

*Easy Rider* (film), 123
Eichmann trial, 101, 140
Eliot, George, 148, 150–2, 159, 160
Ellmann, Maud, 13–14
eroticism, 38, 40, 41, 74, 77, 89–90, 92, 94
'Every Cripple Has His Own Way of Walking' (Quin), 33, 34
experimental fiction, critical reconsideration of, 4–5
'Eyes that Watch Behind the Wind' (Quin), 53, 115, 138

Felman, Shoshana, 152, 156, 159, 160, 166
Figes, Eva, 5
Fiore, Quentin, 121, 128, 134
free love, 88
Freud, Sigmund, 27–8, 56–7, 157

gaze, 16, 65, 106, 107, 122
    female gaze, 88–92, 96, 99, 101, 109, 133
    oblique/indirect gaze, 11, 111n41
'Gentile Jewesses, The' (Spark), 105
'Ghostworm' (Quin), 138, 169

*Girl Is a Half-formed Thing, A* (McBride), 5
glossomania, 11, 20n32, 167, 169–70
Goffman, Erving, 171n19
Goldsmith's Prize, 5
Goodell, Larry, 116
Gordon, Giles, 152, 171n22
Greek myths
   Antigone, 100, 101
   Cassandra, 159
   Medusa, 98–9, 101
   Oedipus, 25–9, 68–9
Greene, Graham, 37
Guattari, Félix, 130–1, 134

*Ha-Ha, The* (Dawson), 152
*Hair* (musical), 123
Hall, John, 143n29
Hamilton, Patrick, 37
*Hamlet* (Shakespeare), 27, 28
*Hangover Square* (Hamilton), 37
Hansen, Denise Rose, 80n15
Hardy, Thomas, 79n8
Harrison, Jane, 97, 98, 99–101
Hassam, Andrew, 61, 80n17
H.D. *see* Doolittle, Hilda (H.D.)
*Helen in Egypt* (H.D.), 100
Hillcroft Women's College, 148
Hodgson, Jennifer, 33
Home, Stewart, 5
Horkheimer, Max, 120
*How to Be Both* (Smith), 5
Huxley, Aldous, 123

ICA (Institute of Contemporary Arts), 147
identity, 6
   class identity, 7, 8
   cultural identity, 12
   gender identity, 42, 58
   group identity, 82n49
   Jewish identity, 104
imagery, 98
   bird metaphors, 168–9
   drowning at sea metaphors, 53
   journey metaphors, 107–8
   knitting/knotting metaphors, 167

rain metaphors, 9–12
window metaphors, 30, 31
*see also* 'Metaphor of the Eye, The' (Barthes)
incompletion, 30
Institute of Contemporary Arts (ICA), 147
irony, 132–6

Jacques, Juliet, 5, 55–6, 71
Jameson, Fredric, 131, 138
jazz, 91, 92
Jewishness, 101–5
Johnson, B. S., 5, 18n4
Jordan, Julia, 5, 28, 36, 46, 66–7, 145n61
Josipovici, Gabriel, 4
*Jules et Jim* (film), 64
Jung, Carl, 28

Kavan, Anna, 5–6
Kerouac, Jack, 141n3
knitting, 158, 166, 167, 168
knotting, 167
Kohn, Jesse, 5, 108
Kovacs, Andras Balint, 64
Kushner, Tony, 102, 105

Laing, R. D., 134, 163, 167
landscapes, unfamiliar, 106–7
*Last Year in Marienbad* (film), 64–5, 67, 68
*Last Year in Marienbad* (Robbe-Grillet), 64
Lawrence, T. E., 12
Leary, Timothy, 123
'Leaving School – XI' (Quin), 22
letters
   to Boyars, 116, 150
   to Carol Burns, 28, 64, 101–2
   to Calder, 115, 116
   New Mexico letters, 106
   to Diane Sward, 101
   to Robert Sward, 9
Levy, Deborah, 4, 14, 19n6, 24n1
libertinism, 88, 90
*Little Birds* (Nin), 89
*Lolita* (Nabokov), 131
'Lost Seagull, The' (Quin), 22

McBride, Eimear, 5
MacCabe, Colin, 31, 151
McCarthy, Tom, 5
McHale, Brian, 128
Mackrell, Judith, 27–8, 46
McLuhan, Marshall, 121, 128, 134
madness, 152
  failure of articulation of, 153–6
  iterations of, 165–70
  stereotypes, 156–9, 161–2, 163, 165, 166, 169–70
Magritte, René, 157
make-up, 41–2, 44–5
Man Booker Prize, 5
'Matters of the Heart' (Quin), 143n27, 148
  religion, 163–4
  CHARACTERS
    Linda, 150, 162, 163–4
melodrama, 67, 140–1
metalanguage, 31
'Metaphor of the Eye, The' (Barthes), 93–4
Miller, D. A., 159
Miller, J. Hillis, 20n28
Moore, Nathan, 126
Morley, Lorraine, 19n11, 25, 42, 57–8, 63
Morrissette, Bruce, 91
*Mrs Dalloway* (Woolf), 169
Munch, Edvard, 138, 139, 140
Murdoch, Iris, 102
music, 91, 92

Nabokov, Vladimir, 131
*Nausea* (Sartre), 45
Nelson, Maggie, 6
'Never Trust a Man Who Bathes with His Fingernails' (Quin), 10–13, 89, 106
Ngai, Sianne, 133
Nicolls, Peter, 61
Nin, Anaïs, 89
'Notes for a Theory of 1960s Style' (Carter), 37–8
nouveau roman form, 63, 64, 70, 91
nouvelle vague techniques, 63–7, 70
'Nude and Seascape' (Quin), 53
Nye, Robert, 49n35, 97, 140, 150

obliquity, 11, 13, 20n30, 99
  oblique reading, 14, 17–18, 101
Oedipus complex, 27–8
*Oedipus Rex* (Sophocles), 27
*On the Road* (Kerouac), 141n3
'One Day in the Life of a Writer' (Quin), 24
onomatopoeia, 11–12
otherness, 10, 12, 101, 102, 104

*Passages* (Quin), 16, 87–109
  ambivalent desire, 101–5, 109
  eye-sleep-blindness-death connotations, 98–9
  female gaze, 88–92, 99, 101, 109
  Jewishness, 101–5
  man's journal sections, 87, 96–101, 106, 108–9
  missing person quests, 2
  mythologies, 96–101
  narrative perspective, 87, 108
  political situation, 105–6
  sea, 52
  sex scenes, 89–90
  sexual fantasy, 88
  vibrating prose, 92–6, 107
  violence, 106
  woman's sections, 87, 90–1, 92–6, 106–9
patricide, 25
Patterson, Ian, 5
pet animals
  *Berg*, 26, 43–4
  *Three*, 43, 74–5
Piette, Adam, 162
Plath, Sylvia, 152
pop art illustrations, 119, 127–8, 129, 137
pornography, 89, 90, 92
precariousness, 6–7, 8, 15
*Principe du Plaisir, Le* (Magritte), 157
*Prolegomena to the Study of Greek Religion* (Harrison), 97, 98, 99–101

Quin, Ann
  accommodation, 23–4
  breakdowns, 147–8

death by drowning, 52–3, 54
education, 22, 148
first job, 22
Lansdowne Road, Notting Hill, 23
secretarial jobs, 22–3
sexuality, 84–5
Soho, 23
travels abroad, 115–16, 147

RADA (Royal Academy of Dramatic Art), 22
recuperation, 14
religion, 110n32, 125, 135–6, 138
  visions of God, 163–5
Resnais, Alain, 64
Riley, Denise, 133, 169
Robbe-Grillet, Alain, 64
*Room of One's Own, A* (Woolf), 23
Roszak, Theodore, 124, 134, 135
Rourke, Lee, 5
Royal Academy of Dramatic Art (RADA), 22
Royal College of Art, London, 22–3

Sade, Marquis de, 89
*Sadeian Woman, The* (Carter), 90
St Dunstan's, Brighton, 22–3
Sarraute, Natalie, 80n18
Sartre, Jean-Paul, 45, 104
Sass, Louis, 171n18
Schor, Naomi, 36
sea
  and drowning, 52–4
  and sex, 52, 77
'Second Chance' (Quin), 148
*Severed Head, A* (Murdoch), 102
Sewell, Brocard, 2, 54, 85
sexual violence, 20n23, 75–6, 78
Shakespeare, William, 27, 28
Sharp, Ellis, 5
Showalter, Elaine, 156
*Silence* (Cage), 147
*Slice of the Moon, A* (Quin), 23
Smith, Ali, 5
Sophocles, 27
Spark, Muriel, 57, 105
Stallybrass, Peter, 36
*Sterling Karat Gold* (Waidner), 5
Stevens, Jay, 123

stereotypes, 12, 74
  gendered, 54, 68, 90, 92
  Jewish, 101–2, 104, 105
  of madness, 156–9, 161–2, 163, 165, 166, 169–70
Stevick, Philip, 32, 38, 40, 52
Stonebridge, Lyndsey, 140
*Story of the Eye* (Bataille), 93–4
'Struggle with the Angel, The' (Barthes), 97, 99
stuttering of language, 12–13, 16, 17, 95, 96, 106, 167
suicide, 54, 55–6
Sward, Diane, 84, 101
Sward, Robert, 2, 9, 84, 116
Sweeney, Carole, 5, 6, 19n11

*Tess of the D'Urbervilles* (Hardy), 79n8
*Three* (Quin), 15, 16, 54, 55–79
  classism, 70–4
  collage form, 58–63, 70
  coupledom deconstruction, 67–70
  death drive, 55–8
  Grey House, 65–6, 67, 71–2
  knitting, 167
  missing person quests, 2
  narrative perspective, 59–60
  nouvelle vague techniques, 63–7, 70
  pet animals, 43, 74–5
  sex scenes, 89–90
  sexual violence, 75–6
  silent scream, 138
  trinary logic, 56, 68–9, 77–9
  violence, 73–4
  CHARACTERS
    Leonard, 55, 56, 58, 59–60, 62–3, 66, 67–70, 73, 75–6, 77, 78, 87–8
    Ruth, 55, 56, 58, 59–60, 66, 67–70, 72, 73, 75–7, 78, 87–8, 167
    S, 55–6, 57–8, 59–62, 66, 67–9, 70–1, 72, 73–4, 76–8
*Through a Glass Darkly* (film), 63–4
*Times Literary Supplement*, 106–7
*To the Lighthouse* (Woolf), 167
*Tripticks* (Quin), 16, 116–17, 118–41
  clichés, 129–32
  counter-culture critiques, 122–5

*Tripticks* (Quin) (*cont.*)
  cut-up technique, 126–31, 133
  drugs and drug-taking, 122–5
  irony, 132–6
  pop art illustrations, 119, 127–8, 129, 137
  screens, 118–22
  silent scream, 136–41
  television, 119–21
  CHARACTERS
    Nightripper, 125
'Tripticks' (Quin and Sward), 122
Truffaut, François, 64

*Unmapped Country, The* (Quin), 16–17, 33, 138, 148, 150–70
  bird metaphor, 168
  glossomania, 167, 169–70
  knitting, 158, 166, 167, 168
  madness, 152
  madness, failure of articulation of, 153–6
  madness, iterations of, 165–70
  narrative perspective, 156, 157, 158, 159, 160
  signs, interpretation of, 159–63
  stereotypes, 156–9, 161–2, 163, 165, 166, 169–70
  visions of God, 163–5
  writing mind, 150–3
  CHARACTERS
    Annie Carr, 163
    Clive, 153, 160–1
    psychiatrist, 153–5, 157

    Red Queen, 156, 162
    Sandra, 150, 153–7, 159–63, 164, 168, 169
    Thomas, 163

Valman, Nadia, 102
Van Hove, Hannah, 2, 109n3, 110n18
'Ventriloquist, The' (Zabreno), 122
Vietnam War, 134–5
violence, 73–4
  against animals, 44, 45, 74
  creation as, 20n23
  domestic violence, 40–1
  *Passages,* 106
  sexual violence, 20n23, 75–6, 78
visual eroticism, 90, 92
von Hallberg, Robert, 121

Waidner, Isabel, 5
Wallace, David Foster, 132
Walsh, Joanna, 5
White, Allon, 36
White, Hilary, 128–9
Wilde, Alan, 134, 140
Williamson, Henry, 85n4
Wilson, Leigh, 7
windows as framework, 90–1
Winnicott, Donald, 139
Wood, James, 132
Woolf, Virginia, 23, 24n1, 50n52, 167, 169

Zambreno, Kate, 5, 25, 44, 122
Zarestky, Eli, 123

EU representative:
Easy Access System Europe
Mustamäe tee 50, 10621 Tallinn, Estonia
Gpsr.requests@easproject.com

www.ingramcontent.com/pod-product-compliance
Lightning Source LLC
Chambersburg PA
CBHW051127160426
43195CB00014B/2369